A HISTORY OF SIND

SELECTIONS FROM THE RECORDS OF THE BOMBAY GOVERNMENT
No. XIII.—New Series

A HISTORY OF SIND,

EMBRACING THE PERIOD FROM A.D. 710 TO A.D. 1590;

WRITTEN IN PERSIAN, AT THE CLOSE OF THE SIXTEENTH CENTURY,

BY

MAHOMED MASOOM;

AND TRANSLATED INTO ENGLISH, IN THE YEAR 1846

BY

CAPTAIN GEORGE GRENVILLE MALET,
SRD REGIMENT BOMBAY LIGHT CAVALRY,
RESIDENT AT KHYRPOOR.

ASSISTED BY PEER MAHOMED,
RESIDENCY MOONSHEE.

EDITED BY A. HUGHES THOMAS,
ASSISTANT SECRETARY, POLITICAL DEPARTMENT

GYAN

Published by

GYAN

Gyan Publishing House
5, Ansari Road
Daryaganj, New Delhi-110002
Phone: 011-47034999, 9811692060
E-mail: books@gyanbooks.com

Distribution Network
gyanbooks.com
India, USA, Canada, UK, Australia, France

ISBN : 978-81-212-2148-1 (PB)
First Published, 1855

2nd Impression 2021

Printed at: Gyan Press, Delhi.

A History of Sind
Author: Mahomed Masoom

SELECTIONS FROM THE RECORDS OF THE BOMBAY GOVERNMENT.

No. XIII.—New Series.

A HISTORY OF SIND,

EMBRACING THE PERIOD FROM A.D. 710 TO A.D. 1590;

WRITTEN IN PERSIAN, AT THE CLOSE OF THE SIXTEENTH CENTURY,

BY

MAHOMED MASOOM;

AND TRANSLATED INTO ENGLISH, IN THE YEAR 1846,

BY

CAPTAIN GEORGE GRENVILLE MALET,

3RD REGIMENT BOMBAY LIGHT CAVALRY,

RESIDENT AT KHYRPOOR.

ASSISTED BY PEER MAHOMED,

RESIDENCY MOONSHEE.

EDITED BY R. HUGHES THOMAS, ASSISTANT SECRETARY, POLITICAL DEPARTMENT.

Bombay:

PRINTED FOR GOVERNMENT

AT THE

BOMBAY EDUCATION SOCIETY'S PRESS.

1855.

SELECTIONS FROM THE RECORDS OF THE BOMBAY GOVERNMENT.

NO. XIII.—NEW SERIES.

A HISTORY OF SIND,

EMBRACING THE PERIOD FROM A.D. 710 TO A.D. 1590;

WRITTEN IN PERSIAN, AT THE CLOSE OF THE SIXTEENTH CENTURY,

BY

MAHOMED MASOOM;

AND TRANSLATED INTO ENGLISH, IN THE YEAR 1846,

BY

CAPTAIN GEORGE GRENVILLE MALET,

3RD REGIMENT BOMBAY LIGHT CAVALRY,

RESIDENT AT KHYRPOOR.

ASSISTED BY PEER MAHOMED,

RESIDENCY MOONSHEE.

EDITED BY R. HUGHES THOMAS, ASSISTANT SECRETARY, POLITICAL DEPARTMENT,

Bombay:
PRINTED FOR GOVERNMENT
AT THE
BOMBAY EDUCATION SOCIETY'S PRESS.
1855.

A HISTORY OF SIND,

FROM THE COMMENCEMENT OF THE EIGHTH TO THE END OF THE SIXTEENTH CENTURY;

BY

MAHOMED MASOOM NAMÉ.

TRANSLATED, IN THE YEAR 1846, FROM THE ORIGINAL PERSIAN,

BY

MAJOR GEORGE GRENVILLE MALET,

3RD REGT. BOMBAY LIGHT CAVALRY,

RESIDENT AT KHYRPOOR,

ASSISTED BY PEER MAHOMED,

RESIDENCY MOONSHEE.

NOTE BY THE TRANSLATOR.

THIS "History of Sind" affords the following information relative to its Author:—

His name was Mahomed Masoom, with the titular name of Namé: his father's name was Sufaee Hoosainee, who, leaving his native place Tirmaz, came to Bukkur, where he died and was buried. His descendants are now to be found living on a limited portion of the lands which were presented in Jageer by the Emperor Akbar Shah to the Historian, on the occasion of his visiting and paying his respects to His Majesty in the district of Bukkur.

"*He is a fool who lends a book— he is a greater who returns it!*"

is an Eastern saying. Acting up to this, the Natives in general have a great repugnance to lend their MSS.; but I had the good fortune to obtain the loan of a copy of this work from His Highness Meer Ali Morad Khan Talpoor, another from Peer Ali Gohur, and a third from Goolam Ali Shah (these two last-named are Syuds of respectable families in Upper Sind): with these before me I executed this translation.

PREFATORY, REMARKS BY THE AUTHOR, MAHOMED MASOOM.

"BE it known to the hearts of those having knowledge: this book is such, that by it is shown how Sind was conquered; also how the Musulmans fought with the Kafirs of the country; also how, and for how many years, the agents of the Khaliphs, Bunee Oomaiyuh and Bunee Abbas, governed it; likewise how the Hakeems, who succeeded these agents, ruled over it. There is also described in this the government of the Urghooneeyuhs, and the times of their rule, their battles, the districts and towns which they took, and all that they did till the time of their departure; after which the country came into the possession of Julal-ood-deen Mahomed Akbar, Badshah; and it is also shown who of his Ameers came to Bukkur, Sehwistan, and Tatta.

This book is divided into IV. Chapters.

In the I. Chapter, is mentioned the conquest of Sind, and the times of the government of the agents of the Khaliphs, Bunee Oomaiyuh and Bunee Abbas.

In the II. Chapter, is mentioned the Kings of Hindoostan, in whose agents' hands the government of Sind was placed; also how Soormah and Summah governed it.

In the III. Chapter, is mentioned how the Urghooneeyuhs ruled this country.

In the IV. Chapter, is shown how this country came into the hands of Akbar Shah, and what Ameers and Hakeems were appointed to, and came to govern, this country, by and from him, till the date of the commencement of this book.

This book is named "THE HISTORY OF SIND."

God is the giver of help to all; all have confidence in Him!

Praise is due to the Ruler of all the world; by whose wisdom the good of the people of the earth is secured by the justice of kings, the proof of which is, that if there were no kings in the world, of course some men would devour each other!

"God is such, that there is no other like Him.
"By His omnipotence, He is King above all other kings.
"He is such a God, that there is no other like Him.
"Everything on earth gives evidence that there is a God.
"He has given the arrangement of things on earth to kings.
"He has given the justice of kings to be the ornament of the world.
"If there were no kings on earth, this world would become desolate by misfortunes!"

Offer sincere prayers to Mahomed!

The elevation of the flag of Mahomed's prophecies is known from the following:—

"I was the Prophet when Adam was in the earth and water!"

The high flag of his prophecy is known from this:—

"I do not send you, were it not for mercy to the world!"

The blessing of God on him, his family, all his friends, and his posterity, as long as the world exists, until the Resurrection:—

"Mahomed's existence comes from the first. By his kindness the world was created.
"All the world, he took, and to heaven, by his majesty.
"For upon high heaven he beat five Nobuts.
"Earth and heaven; honour is from him.
"His exaltation exalted the world.
"To the foundation of religion he gave such strength, that it will flourish to the last day!"

The Writer of this Book, Mahomed Masoom, whose Titular Name is Namé, the son of Sufaee Hoosainee.— The original place of residence of my father is Tirmaz; his house and tomb are at Bukkur; related to Syud Sher Kulundur, the son of Baba Husun Abbal, who was born at Subzwar. He lived and was buried at Kandahar. It has been my intention for a long time to write a short account of the conquest of Sind, describing the doings of the Hakeems of that country, and to gather and select such information as I could obtain; but on account of bad fortune, and the displeasure of Heaven, there was all the will, but the power was wanting. Everything takes place at its proper time; therefore it was delayed until the days when I wrote it on account of my son, the cooler of my eyes, the flower of my heart, Meer Boozoorg! O God, make him after yourself! On his account I wrote this book. Another final cause of my writing this book was, that by reading it my son may learn what the good men of old did, that he may know what is good, what is bad; that which is advantageous, that which is the contrary; so that he may follow the paths of good men; that, following the ways of good men, by that means he may avoid the ways of bad men. From God we obtain the completion of our wishes, protection, and assistance!"

A HISTORY OF SIND,

EMBRACING THE PERIOD FROM A.D. 710 TO A.D. 1590

BY

MAHOMED MASOOM;

CONTENTS.

THE HISTORY OF SIND.

CHAPTER I.

THE CONQUEST OF SIND.

IN this appears the ordering of the Musulman armies from Bagdad to Sind, in the time of the Khaliph, the son of Abdool Mulik, and the circumstances of the wars of the Musulmans with the Kafirs; also the times of the governorship of the agents of Bunee Oomaiyuh and Bunee Abbas, Khaliphs.

It is proper to give the greatest praise to the glory of the Maker, that He has made a difference in the attributes and natures of men; and the intentions of the heart He has made different in the hearts of kings: from some of these kings injury comes upon themselves, and others send their good deeds in advance!

Men of understanding will know, that all historians are agreed that Sind was conquered in the Khaliphat of the son of Abdool Mulik, by the exertions of Hujjaj the son of Yoosoof Sukafee, as Ali the son of Hamed, the son of Aboo Bukur Koofee, wrote in the Chuk Namé, which is a history of Sind. The writer of this book has omitted to include that which was useless in that work; he takes out only that which is useful and necessary.

A SUMMARY OF THE LIFE OF THE SON OF ABDOOL MULIK.

Some historians say that the son was an oppressor: a few think he was such; but the greater number say, that of all the Bunee Oomaiyuh Khaliphs he was the most excellent, because he made the Jooma Musjid at Damascus, that is called the Bunee Oomaiyuh Musjid; and in the Goozeeduh history it appears that he spent 1,000 Dinars six times over on this Musjid, and that every day 1,000 men were employed on this building. At Medina he enlarged Mahomed's Musjid, and in Jerusalem he built up anew the Musjid Aysa, and those who were blind he fed in charity; those who were holy men he selected from the crowds, arranging for their food. In the days of his Khaliphat many cities of Mawraun Mehr (beyond the river Oxus), and to Furghunah, and to the countries of Kabool and Mooltan, were conquered.

In the Mirat-ool-Jenan history it is written, that notwithstanding his oppression, he was a great reader of the Koran, as every third day he read it through, and in the month of Rumzan he read it through seventeen times.

It is also written in the Goozeeduh history, that in the Khaliphat of the son of Abdool Mulik, on the Badeeuh road he made many reservoirs for water; in Damascus he built a hospital and a Karavanserai. He was the first inventor of these places; and amongst all the other things which he did, he pointed out the proper position of the Minars, from the tops of which the summons to prayer is called.

His death took place in the month of Jumad-ool-Awul, Hijree 96 (A. D. 714). He lived on earth forty-nine years; out of that he reigned nine years and eight months.

The title of the son was "MOOSTUKEEM BILLAH" (the Faithful to God).

God only knows the truth of this! I now describe some of the events, and some of the reasons why the Musulman forces came from Bagdad.

It is written in the histories of Sind, that in the time of the Khaliphat of Abdool Mulik, he gave orders to some of his servants to go to Sind to buy Hindoostan female slaves, and other things. Some merchants of Egypt having joined them, they came to Sind. They bought and collected female slaves, and other things, as ordered, and having made their arrangements, started on their return by the sea route. When they got to Daiwul Bunder (now called the Tatta and Luheree Bunder), a band of highway robbers came upon them, killing many, taking a few prisoners, looting the whole of their property; and the remaining few escaping, they returned to, and made their complaint before, the Khaliph, who was so incensed, that the perspiration issued from his body: he warned an army to go to that country, and then he died, the force remaining stationary, when his noble son succeeded to the Khaliphat. Hujjaj the son of Yoosoof was sent by him to govern Koofa. He arranged affairs in Bagdad and Koofa, and then in Karmania, Khorasan, Sejistan (Sehwistan). He then heard some of the circumstances of Mukran and Sind, which he reported to the Khaliph: "That formerly some of the Khaliph's servants went to buy things, and that the people of Sind had looted them of all they had, killing many of the party, keeping some as prisoners; and that the deceased Khaliph had warned a force to go and take revenge. In the mean time the Khaliph was taken ill, and died: thus to this time the Mahomedans are still in confinement in the hands of Kafirs. If ordered, it is possible that these people shall be released, and the property which was looted recovered."

It is the custom of good, clever men, first of all to gain intelligence of the circumstances of their enemies, and their condition. Previous to receiving a reply to his petition, Hujjaj warned two clever men to go as spies, to ascertain the circumstances of Sind, and the strength of its armies. He gave them a Firman, as if from the Khaliph, and dismissed them. At that time, Daher, the son of Chuk, was the King of Sind: they gave the Firman to him, he receiving it with much honour; he read, and understood its contents. He denied that his men had done as alleged, saying that he was clear of the matter. His tongue was full of enmity, but with it he spoke in terms of friendship before these persons: asking his attendants about the occurrence, he said he would send people to find out who had behaved in this way towards the Khaliph's servants, declaring, that if caught, he would punish them; that he would recover the stolen property from them, and send it to the Khaliph. He sent his people to inquire into it, detaining the two men for some time by cunning artifices. He wrote a reply to the Khaliph, full of excuses, saying that at the Daiwul Bunder bands of thieves always remained; that these were the people at whose hands his (the Khaliph's) servants had been maltreated, and that he had not sufficient strength to catch these men. The two spies discovered the condition of the country, and troops, and, returning to Hujjaj, told him all they knew.

In the mean time Hujjaj had received from the Khaliph a reply to his petition. In this it was ordered as follows: "That he should send his cousin Mahomed the son of Kasim to occupy Sind; that Hujjaj should draw upon the royal treasury at Bagdad for the expenses of the army." In the space of one month Hujjaj had got ready a force of 15,000 men: of these 6,000 were horse; 6,000 were on camels, and 3,000 were footmen. These he sent towards Sind, and with them 30,000 Dirhams for expenses, that, when necessary, it should be expended. This took place in Hijree 92 (A. D. 710).

A SUMMARY OF THE CIRCUMSTANCES OF RAIS SUHEERIS, THE SON OF SAHSEE, KING OF ALORE.

Many historians write that Alore was a very large city on the bank of the Mihran (the Indus); that there were many very fine buildings in it; that outside and around the town there were gardens full of trees, having good fruit, and that everything was to be found there that the inhabitants and travellers might desire. The name of the ruler of that city and the surrounding country was Rais Suheeris, the son of Sahsee. He was a good, just king. By his kindness, all the men of consequence were obedient to him, the nobles and plebeians were under his control. The boundary of his country extended in an Easterly direction to Kashmere and Kanoge, to the West to Mukran and the sea side (Daiwul, now called the Tatta and Luheree Bunder); to the South to Surat and Diu Bunder; to the North to Kandahar, Sejistan (Sehwistan), the Sooliman Mountains, Karmania, and Keekanan. He divided this country into four divisions; in each division he placed a friend as governor, and he fixed upon Alore as his own place of residence. For a long time he reigned over this country in such a manner, that no one was rebellious; all obeyed his orders.

Suddenly a large Persian force from the King Neemroz came to Kuch and Mukran, by the way of Karmania. After looting those countries, and taking many prisoners, they returned. When Suheeris heard of this, he prepared a large army, and went to Kuch and Mukran, sending word to King Neemroz, who, also getting ready, went to fight him. In a few days they met, and fought from the morning till midday. At the end, Neemroz was the conqueror. He defeated the Sind army. As these were retreating, a Nawuk (a sort of arrow) struck Suheeris in the neck, and he died. The army of Neemroz looted the enemy till midnight, when they proceeded to return. The Sind army, which was dispersed that night, collected and went to Alore. When they got there, they all agreed to place Rais Sahsee (the son of Suheeris) on the throne. He gave great festivals, distributing in charity much gold and pearls. He made no alteration in the mode of ruling the country: he governed with justice. He had a good disposition, treating all with kindness: full of mildness and humility, as he sat in judgment he displayed these qualities. All his subjects were very happy under his rule. After he had reigned one year, he took his army for exercise, and went to see the districts of his country. Wherever he found any disobedient, he took them out by the roots.

When he had satisfied himself with regard to the state of his country, he came to Alore, and he and all his people lived very happily.

He made four laws, relating to the country, and to property:—

The first Law, on the Army.— "To whom pay is due, he receives it at once; there must be no delay."

The second Law, on the Ryuts.— "The proper rent which is fixed is to be brought by the Ryut in three instalments, without his being sent for. The sign of his great justice is this, that the Ryuts are ordered to be excused paying duty on grain, and money, on condition that they build six forts— Alore, Sehwistan, Ooch, Mattehlath, Mode, Suvraee." These were built of mud, and some of them are standing at the present time.

The third Law, on the Merchants.— "Whatever tax has been fixed on these, they are to pay it to the collector of taxes, without his asking for it."

The fourth Law, on the Trades.— "Whatever duty for the Sirkar is imposed upon each of these, they have done it."

Rais Sahsee had a Wuzeer, by name Rais Ram, to whom he gave the reins, placing everything, large and small, in his hands. In all his arrangements he displayed such tact, that the most minute thing did not escape him. On this account, Rais Sahsee was at his ease, spending his days and nights in the bedchamber of happiness, and passing his life there. If at any time there were matters of consequence, or if any letters came from the rulers of the boundaries, then Rais Ram, going to the door of the Harem, represented it.

One day Rais Ram had an assembly, at which many Bramins and men of genius were collected. In the mean time a very handsome, clear-spoken, eloquent young man came in. Those who composed the assembly were astonished at the eloquence of his tongue. Asking him from whence he came, and what his name was, he said his name was Chuk, that his father's name was Seelaj (Seelaj was a Bramin of note in that city). Rais Ram approved of his conversation, taking him into companionship, giving him great presents; and he took him to assist him in the affairs of the State. He was well versed in accounts, clever in speaking and writing the Hindee language. Day by day he attained great knowledge in the business of the country, and property, and his arrangements in these were very good. His good fortune was so great, that he conducted all the duties of the Wuzeer; the name of Rais Ram alone remained. Suddenly, Rais Ram was prostrated with sickness. At that time Rais Sahsee gave a festival in his Harem: he was sitting there very happy. In the mean time many letters came from Daiwul, which, being very important, the Chobdars went and at once gave them to the king. He was unwilling to rise, so he gave orders for a curtain to be placed before the throne, and to summon Chuk. The queen then remarked that he (Chuk) was a Bramin— why have a curtain with him; it is better to have him as it is. Chuk approached the king's throne, offering benedictions, and scattering praises. He then read the letters which had come, and making known their contents, the king gave his replies. He (Chuk) then wrote such a letter, that on hearing it the king presented him with a valuable Khilat, giving directions, that when any business of importance occurred, he should bring it into the Harem. But from seeing him the queen had become distracted. Wishing to have a meeting with him, she sent a procuress to Chuk, acquainting him with her heart's desire. He stood on the ground of denial, saying he was a Bramin, and could not commit such perfidy, particularly in the king's house, from which there was fear for his life, and the destruction of his family. But the god of love was strong in the breast of the queen. On this account happiness left her heart, and from unhappiness she rolled about like a half-killed bird. In a short time this matter was known to every one. Some tale-bearers mentioned it to Rais Sahsee: he replied that Chuk was a faithful Bramin, and would not commit such an act. In short, matters remained in this way some time. Rais Sahsee then became sick: many doctors did all in their power, but without effect. The queen then saw that the king would die, so she sent to call Chuk. When he came, she told him of the condition of Rais Sahsee, and to get him (Chuk) named as vicegerent, formed this stratagem: calling all the Chobdars, she told them that it was Rais Sahsee's order that they should make it known to all, that there would be a grand Durbar the following day, when all, great and small, must be present. On the morning of the next day, the queen gave orders that Rais Sahsee's throne should be placed in the Hall of Audience, and it was done as she directed. The Chobdars, being instructed by her, then went and told the people that the king said, that in consequence of weakness he was unable to come forth; for this reason he had put Chuk in his place, having given to him the royal seal. Helpless, all the people obeyed this order, and a few days afterwards Rais Sahsee died. Then the Ranee, calling Chuk, said: "The time has now come when we can be one; we must arrange to get rid of those who may not approve of this." Chuk replied that he was willing to do as she wished. The queen said: "Rais Sahsee has no son, but there are many of his relations who will lay claim to the heritage of his country and property: it is better to make arrangements before they do so." She then instantly collected fifty chains, which she had placed in one of the rooms of the Harem. She then sent word separately to each of the relations of consequence, that Rais Sahsee was calling them to bequeath his country. Such of these as came, and went inside, were seized, and made secure with the chains. Having done this, she gained confidence, and calling the more humble relations, she said to them: "Those who were perverse towards you I have in confinement; such of you as destroy any of them shall become the masters of their property." They each killed such as had been unfriendly towards them; the whole were destroyed. After this, the following day the queen had the coffin of Rais Sahsee taken out, and, according to custom, burnt his remains; and Chuk succeeded him as king.

THE PLACING OF CHUK ON THE THRONE OF THE KINGDOM, AND HIS MARRIAGE WITH THE QUEEN.

When Chuk, with the concurrence of the Ameers, sat on the throne of the kingdom, he opened the doors of the treasury, announcing to all that largess would be given. He made the nobility and the mobility rich, so these became his, obliged by favours; he increased the pay of the army, and he lowered the rents of the Ryuts— on this account cultivation increased. He married the queen according to the forms. When the news of this went abroad through the country, the relations of Sahsee about Jodhpoor and Jetpoor prepared to attack the country, to obtain their heritage. They collected a large force, and made arrangements for fighting. The chief Sirdar of this army was Rana Muhurut. When this force got near Jaisulmere, he (Rana Muhurut) wrote a letter to Chuk, saying: "You are a Bramin, and not calculated to be a king; you will not be able to fight: for you it is more fit that you go and sit in a corner, and do not bring yourself into a field of battle." Chuk, taking this letter to the queen, explained its contents to her, saying— "A very strong enemy has come; what is your advice?" The queen said— "Men are best acquainted with the councils of war: if you are afraid, give me your clothes, and you shall take mine; then I will go to fight the enemy." Chuk, becoming ashamed, bent his head downwards. At that time the queen said: "Great wealth and much hidden treasure came to you; it is proper that you now give it to the people, that they may be your well-wishers, and all shall come beneath your crown." Chuk, upon this, again opened the treasury, giving much money to the troops, preparing them for war. He also put in proper order a field of battle. By this time Rana Muhurut approached Alore. Chuk, hearing of this, took his army to the field of battle. The two armies fronted each other. Then Rana Muhurut, raising his voice, exclaimed: "O Chuk! why do you bring this force to be destroyed? The dispute is between you and me; it is better that we both come into the plain and fight with each other: if you kill me, you will obtain your desire— all who are with me shall become yours; if I am victorious, the country and property shall be mine." Chuk agreed to this— the foot of his bravery was in front. Rana Muhurut, advancing in front of his army, dismounted from his horse. Chuk likewise got down from his horse, giving orders to his stirrup-holder to bring his horse gently after him. When the two drew near each other, and were thinking of drawing their swords, at that moment the stirrup-holder brought up the horse, and Chuk, quickly mounting, drew his sword, and slew Rana Muhurut— with one blow his death came. The army of Rana Muhurut, seeing this, the thoughts of flight entered their breasts, and they fled. Chuk pursued them, killing great numbers; those who escaped might be counted. Chuk, returning that day, halted on the field of battle. The day following, the people of the city dressed up the town, and Chuk came into Alore with great state. From that time he became the sole ruler of the kingdom, and property. That same year, taking his army for exercise, he visited the limits of his country. Seeing that all was settled, he became free from apprehension, and, coming to Alore, he remained there. Chuk had two sons by the queen— one called Daher, the other Daher Seyn. He had also a daughter by her. Some years after this, Chuk folded up the carpet of his life, and his eldest son succeeded him.

THE ASCENDING OF THE THRONE OF HIS FATHER BY HIS SON DAHER.

When by universal assent Daher sat on the legitimate throne of his father, he followed the path of justice. By giving much money to the troops, and by protecting the Ryuts, he pleased them. All the people of the country bowed their heads on hearing his orders; they girded the waist-belt of obedience around their loins. When he had been on the throne one year, Daher went to the east country. On the eastern boundary he placed a man in whom he had confidence, and setting his mind at ease, he went to Jetpoor. From thence he went to the west, where he did that which he had to do, and then he came to Braminabad, stopping there some days, and leaving his younger brother, Daher Seyn, the son of Chuk, as its governor. He remained six months on its boundary, making friendship with the Governor of Karmania. He then returned towards Alore. When he drew near Alore, the great and small of the city came in front to meet him, and to offer their congratulations to him, on his return. They made their obeisances, and he distributed largess amongst them. The Bramins and astrologers were present, and discovering the fortunate hour for the king to enter the city, made it known to him, saying— " We have seen your fortune, and that of your brother, as also that of your sister: now, in the future fortune of you and your brother there is no bad presage, but in that of your sister Baee Ranee, it appears that she will be the wife of the man who will be the king of this country, and this throne, and she (Baee Ranee) will not go out of this city." Rais Daher, on hearing this, became much oppressed. In the end, he entered the city. For many successive days he held Durbars, and putting in order the affairs in the neighbourhood of the throne, he became at leisure; but when the thorn of the astrologers' word pricked his heart, he was unhappy. He again called the astrologers, asking them the situations of the good and bad stars, and the fortunes of his sister and brother. The astrologers showed him their exact state by explanations. Rais Daher, all his father's ministers, and his men of note, came before the astrologers, laying before them the carpet of inquiry, saying: "It is a very difficult matter to part with country and government: to my understanding it would seem that I should take my sister in marriage— thus my government will remain in my hands, and no dissensions will arise in the country." Immediately on hearing this, his relatives turned away their heads, vehemently exclaiming, and calling out, saying— "Never go near to such a desire, for by such means a spot will come upon our family; the whole world will curse and reproach us; they will turn us out of our religion, and from under our laws: besides, from this there will be such dissensions in the whole country, that they will never be allayed." Rais Daher did not approve of what they said. A few days after this, Rais Daher, summoning his nobles, got them to be of his opinion, and then they agreed to give his sister to him in marriage. After this, on a certain night, Rais Daher collected the Bramins secretly in retirement, and, according to the custom, he tied with a knot the corner of his sheet to the corner of that of his sister; they then both walked in a circle round fire, and, ascending, sat on the throne. Rais Daher then drawing his sword, he saw both their faces on the blade. He then gave away much gold and pearls. They remained there the whole night, but there was no consummation of the marriage. When the day broke, Baee Ranee was taken to her house. When his brother Daher Seyn, at Braminabad, heard of what had taken place, he wrote a letter to him, full of cursing and reproaches, saying: "I have heard that you have committed this bad act; you have given the name of our family to the winds." Rais Daher wrote to him thus in reply: "To avoid the predictions, this has been done by me; if it had not been for these, I would never have agreed to such a bad act." Daher Seyn wrote another letter, saying— "Leave this business alone." Rais Daher said in reply— "It is impossible to turn our destiny by deliberation." After this, the custom of writing letters was left alone, and the fire of enmity began burning between them. Daher Seyn placed the thoughts of fighting with his brother before his mind. He prepared a large army, and went with it towards Alore. When this news reached Rais Daher, the sweat of his anger broke out on his body: he collected a large force, prepared a battle-field, and looked for his coming. After waiting for some days, he went to the jungle to hunt. Some days after this Daher Seyn approached Alore. He was anxious to get into the fort at once; but the people of the city shut the gates, taking their fighting weapons in their hands. Some men then went between, and induced Daher Seyn to desist, showing him a place for his camp to the eastward of the town. They also sent a man to Rais Daher, to give him the news of the arrival of Daher Seyn; on hearing which, Rais Daher left his hunting, and quickly returning, reached the fort. The next morning, he had prepared all the requisites for a feast and for a dwelling, sending them to his brother by his men of consequence. Daher Seyn rejected these, and sent them back, turning his head from the agreement to accept them. In the afternoon, his mother, and the nobles of the city, went to visit Daher Seyn, comforting him by counsel, saying: "Sensual pleasures were not the intention of Rais Daher, but that he had adopted this stratagem to escape from the imagination of misfortune, which the artrologers had foretold in the fortune of Baee Ranee. All approved of this excuse; do you also agree to it, leaving the jungle of your brother's enmity, and turning your heart to obey his orders, as formerly." Daher Seyn agreed to what his mother and relations said, and on the following day, mounted on an elephant, he went underneath the fort, and standing opposite the palace of Rais Daher, made his Salaam, and showed his respect for him. Rais Daher called him inside. Daher Seyn replied, that he had sworn an oath never to enter his house, nor to sit down with him, adding— "if you will come to me, and do me the honour to sit by me, it will be kindness." Rais Daher was anxious to go at once to meet him, but the time was unseasonable, so he determined on the following day for the meeting. In the morning Rais Daher went out with many people to meet his brother. When Daher Seyn heard of his approach, he went forth to meet him in front, and when he was close to him, he dismounted from his horse, and kissed his (Rais Daher's) foot. Rais Daher also did such acts of kindness as are usual between brothers: getting off his horse, taking him in his embrace, kissing him on the face and head, and taking his hand, went inside the tent. They sat talking together for some time, laying open particular subjects. In the afternoon Rais Daher returned to his house, and after he had left, signs of fever were felt on the body of Daher Seyn. These increased every minute to such an extent, that blisters came over his whole body. On the fourth day he quitted the house of sickness, going to that other country where sickness never comes. When the news of his brother's death reached Rais Daher, he became very sorrowful; and quickly getting up, hasted to the place where he was, sending messengers on in front, to find out the true news, and come and tell him. When these arrived at the tents of Daher Seyn, they saw the princess with her head uncovered. The attendants took the messengers inside the curtain, and lifting the covering from off the face, displayed the corpse. Upon this, seeing he was dead, they cried out loudly, running to meet Rais Daher. Rais Daher, uncovering his head and feet, entered the tent of his brother, and, lifting up his body, took it to the place set apart for the purpose of burning their dead, and there burned it. He performed all the necessary mournings, and after these, he went to the place of residence of Daher Seyn, at Braminabad. Taking away with him all his (Daher Seyn's) servants, and leaving those of his own in whom he had confidence, he returned, and came back to Alore.

For many years he held the reins of government in his hands, with absolute power.

THE RELATION OF THE CONQUEST OF SIND BY AMEER IMAD-OOD-DEEN MAHOMED, THE SON OF KASIM SUYFEE; AND THE DESTRUCTION OF RAIS DAHER.

Kazee Ismael, the son of Ali, the son of Mahomed, the son of Moosa, the son of Taiee, has written as follows of the history of Sind. That in the Khaliphat of the son of Abdool Mulik, Hujjaj, the son of Yoosoof Sukfee, sent Mahomed the son of Haroon, with a body of men, from Darul Islam (the Mansion of Islamism), Bagdad, to Mukran. This force took all the country around Mukran, and about the sea side. It was also their intention to take Sind. On this account, they were always inquiring about the people of that country; and those people who had formerly come from Bagdad to buy slaves, and other things, and who had escaped, as I have previously mentioned, these were with them; they were their guides. In short, in the year Hijree 92 (A. D. 710), Mahomed the son of Kasim (the cousin of Yoosoof, and the son-in-law of Hujjaj) left Bagdad with a very fine army, to take revenge on Sind. He came to Karmania, where he halted a short time, to prepare the arms, set the army in order, and get ready the implements for opening forts. He then came to Kuch and Mukran. From thence he intended to take Sind. When the news of the approach of the Mahomedan force reached Rais Daher, he proposed to go to the borders of Mukran to fight them. His nobles said: "This is an Arab force; they have come on account of the enemies of their religion: it is right to be patient. If they make excursions here and there, and in this way leave our country, it will be good; if not, we must deliberate, and it will be necessary to give them much money from the treasury, to save our country from their mischief." Rais Daher approved of this advice, deferring his march until they (the enemy) came to Neerunkot,* where they set a light to the war, surrounding the fort, and after much fighting they were victorious, slaying many Kafirs. The remains of the sword fled, turning their heads to Alore. The Mahomedan armies, with victory, turned the bridle of their intentions to take Tatta. In a short time they subjected Tatta, and taking out the Musulman prisoners, sent them to Hijaz (Arabia). From thence, proposing to go to the royal residence of Alore (Darul Moolk Alore), they came to Sehwistan, where there was so much fighting that it is not possible to describe it. In short, the Kafirs were the victors in two battles; but in the third fight the wind of victory struck the tassels of the Mahomedan flags, and the Kafirs, being overcome, fled. Mahomed Kasim, after taking the fort of Sehwistan, made arrangements for the surrounding country. He sent Boodhnum, Wuzeer (who had asked for, and received quarter from, the forces of Islam,) with some of his own people, to Tatta, and Neerunkot, placing in his hand all the matters of those countries.

The men of Chinuh, hearing the news of the forces of Islam, brought great and fitting presents for, and met Mahomed Kasim; and having agreed to obey his orders, and to pay tribute, they were given their leave and went away. This is the reason why the theologians of Islamism called the country on that side of the river, which was in the hands of the Chinuhs, "Ooshree" (the land which pays one-tenth as yearly tribute.

A DESCRIPTION OF WHEN MAHOMED THE SON OF KASIM WAS IN THE PROVINCE OF SEHWISTAN.

The men of Chinuh sent a man as a spy to the army of Mahomed Kasim. He arrived at the force at the time of the summons to prayer. He was noticing the condition of the troops. At that time the congregation was drawn up in lines for prayers, and Mahomed Kasim was conducting the duties of chief priest; the imitators were all following the motions of the chief priest. The spy, seeing this occurrence, returned, and, explaining to the men of Chinuh, said— "By the oath of God! I have seen those people so united, that to whatever business they turn their heads, they will assuredly accomplish it." He also told them the circumstance of the imitation of the priest by the people at prayers. On hearing this, the Chinuh people had a wish to go to them; so they came, and submitted to the orders of Islamism. Of the people of Sind, the first to become Musulmans were the Chinuhs. It is said, that when the Chinuh people came to submit to Mahomed the son of Kasim, they brought trays full of victuals as a banquet for Mahomed Kasim. He said: "These people provided for" (Murzoog). On this account the Chinuhs are called Murzoog.

When Mahomed Kasim had accomplished the conquest of the province of Sehwistan, some people said that he should now go to Braminabad (now this is called Bramin, or Bahna-ka-Thool), and that after overcoming that fort he should proceed to Alore. Mahomed Kasim said that it was better first to go to take Alore, and, after overthrowing Rais Daher, then to proceed to take other countries. All approved of this, and they crossed the river opposite to Tuluhtee, and marched towards Alore.

When Rais Daher heard of this, he made preparations to march forth. Then the astrologers and magicians collecting, went to him, and explained, "that from the appearance of the stars, it appears your destiny is very weak, and the strength of the fortune of Islam is in the ascendant. At this time it is not proper for you to go forth." Then Rais-Daher, preparing many troops, sent them in front of the forces of Islam. They halted on the bank of the Kuchhuree Kolab (lake). The following day Mahomed Kasim, at Rufyan, gave orders to Abdoola the son of Ali Sugfee to go to fight the Kafirs. Abdoola, agreeably to orders, went against the Kafirs. The two armies met on the banks of Kuchhuree, and the fire of battle commenced burning between them. In short, there was much fighting, after which the Kafirs ran away. Of them many men died in the waters of death.

Some historians say, that the reason why the Kafirs fled from the battle is this, that in the middle of the fight the commander of their army lost his presence of mind— the reins of his will left his hands. In such a state, his horse threw him on the ground, and ran amongst the troops. The men of the army, seeing the horse without his rider, thought that he had been killed. On this account, leaving the fight, they turned their heads in the direction of the jungle of flight. In short, Abdoola returned to Mahomed Kasim with victory. After this, Mahomed Kasim, leaving that place by successive marches, without halting (Billa Fusul), drew near Alore. Rais Daher retired into the fort with fear. Mahomed the son of Kasim did what was necessary for the investment of the fort. He brought into play the battering rams (Munjneeg), and he threw fire in the manner the

Musulmans had seen it in done in Turkey and Persia. On both sides there was constant fighting, so much so, that in ten days there were seven battles. In all these battles, the breeze of victory struck the flags of Islam, and the Kafirs, discomfited, ran away. On Thursday, the 10th day of Rumzan, in the year Hijree 93 (A. D. 711), Rais Daher, having prepared all his elephants, and all his forces, went forth to battle against the Mahomedans. It is said that 10,000 men in armour were with him, and 30,000 footmen: these were in front. Rais Daher sat in a litter with a canopy on an elephant, wearing on his head a crown, covered with gold. He placed his troops on his right and left hand, and the foot of his courage advanced into the plain. In his litter there were two female slaves of great beauty with him: one of these handed him cups of wine, the other helped him with Pan.

The battle raged from the morning till the evening: then the Musulmans, fixing their feet firm on the ground, and drawing their blood-drinking swords from the scabbard of revenge, slew many Kafirs.

Mahomed Kasim, with his ferocious spirit, taking a body of men, went against the troops in front of the elephants, driving them away. At that time, a few Musulmans in the rear threw rockets in the direction of the litters on the elephants. When the fire began to ignite the litters, the elephants, breaking their ranks, fled towards the water. When they got near it, there was mud, in which Rais Daher's elephant sat down. At this time, the Musulmans were shooting arrows, and of these one arrow struck Rais Daher in the throat. The bird of his life, being freed from the cage of his body, flew away. This took place at that time when the sun had set. When Rais Daher was dead, those Bramins who were in the litters on the elephants behind him took him out of his seat, and hid him in the mud, and then they fled towards the city. But the Musulmans had so securely guarded the approaches to it, that, if a bird had wished to go there, it could not have done so. Thus these Bramins were endeavouring to pass, when by chance they fell into the hands of Kais, who secured them. Kais intended to kill them, but they begged for quarter, giving intelligence of the death of Rais Daher; so he gave them quarter.

At that time, some people of the force brought the two slaves who were in the litter with Rais Daher to Mahomed Kasim. On seeing them, it came into his mind that Rais Daher had escaped. With this idea, he gave orders to have it proclaimed to the troops, that "Rais Daher the accursed had got away, and that it was not known that he was dead: therefore that by no means they (the troops) should occupy themselves in plundering, lest he comes and takes us by surprise." At the time of hearing this proclamation, Kais took the Bramins to Mahomed Kasim. When he heard their news, he said— "God is great!" (Allah-ho-Akbar.) On the troops hearing this, the exclamations of those who fight against the infidels reached the heavens. Mahomed Kasim, taking a few brave men, went with the Bramins to near the water. He ordered the body to be taken out, and when it was taken out, he had the head cut off, and placed it on the point of a spear. He first showed it to the slaves, who, recognising it, said it was the head of Rais Daher. Mahomed Kasim gave orders to his forces to stop all around the fort, and it being the night of Friday, the men of the army kept awake, spending it in prayer, and calling upon God.

When it was morning, Mahomed Kasim sent the head of Rais Daher, with the two slave girls, in front of the gate of the fort, the people of which, seeing it, denied it. When the news reached the ears of Rais Daher's wife Ladhee, she instantly ran to the gate, and asked the slaves concerning Rais Daher. These, weeping, pointed out his head, on seeing which she threw herself off from the gateway. There was then great lamentation through the fort, and the Kafirs, being helpless, opened the gates.

On that day, which was Friday, the 11th of Rumzan, the Mahomedan army entered this fort; and Mahomed Kasim took possession of the treasure, and all the hidden wealth; the army and servants giving them in charge to Kais.

In the court-yard of a temple the Musulmans made a pulpit, a sermon was read, and then prayers. In the beginning of Shuwal, Mahomed Kasim took an inventory (written) of the treasure, and property of all sorts, also of the prisoners, and sent the whole in charge of Kais, with 200 horsemen, by the way of Kuch and Mukran, to Darul Islam (Bagdad). Hujjaj, hearing of this, was exceedingly happy, and he sent everything on to the Khaliph in Syria. When Kais reached the Khaliph, and gave him the news about Rais Daher, and all concerning the fights and victories, separately, he became very happy, and presented him with a sumptuous Khilat, and a valuable present for Mahomed Kasim; and he wrote him a Firman, saying: "It is not proper for the armies of Islam to be content with the conquest of Sind alone; they must now proceed to the countries to the east. It is necessary for you to take possession of all the territory held by Rais Daher." When this Firman reached Mahomed Kasim, he marched to Braminabad, and, conquering it, he settled the taxes of the people of Sind.

The Bramins he placed, as before, in charge of the revenues, and appointed them to listen to suits of law.

The Summah people, who resided about Loharee, collected, and came to Mahomed Kasim, with drums beating, and blowing horns. He, inquiring who these were, was told by the Bramins that they were a tribe of the country, and that it was customary with them, on approaching the ruler, to go in this way. Mahomed Kasim, fixing a settlement for them, gave them their leave.

Then the Loharees, the Suhtuhs, the Chundars, the Machees, the Halas, the Ghorachas, also came bare-headed and bare-footed, through the introduction of Abee, the son of Abdoor Rayman, Suhleetee, to Mahomed Kasim, for safety. He gave them protection, issuing orders, that upon these people should rest this business, "that whenever any Musulman went from this to the residence of the Khaliph, or when any should come from thence to Alore, these should show them the road."

In the beginning of the year Hijree 94 (A. D. 712), the sons of Rais Daher collected some men in the fort of Sekunder (this was a strong fort), and from this they looted the villages of Sind. When this news reached Mahomed Kasim, he went there, surrounding the fort. After some time, there was great distress from a scarcity of provisions; there was nothing to be got to eat but flesh alone. Mahomed Kasim then sent a good man to the sons of Rais

Daher, telling him to say, that if they wished for his friendship, he would give it to them. They sent back for answer that they were certain that Rais Daher was still alive, and that they expected he would shortly come with an army from Hindoostan to take his revenge. When Mahomed Kasim heard this, he ordered the wife of Rais Daher to be brought from Alore to her sons, when this absurd idea would leave them. She was brought, and sent in front of, and close to the gate. The garrison got on the walls; when the wife of Rais Daher told them all the circumstances of the fight, and of the death of Rais Daher, also of that of the Sirdars, separately. She then wept. The people, saying she spoke false, commenced throwing stones and mud at her, declaring she was in league with the enemy and not worthy of credit. She was then taken away.

In a short space, by the battering rams and other implements for breaking down walls, this fort was conquered. Mahomed Kasim destroyed numbers of the Kafirs; some few of them came under the rules of Islamism. Much money and other things fell into the hands of the Mahomedans. There was in the fort a large temple, which they destroyed: from it they obtained great riches, which Mahomed Kasim put on one side for the Khaliph, and one-fifth of all the prize he took and spent in building Musjids; then he returned to Alore.

In the beginning of the 3rd month of the year Hijree 94 (A. D. 712), he made Ahnuf, the son of Kais Ussudee, Governor of Alore, and, leaving him there, he himself turned his face to take Mooltan; the leading men of which, hearing of his approach, went to the front to meet him; and getting an interview, he executed a treaty with, and arranged what articles of produce and merchandize should be paid by them yearly to the State. He left this, placing Daood, the son of Nusseer, the son of Ummanee, as governor of it. He also placed Huzeen, the son of Abdool Mulik Bunee Tumeem, as governor at the fort of Burumpoor, on the bank of the water of Jhelum (this fort is also called Shiewpoor).

When Mahomed Kasim marched from Mooltan to go to Delhalpoor, 50,000 men, horse and foot, were under his standard. To whatever country he went, he fixed a force there. In this manner he carried the armies of Islam as far as Kanoge. The Rajas and Hakeems in all that space came under the orders of Islam, agreeing to pay yearly tribute in money and produce, and to convey it to Darul Islam. Mahomed Kasim, having quieted his mind, by placing men of confidence and troops in all places of importance, turned homewards. At that time a letter came, written agreeably to the order of the Khaliph Wulleed, to this effect:—

"After taking Alore, you sent two daughters of Rais Daher, and some prisoners, in charge of Mahomed the son of Ali Tohman, Humdanee, with Seedee servants, to Darul Khaliphat. The Khaliph called these two sisters to the Harem one night, and gave them in charge of the eunuchs, that they might pay them attention. They were to produce them when they had recovered from the toils of travel. Two months afterwards, they were produced before the Khaliph, and an interpreter attended. The two sisters threw back their veils, and the Khaliph, on seeing them, became distracted with their great beauty. He then asked them their names. One said her name was Purmul Dewe, the other said her's was Sooruj Dewe. The Khaliph ordered the attendants to leave one of them there. Then she, rising, said: 'We are not fit for the bed-chamber of the Khaliph, because Mahomed Kasim placed both of us by himself for three days, and he afterwards sent us to the Khaliph.'"

The interpreter explaining this, the fire of anger was lighted in the body of the Khaliph, who gave orders, that as a punishment for this want of respect, Mahomed Kasim should wrap himself up in the raw hide of an ox, and be present at Darul Kaliphat. To show his great anger, and by way of intimidation, the Khaliph wrote in the margin of this letter in his own hand, that "Whenever this reaches Mahomed Kasim, he is to come from thence to Darul Khaliphat, wrapped in the hide of a cow. There is to be no delay in obeying this order."

At that time Mahomed Kasim was at Oodeypoor. When the Chobdar brought this letter (Firman), Mahomed Kasim, on reading it, to obey the orders it contained, said to the Chobdar:— "That which you have been directed to do, do it. He wrapped Mahomed Kasim in a raw hide, and departed. Three days afterwards the bird of his life left his body, flying to heaven. The Chobdar, seeing this, put the body into a box, taking it to Darul Khaliphat. He arrived there on a Durbar day, and took the box to the Khaliph, who, seeing it, inquired if he were alive or dead. The Chobdar replied, that he had wrapped him in a raw skin, but three days afterwards he died. The Khaliph then directed the box to be taken into the Harem, and that it should be opened in his presence. The Khaliph went to the Harem, and calling the daughters of Rais Daher, said, come and see how penetrating my orders are; come and see Mahomed Kasim. They both went forward, and, looking at, recognised him. Offering great praises to the Khaliph, they said:— "Kings of great justice should not do great things in a hurry; they should not use that which is told them by their enemies." The Khaliph asked what was the meaning of this. They replied:— "We raised this suspicion against Mahomed Kasim in enmity to him, because our father was killed at his hands: country and wealth have departed from our father's house, and we have come as prisoners to the land of travellers. The king, in his anger, did not weigh our words, he did not distinguish between our truth and our falsehood, and issued such an order. The truth is, this man was to us as a father or a brother; his perfidious hand never touched the skirts of our purity: it was in our heart to revenge our father; on this account we raised this suspicion upon him. Our wishes have been fulfilled, but in the house of judgment of the king there is great sorrow."

When the Kahliph heard this, for one hour his head was in the pocket of repentance; then the fire of anger became alight in his breast. He gave orders— the two girls were tied to the tails of two horses, and after having been dragged round the city, they were thrown into the Dijlah (the Tigris).

Mahomed Kasim was buried at Damascus. It is said, that two years after the death of Mahomed Kasim, the people of all the countries he had conquered refused to obey orders; only those from Daibulpoor to the salt sea remained under the hands of the agents of the Khaliph.

In the year Hijree 96 (A. D. 714), Khaliph Wulleed went to the country of heaven, and his successor, Sooliman the son of Wulleed, sat on the throne of the Khaliphat. He sent Ahmir the son of Abdoola as the Governor of Sind.

After the death of Sooliman, Murwan the son of Mahomed, whose title was Kadir Billah (the Strong by the power of God), succeeded to the Khaliphat. He sent Abdool Khuttab to take the government of Sind.

In the year Hijree 133 (A. D. 750) Abdoola the son of Mahomed, the son of Ali, the son of Abdoola, the son of Abbas (commonly called Sifah), having taken the Khaliphat from the Khaliph of the Bunee Oomaiyuh, became the first Khaliph of the Bunee Abbasee. He sent a force from Darul Khaliphat to Sind, which drove the agents of the Bunee Oomaiyuh out from that country.

Four years after this Junfur Munsoor Abbasee sent an army to Hindoostan; and in the year Hijree 170 (A. D. 786) the Khaliph Haroon Reshid, the son of Muhdee, sent Abool Abbas to govern Sind, who stayed there a long time.

END OF CHAPTER I.

CHAPTER II.

A RECITAL OF THOSE KINGS WHO, AFTER THE GOVERNMENT OF THE AGENTS OF THE KHALIPHS OF BUNEE ABBAS, RULED THE COUNTRY OF SIND.

The historians have written, that after the monarchy of all of the denomination Bunee Oomaiyuh, the agents of the Khaliphs of Bunee Abbas, having come to Sind and Mooltan, held the government in the time of the Khaliphs Hurroom and Mamoon. A portion of the country of Hindoostan came into the hands of their agents.

At the termination of the rule of the agents of the Khaliphs of Bunee Abbas, came the time of the Khaliphat of Kadir Billah Abool Abbas Ahmed, the son of Ishay, the son of Mooytedir Billah.

In the middle of the month of Rumzan, in the year Hijree 410 (A. D. 1019), Sooltan Mahomed Gazee left his seat of government, Ghuznee, to take Hindoostan. On reaching Mooltan, he took it, also Ooch, dismissing the agent of Kadir Billah. He appointed the Wuzeer, Abdoor Ruzay, to take a force to conquer Sind. In the year Hijree 417 (A. D. 1026), he (the Wuzeer) had arranged everything at Bukkur, and departed for Sehwistan and Tatta, from whence he sent away many Arabs. Those who had families, and those of learning, he placed in the law offices, and having done this, he settled their rates of pay.

When, in the year 422 (A. D. 1030), Sooltan Mahomed Gazee died, his son Sooltan Musnood, brought up in the ways of God, sat on the throne of Ghuznee. He took into his hands all the hereditary possessions of his father, as well as Hindoostan and Sind. The people conveyed to Ghuznee the yearly tribute of produce and property, which had been laid upon them, as by custom. When, in the year 433 (A. D. 1041), he left this transitory world, and turned his face to the world of life, his son, Sooltan Mondood, adorned the throne of the kingdom, by sitting upon it. He took into his hands all the hereditary possessions. In the year 441 (A. D. 1049), turning his face to the world of futurity, Sooltan Mujdood succeeded him, who held all the hereditary lands. When the angel of death sought to take his life, then at Lahore, the apparatus of his being was taken to heaven.

After him, the turn of sovereignty came to Khoosruwi Moolk (he was of the family of the Kings of Ghuznee). The cup of prosperity remained with him for a long time; till the year Hijree 583 (A. D. 1187,) when Sooltan Ghuyas-ood-deen Ghoree came to Lahore with conquest, and, taking prisoner Khoosruwi Moolk, sent him to be confined at Ghuznee. After this, if any of the family of the Kings of Ghuznee came into the hands of Ghoree, he gave them to drink the sherbet of death.

AN ACCOUNT OF THE SOOLTAN SHUHAB-OOD-DEEN MAHOMED, THE SON OF SAM GHOREE.

After Sooltan Ghuyas-ood-deen had turned his face from Hindoostan, and reached Khorasan in the year Hijree 599 (A. D. 1202,) he died at Herat. He was buried in the tomb which had been made for him in the Jooma Musjid of that city.

In this good garden, two doors are placed. These two doors are not closed. You come in at one door of the garden, and you go out at the other door.

In the year Hijree 591 (A. D. 1194), Sooltan Shuhab-ood-deen (the brother of Ghuyas-ood-deen) came to Hindoostan with an army, as the vicegerent of his brother. He took Mooltan and Ooch, and he sent a force, under Kooth-ood-deen Abeek, to take Sind, who, having in three months taken possession of all that country, and leaving Sasfool Muloog there, he went towards Delhi. Shuhab-ood-deen was at that time marching gently from Mooltan to Hindoostan. He took all the forts and cities as far as Delhi (the seat of the government of Hindoostan), which he conquered, and from that date Delhi became the royal residence.

Shuhab-ood-deen, appointing Kootub-ood-deen as his successor, went to Khorasan. In the mean time, the news of the death of his brother Sooltan Muz-ood-deen reached him. At hearing this he was very sorry, and at once pushed on. After reaching Ghuznee, he issued orders to all his troops to prepare everything requisite for three years, to go to Toorkistan. He then heard that a body of men of the Khokur tribe was on the road of violence near Lahore. Thinking it best to root these out, he marched in that direction, and after killing numbers of them, as he was on his return, he fell a martyr to the knife of one of the Khokur robbers, at Doomyuk encampment.

Shuhab-ood-deen, the king of earth and water— from the beginning no one had been like him!— he fell a martyr on the 3rd of Shuban 602 (A. D. 1205). It occurred at Camp Doomyuk, on the Ghuznee road.

His reign to the time of his death was thirty-two years and some months. He only left one daughter as his heiress. It is said that he had collected vast treasures of gold, silver, and precious stones. Of this there were five hundred maunds of diamonds, the most valuable of all stones— from this may be inferred the quantity of other treasure. He came to Hindoostan nine times: he was beaten twice, the other times he was victorious. He was a just king, fearing God, kind to the people, giving honour to the learned and good, and full of charity.

AN ACCOUNT OF SULTAN KOOTB-OOD-DEEN ABEEK.

Sultan Shuhab-ood-deen, leaving Kootb-ood-deen Abeek in his place at Delhi, marched towards Khorasan. On the news of his death reaching Kootb-ood-deen, he raised the royal standard, and read his own name in the sermon (Khootbah). From that date he was styled Sultan Kootb-ood-deen. The whole country of Hindoostan and Sind came into his hands, and thus they remained until the year Hijree 607 (A. D. 1210), in which year, at Lahore, he was engaged in games on horseback in the plain, when, being thrown from his horse, the ready money of his life was won by death. For four years his name was read in the sermon.

AN ACCOUNT OF ARAM SHAH, THE SON OF KOOTB-OOD-DEEN ABEEK.

After the death of his father, at the suggestion of the Ameers, Aram Shah ascended the throne of Delhi; but on account of his want of ability, he did not find ease (Arain) on the throne of royalty. The Ameers, seeing that he was not fit to govern the kingdom, sent a man to Sultan Shums-ood-deen Elthemis, to summon him, and having called him to Delhi, they gave the kingdom to him. At that time all the countries of Hindoostan became divided into four shares:—

Sultan Shums-ood-deen Elthemis took the seat of government, Delhi.

Ooch, Mooltan, and Sind came into the hands of Nasir-ood-deen Kebachuh.

Luknootee* went under the rule of the Kings of Khuluge.

The agents of Taj-ood-deen Yulzur took possession of Lahore and its districts.

Mulik Nasir-ood-deen Kebachuh was from among the purchased slaves of Sultan Shuhab-ood-deen; but his wisdom and knowledge were great. He was well acquainted with the duties of kings, and versed in the matters of the country: on this account, after the death of Shuhab-ood-deen, being fixed firmly in Ooch and Mooltan, he took possession of Sind.

In the year 621 (A. D. 1224), a Sirdar brought a force from Gungeez or Jinghez Khan to fight against Nasir-ood-deen, who, not having strength to meet this force, on this account he sat down in the fort of Mooltan, which the enemy surrounded. Thus matters remained for forty days. Mulik Nasir-ood-deen having opened the doors of his treasury, gave money to all; and, with them, showing opposition to the enemy, they retreated without gaining a victory.

When Nasir-ood-deen took possession of Sind, many Sirdars of Khorasan, Ghore, and Ghuznee, on account of the oppression of Gungeez Khan, came to him, to all of whom he gave great honour, and money.

In the year 623 (A. D. 1226), Mulik Khan Kailchee and his brethren came against Sehwistan. Mulik Nasir-ood-deen Kebachuh marching against these, there was a great battle between them, in which Mulik Khan was slain.

As the time drew near for the termination of the Sultan of Mulik Nasir-ood-deen Kebachuh, in the year 624 (A. D. 1226), Sultan Shums-ood-deen Elthemis himself marched an army against Ooch, but Nasir-ood-deen ran away, and got into the fort of Bukkur. On hearing of this, Sultan Shums-ood-deen ordered his Wuzeer Nizam-ool-Moolk Mahomed, the son of Usu-ud, to besiege Ooch, and he himself went to Delhi.

On Tuesday the 28th day of Jumadee-ool-Awul, in the year Hijree 625 (A. D. 1227), Nizam-ool-Moolk entered Ooch without opposition. He then went towards Bukkur, hearing of which, Mulik Nasir-ood-deen Kebachuh, getting on board a boat, fled. When he reached the ocean, the boat of his life fell into the whirpools of death.

AN ACCOUNT OF SULTAN SHUMS-OOD-DEEN ELTHEMIS.

When, in the year 624 (A. D. 1226), Wuzeer Nizam-ool-Moolk came to Sind by order of Sultan Shums-ood-deen, he made such arrangements for the country as were necessary. He took great pains to people cities, and to do good to the Ryuts. In the year 630 (A. D. 1232), having placed Noor-ood-deen Mahomed in the government of the country, he returned to Delhi. On Monday the 26th of Shaban, in the year 633 (A. D. 1235), Sultan Shums-ood-deen, at Delhi, turned his face to the country of life.

AN ACCOUNT OF SULTAN MUSOOD SHAH.

When Sultan Musood, the son of Rookn-ood-deen Pheroz Shah, the son of Sultan Shums-ood-deen Elthemis, in the year 639 (A. D. 1241), sat upon the throne of Delhi, he took possession of all hereditary countries. One day, in the month of Sufur 643 (A. D. 1245), the news of the Mogul armies having crossed the river of Sind, and surrounded Ooch, reached Delhi. Musood Shah went forth against his enemies. The Moguls, hearing of this, broke up from Ooch, and taking the way of Bukkur, retreated to Khorasan. Sultan Musood Shah came to Bukkur, and removing Noor-ood-deen Mahomed from the government of Sind, gave it to Julal-ood-deen Husun, and from thence he marched towards Delhi. When he arrived at Mooltan, some young men, addicted to drinking wine, found their way into his assemblies. These talked of the pleasures of drinking; and he, who was always in the habit of indulging, from what these said drank more. On this account, dissensions arose in his country. Then the Ameers, seeing this, sent a Kosid secretly to his uncle, Sultan Nasir-ood-deen Mahomed, who was at Buhraiyuch, inviting him to come. Sultan Nasir-ood-deen, with all speed, proceeded to Delhi, and having ascended the throne on Sunday the 23rd day of Mohurrum, in the year Hijree 644 (A. D. 1246), he seized and confined Musood Shah, whose remaining days of life were spent in prison.

AN ACCOUNT OF SULTAN NASIR-OOD-DEEN MAHOMED, THE SON OF SULTAN SHUMS-OOD-DEEN ELTHEMIS.

On Tuesday the 25th of Mohurrum, 644 (A. D. 1246), Nasir-ood-deen ascended the throne of the kingdom of Delhi, in the Kusre Pherozuh. For many years he ruled with great power. On Monday the 22nd Shuwal, 649 (A. D. 1251), he marched with the intention of going towards Lahore, Mooltan, Ooch, and Bukkur. When he left Ooch, and entered Sind, he appointed Kulugh Khan to the district of Sehwistan, and Mulik Sunjur to Ooch and Mooltan; he himself returned to Delhi. He then proposed going to the country of Luknootee; but the Ameers were averse to his proceeding in that direction: therefore a force under Mulik Julal-ood-deen was sent there, to punish the breakers of the law. In the latter months of 656 (A. D. 1258), a Mogul force came towards Ooch and Mooltan. The king, hearing of this, marched from Delhi to expel them, but the Mogul army went away without fighting. The Sultan then returned back again. It is said that Sultan Nasir-ood-deen wrote with his own hand two Korans every year. The money realized by their sale he expended on his food. Besides this, he did not spend any other money on his food. At one time, this incident occurred: the king, having written a Koran, an Ameer on this account gave more money for it than the usual price. The king was displeased on hearing of this, and he gave orders to his servants, that from that time, the Korans which were written by him should be sold without making this known, and that nothing above the usual price should be taken for them. It is also said, that in the royal palace there were no female slaves, or any female domestics for his wife, who always cooked the king's bread with her own hands. One day she said to the king, that there would be nothing wrong if one female slave was brought to cook the food. He replied that the public revenue was the right of God's poor and humble, that it would not be becoming in him to expend any of it in buying female slaves, and that if she (the queen) would have patience, the Almighty would reward her after death.

"The world is a dream in front of open eyes; with such a dream the hearts of the good will not mingle!"

In the year 663 (A. D. 1264), Sultan Nasir-ood-deen became sick, and on the 11th Jumadee-ool-Awul, 664 (A. D. 1265), from this world he went to the other world. He had no offspring. He reigned nineteen years, three months, and some days.

AN ACCOUNT OF SLUTAN GHUYAS-OOD-DEEN BALBUN.

This king was from among the bought Chihulganee slaves of Sultan Shums-ood-deen Elthemis. After the death of Sultan Nasir-ood-deen, in the year 664 (A. D. 1265), he ascended the throne of Dehli. He conducted the affairs of state in a way similar to foreign kings. He brought into his hands all the country that Sultan Shums-ood-deen had held; he spread the carpet of justice, giving justice according to Mahomedan law. He fixed the orders of government so securely, that no one could move them. In a short time all his country became flourishing; on the highways there was no fear; the sepoys and Ryuts lived happily. He was a very good king. With great honour, he was strong in experience, and he did everything well.

How good a thing is wisdom! Oh God! do not deprive this world of it.

At the commencement of his reign, he gave Lahore, Mooltan, and Sind, in charge of his son, Sultan Mahomed, whose heart was much given to mix with religious men. On this account he always visited Shaikh Buha-ood-deen Zukreeya, and Shaikh Fureed-ood-deen Gunj Shukur. He was a most valiant man; his disposition was bountiful; he was the friend of the wise, such as Ameer Khusrow, and Ameer Husun, inhabitants of Delhi. These two men were always present in his service. They received pay and presents in the rank of courtiers. The Sultan greatly approved of their poetry and prose. Sultan Mahomed was so well bred, that if he sat the entire day and night in the assembly, he would not raise one leg above the other. His oath was, "By God!" (Hukka!) His heart was always upon the priests and men of learning. It is said that Shaikh Oosman Murwundee was among the priests of Sind. He went to Mooltan, when the Sultan showed him great respect, making him an offering. He asked him to settle in Mooltan; to this the priest would not agree.

It is related that one night Shaikh Oosman, and Shaikh Sudr-ood-deen the son of Shaikh Buha-ood-deen Zukreeya were in an assembly, where, by the extacy occasioned by hearing the song of poetry, they became transported, and all commenced capering. The Sultan, arising, put his hand to his breast, and cried. They say that a daughter of Sultan Shums-ood-deen was his wife at that time, and in this condition he (the Sultan) three times declared her divorced. After divorce, marriage with her could not again be performed with the Sultan, until she had been married to some one else (Untalah.) On this account she was married to Shaikh Sudr-ood-deen. After she had gone to his house, the king's attendants told him to declare the divorce. The lady then said to him: "I have left the house of that bad man, and come near you: it will not be proper before God for you to place me in his hands again." Sudr-ood-deen replied: "I will not be inferior to a woman"; and he did not declare the divorce. The Sultan, being angry, determined to be revenged upon him.

Sultan Mahomed twice sent men to Shaikh Sundee Shirazee, saying that in Mooltan he would make him a place of residence; that he would buy a village for him, which he might dedicate to pious uses: but Shaikh Sundee, on account of his old age, would not come; and each time he sent his reply in verse, written by his own hand; and he recommended Ameer Khusrow to him. In his time, many good, clever men attended the royal assemblies.

The Sultan went every three years to his father at Delhi, and after remaining there one year he returned.

In the year Hijree 683 (A. D. 1284), Gungeez Khan sent Kutlugh Khan and Taimoor, with a large force, towards Hindoostan, which, having crossed the river Neelab, entered the boundary of Lahore. Sultan Mahomed, with 30,000 horsemen, went towards Lahore. A battle was fought by the two armies. By the desire of God, in that battle Sultan Mahomed drank the sherbet of death, and he went to the Garden of Paradise. Notwithstanding this, defeat came to Taimoor and Kutlugh Khan, and they fled.

Sultan Balbun then appointed Kaikhusrow, the son of Sultan Mahomed, to Mooltan and Sind. The Sultan always remained in sorrow for his son; so much so, that in the year Hijree 685 (A. D. 1286) he departed to the world above.

A HISTORY OF SULTAN JULAL-OOD-DEEN KHULJEE.

He was the son of Pheroz Kuluj, and in the service of Sultan Ghuyas-ood-deen. The tribe of Kulaj came from the race of Khalij Khan, and he was the son-in-law of Gungeez Khan.

Julal-ood-deen was superior to all in bravery and generosity; in wisdom and deliberation there was no one equal to him. By degrees he ascended and sat upon the king's throne. In the year 688 (A. D. 1289), in Delhi, his name was read in the sermon; and by their own free will, or by force, he got the Ameers under him. In 693 (A. D. 1293), Julal-ood-deen having gone to Lahore, he gave Mooltan and Ooch to Urkulee Khan, his centre son. He appointed Nusrut Khan to Sind, settling the revenues of that country upon Urkulee Khan. Urkulee Khan was of happy temper, and a brave man. During his stay at Mooltan, he twice visited Sind, where he punished with his own hands all robbers and disturbers of the peace. The whole of Sind remained under him. In the year 695 (A. D. 1295), he drank the sherbet of martyrdom at the hands of Sultan Ula-ood-deen, his nephew and son-in-law.

AN ACCOUNT OF SULTAN ULA-OOD-DEEN.

In the latter days of the year 695 (A. D. 1295), he sat on the throne of the Sultan of Delhi, reading his name in the sermon. He distributed jewels, horses, and elephants, to so many, that the people, struck with his generosity, became submissive to him; but he having slain his uncle and father-in-law, they looked upon him with disgust. In the beginning of the year 696 (A. D. 1296), putting everything else on one side, he turned his mind to Mooltan, because Urkulee Khan was there. He sent his brother Ulug Khan, with 40,000 horse, there by forced marches. On his arrival, he surrounded the city. After three months, the people of the town became much alarmed from distress, and one night the Mooltanees, leaving Urkulee Khan, went outside the city, and had a meeting with Ulug Khan. Urkulee Khan, driven by compulsion, asked for quarters through a priest, Shaikh Rookn-ood-deen, and he left Mooltan. Sultan Ula-ood-deen retained Nusrut Khan in charge of Mooltan, Ooch, Bukkur, Sehwistan, and Tatta, with 10,000 horsemen, giving orders that he should go through the whole country under his charge, and root out all disturbers of the peace, and thus give confidence to the people. He was also ordered to leave a man of trust in every city, and to make Mooltan his own head quarters. In the commencement of 697 (A. D. 1297), news came that the Moguls from Sijestan had arrived at Sehwistan, looting all property, and surrounding the city; the men in Sehwistan were unable to fight, and placed their faces in the direction of flight. The Mogul force, having taken the place, strengthened it. Nusrut Khan, hearing this news, immediately shipped in boats a large force, with war apparatus, and arrived with these at Sehwistan. The Mogul force, coming forth from the fort, set a light to the fire of battle. In short, they fled, and then the royal army returned, arriving at Bukkur. At that time an order came from Sultan Ula-ood-deen, to say that Ulug Khan being nominated to take Guzerat, he was to march with half the Sind army to that country, by the way of Jaisulmere. When Ulug reached that city with his force, he conquered it, slaying many Kafirs. Leaving 200 men in the fort of Jaisulmere, with the rest of his force he joined the Guzerat force. In the year Hijree 700 (A. D. 1300), Sultan Ula-ood-deen drew the sword of his sovereignty, cutting down all the evil-minded of his country. The borders of the territories under his government to the east, west, and south, extended to the ocean, viz. Bengal, Deccan, Guzerat, and Sind, in a northerly direction to the waters of Neelab. In each province he settled a Hakeem, a Dewan, Ameen, and a Kazee. He made such arrangements, that fresh news came every week from all the provinces to the king. When all the affairs of the State had reached such a degree of perfection, then, in like manner as when things have reached the height of perfection, it may be expected that they will decline, so, on the 6th of Shuwal 710 (A. D. 1310), he tied up his requisites for the journey.

AN ACCOUNT OF SULTAN GHUYAS-OOD-DEEN.

Towards the end of his reign, Sultan Ula-ood-deen placed Ghazee Mulik, with 10,000 horse, in Daibulpoor, to expel the Moguls of Gungeez Khan. He had given to him (Ghazee Mulik) in Jageer, Mooltan, Ooch, and Sind: when the Sultan died he was there.

After the death of Sultan Ula-ood-deen, his sons, by their excessive neglect, indolence, and debauchery, did not turn their hearts to matters of state. On this account, disturbances found their way throughout the kingdom. At the time when neglect has become great, their wealth becomes small. So the wealth of the family of Ula fell. Kootb-ood-deen (the son of Ula-ood-deen) was of weak intellect. By some of his attendants, his head was cut off, at the instigation of Khusrow Khan, and he sat in his place on the throne. Khusrow Khan gave great honours to the Kafirs, and debauched men. He gave amongst these the treasuries of Sultan Ula-ood-deen and Kootb-ood-deen: on this account the Kafirs in Delhi became very strong, oppressing the Musulmans. Then Fakeer Mulik, secretly leaving Delhi, turned his face towards Mooltan. In a few days he got over the road, and finding his father, opened all the condition of Delhi to him. Ghazee Mulik and Fakeer Mulik were both brave men. To give assistance to Islam, and to take revenge on the Kafirs, they drew the sword of battle from the scabbard, and bound the girdle of war round the loins of their lives. They asked God for victory, and collecting the troops in Mooltan and Sind, they marched on Delhi. They arrived near it with 3,000 horse, all of whom had seen much service. When Khusrow Khan heard that they had come so near, collecting a large force, he sent it forth. The two bodies came in front of each other. The secrets of God are revealed!— that is to say, God gave the victory to Ghazee Mulik. The force of the Kafirs was beaten, and fled: many were killed; a few with great difficulty reached the fort. The following day Khusrow Khan, with a large force, went out, and drew up his men in battle array. The force of Ghazee Khan, to fight with their enemies, drew the sword of retaliation from the scabbard, and fought. In about one hour the army of the Kafirs was made grass by the sword of revenge; so much so, that the dead were in heaps. Khusrow Khan, with broken heart, turned his face in the direction of flight. Ghazee Mulik and Fakeer Mulik, from the field of battle, went near the city. At midnight, the governor of the town, the nobles, and the Kutwal, came and delivered the keys of the fort to Ghazee Mulik. The next morning he, with a large attendance, entered the city. In the Dewan Huzoor Sitoon he spread out the bedding of lamentation, in sorrow for Ula-ood-deen and Kootb-ood-deen. For three days he did this, agreeably to custom. He had it proclaimed in the town, that if any of the family of Ula-ood-deen or of Kootb-ood-deen were left and would come to him, he would place him on the throne; adding that he himself would bind the girdle of service round the loins of his life, and do service. After much inquiry, none being found, then the Ameers, the army, the Syuds, the men of letters, the priests, and all the people, agreed that Ghazee Mulik was worthy of the kingdom, because he had erased so many letters of dissension and trouble from the pages of the country, and he had given strength to Islam. In the year 720 (A. D. 1320), the title of Sultan Ghuyas-ood-deen Tughlug Shah was conferred on Ghazee Mulik. All the Ameers agreed to obey him. They placed him on the throne of the Sultanut of Delhi, and his name was read in the sermon. The title of Sultan Mahomed Shah was given to his son Fakeer Mulik. When Sultan Ghuyas-ood-deen left Mooltan to go to Delhi, the Soomrah tribe came and took Tatta. Sultan Ghuyas-ood-deen sent Mulik Taj-ood-deen to Mooltan, Khwaja Khuteer to Bukkur, and Mulik Ali Sher to Sehwistan.

In the year 723 (A. D. 1323), Sultan Ghuyas-ood-deen appointed his son Sultan Mahomed Shah as his heir, resigning the throne to him. He obtained from the Ameers a written deed, by which they agreed to be obedient to Sooltan Mahomed Shah. In the year 725 (A. D. 1324), the lamp of life of Ghuyas-ood-deen was blown out by the cold wind of death.

AN ACCOUNT OF SULTAN MAHOMED SHAH, THE SON OF SULTAN GHUYAS-OOD-DEEN SHAH.

When Sultan Mahomed Shah sat upon his hereditary throne, he spread justice throughout the country. On this account, his goodness was spoken of in all the land. In 727 (A. D. 1326) he appointed Khusrow Khan to Sind. After that he went to Dowlutabad, making his throne there. He remained there two years, during which period Khusrow Khan came to Mooltan from Bukkur, and, assembling the Mooltanese and Beloochees, intended to be rebellious. When Sultan Mahomed Shah heard of this, in the year 728 (A. D. 1327), he quickly arrived at Mooltan. Then Khusrow Khan, who was thus full of ingratitude, went to fight with its patron. When the forces met, that portion of the royal army which was in advance attacked and defeated Khusrow Khan, and cutting off his head, brought it to the Sultan. From fear of the Sultan, all Khusrow Khan's troops dispersed. The Sultan gave orders to make a river of the blood of the Mooltanese. The foot soldiers drew their swords to slay them; when the priest of Islam, Shaikh Rookn-ood-deen, to intercede for them, went to the Sultan's Durbar, and uncovering his head, he stood there. In about one hour the Sultan acceded to the priest's wishes, excusing the blood of the Mooltanese, as a punishment. The Sultan, placing men in whom he had confidence, in Mooltan, Bukkur, and Sehwistan, returned in the latter days of that year. In the year 744 (A. D. 1343) it entered the understanding of the Sultan, that it was not fit for him to reign as the King of Delhi, without the orders of the Abbasee Khaliph. He therefore secretly made homage to him. He exaggerated this subject greatly, directing the Musulmans not to say the special prayers for Friday on that day, until he had sent Mulik Rufeen to the Khaliph in Egypt. When the Khaliph sent him a standard and a Khilat, the Sultan was very happy at this, giving the people who came much honour, and great presents; he had the Khaliph's name read in the sermon, and he directed that his own should follow this.

In the year 751 (A. D. 1350), Sultan Mahomed Shah left Delhi, and turning the reins of his intention towards Guzerat, he quickly came to Gurnal.* There a royal slave, named Tuin, who was in rebellion, ran away, and went to Cambay. When the Sultan, following him, reached that place, he fled to the people of Jhareja. The Sultan, intending to pursue him, went towards Tatta. He halted at Hukree, on the sea side, to collect his troops. He was then taken with fever, and all the difficulties of the road came before his mind. Leaving Hukree, he reached Koondul, and stopping there, the disease left him. At Koondul some of his household joined him, by way of the river. The Sultan was very much pleased at their arrival, giving quantities of many things to his army, and, accompanied by many people, he marched towards Tatta. Tuin, who had fled to, and remained at Tatta, hearing of this, became confused, and at a loss what to do. When the Sultan got 14 kos from Tatta, by chance the Mohurrum commenced. The Sultan halted and fasted. The following day the fever again attacked him; the doctors gave remedies, but they availed not, so much so that on the 21st of Mohurrum, 752 (A. D. 1351), Sultan Mahomed Shah left this transitory world, to go to that country which remains for ever.

ACCOUNT OF SULTAN PHEROZ SHAH.

When Sultan Mahomed Shah saw the signs of death approaching, he named Pheroz Shah, the son of his uncle,— he who bore the marks of nobility on his forehead,— as his heir, giving him his last wishes respecting his country and his army. After this, taking the apparatus of this passing world, he went to that world which is everlasting.

All the courtiers and nobles paid their homage to Pheroz Shah at that place. On the 24th of Mohurrum, 752 (A. D. 1351), he, ascending the throne, summoned all to his presence, making them all happy by his justice and liberality.

Tuin, hearing of the death of Sultan Mahomed Shah, collected the men of Soomrah, Jhareja, and Summah, and got to the rear of the army. Sultan Pheroz Shah, hearing of this, named 2,000 men, and these going all night, crossed the river, and met Tuin, and those who were with him. There was a great fight, when Tuin turned his face towards flight. The following day the Soomrah men again fought, but they met with defeat, many of them being slain. After this, from near Tatta, the Sultan turned his head, and marched towards Delhi, ordering that the troops should not march more than 5 kos a day. He built a fort at Langerah Lake, leaving Nusseer there, with 1,000 horse. He appointed Mulik Behram as the Foujdar of that country. On reaching Sehwistan, he made rulers there, Mulik Ali Shen and Mulik Tuf Kafooree. The Sultan made a pilgrimage to the sacred threshold of Shah Baz Kulundur, and to another holy place. On the attendants at these he settled daily salaries. From this he came to Bukkur, where he remained twenty days. He appointed Mulik Rookn-ood-deen his deputy there; making Mulik Abdool Uzeez Bareed the Dewan, and naming eighty unmarried men to take care of the fort. To Mulik Rookn-ood-deen he gave the title of Ikhlas Khan, and leaving all the arrangements of Sind in his hands, he departed. At every large place he came to he behaved liberally to the people, and made them happy. In this manner he arrived at Delhi in the month of Rujub, 752 (A. D. 1351). When he sat with great power on the throne of the Sultanut, he gave an imperial assembly, when he made all happy, by giving them presents, and to the great and small he afforded justice. On the 5th of Sufur, 753 (A. D. 1352), he went to visit his country. All the great Zemindars of the districts which he went to, came and promised to be obedient. In the year 754 (A. D. 1353), he went to hunt at Kulanoor, in the country near the hills. On returning, he built a handsome palace on the banks of the waters of the Suruswutee. He here gave the title of Shaikool Islamee to Shaikh Sudr-ood-deen, the son of Shaikh Buha-ood-deen Zukreeya, giving him leave to depart to his country. After this the Sultan took Bengal into his hands. In the year 772 (A. D. 1370) he went to Nuggurkot. When he reached the country about the hills, the people brought him ice, which had been made in pans; on seeing which the Sultan said— "When Sultan Mahomed Shah formerly came here, the people brought ice to him, that he might make sherbet; but if I had not been with him, he would not have drank this sherbet, saying that he would only drink it with Pheroz Shah. Thus, as he was so kind to me in those days, I will not drink the sherbet now until I have distributed, in his name, one hundred camel-loads of sugar in sherbet"; and he did so. Having conquered Nuggurkot, he proceeded towards Tatta, on reaching which, Jam Khair-ood-deen, who was the chief, retired to the fort which stands in the water, from which he stopped the royal army for some time. The

Sultan, on account of the scarcity of grain and forage, the floods of water, and the number of musquitoes, left this as it was, and went to Guzerat, remaining there during the rains. Removing Nizam-ool-Moolk, he made Zufur Khan the governor of this country. He afterwards went in the direction of Tatta. Arriving there, Jam Khair-ood-deen asked for pardon, and came into the service of the Sultan, who looked upon him with the eye of kindness, directing that he and the other Zemindars of that country should be taken to Delhi. When Jam Khair-ood-deen reached Sehwistan, he planned in his heart to obtain his liberty in this manner— that when on the line of march, as they went along near the bank of the river, he would get into a boat, and so escape. The men who were in charge of him, finding out this, conveyed it to the Sultan, who gave orders to put irons on the Jam's legs, and so to take him to Delhi, where the Sultan went with his army some time afterwards. He gave a Khilat to Jam Choonah, the son of Jam Khair-ood-deen, placed him over Tatta, and gave him leave to go there. This Sultan, for thirty-eight years and some months, ruled the kingdom with great power. On the 18th of Rumzan, 790 (A. D. 1388), he received death.

AN ACCOUNT OF SULTAN GHUYAS-OOD-DEEN TUGHLUG SHAH, THE SON OF FUTTEH KHAN, THE SON OF PHEROZ SHAH.

On the 18th day of Rumzan, in the year 790 (A. D. 1388), according to the will of Sultan Pheroz Shah, and by the aid of the Ameers, he ascended the throne of the Sultanut, in the palace of Pherozabad, when the people gave him the title of Sultan Ghuyas-ood-deen Tughlug Shah.

Mahomed Shah, the son of Sultan Pheroz Shah, having displeased his father, had been sent to take charge of a distant country. On seeing Ghuyas-ood-deen placed on the throne, he became at enmity with him and the Ameers, and, with the intention of taking the country, he went towards Delhi. The chief nobles, with Tughlug Shah, marched forth to arrest his progress, in the month of Zilhuj. They came to Sirmoor, in the hills. There were with Tughlug Shah one lakh of horsemen. These went in pursuit of Sultan Mahomed Shah, and without doing anything they returned, and when the Sultan got back to Delhi, he still committed errors, from his youth. The country became without arrangement, dissensions began to arise, and from want of ability he imprisoned his brethren.

Aboo Bukur, the son of Zufur Khan, his nephew, from fear concealed himself, and secretly went away. Mulik Rookn-ood-deen, the Wuzeer, and other Ameers, being his friends, went off with him. They killed Mulik Mobaruk Kubeer at Pherozabad, Delhi, near the gateway of the king's palace. Sultan Ghuyas-ood-deen, seeing the strength of these rebellious people, went with Khan Jehan outside the gate, which was over the waters of the Jumna. Mulik Rookn-ood-deen, being there, set upon and seized him, and Khan Jehan killed them both, and placed their heads over that gateway.

This took place on the 21st of Sufur, in the year 791 (A. D. 1389). Sultan Ghuyas-ood-deen reigned for five months and three days.

AN ACCOUNT OF THE REIGN OF ABOO BUKUR SHAH GHOREE.

After these occurrences, the Ameers, being without wisdom, gave the title of Sultan Aboo Bukur Shah to Aboo Bukur, the son of Zufur Khan, the son of Sultan Pheroz Shah. The dignity of Wuzeer was conferred on Mulik Rookn-ood-deen. Shortly after, it became known to Aboo Bukur Shah, that Mulik Rookn-ood-deen had plotted with the nobles of Sultan Pheroz Shah to upset him, and sit on the throne himself. He (Aboo) anticipated him, and, with the concurrence of the nobles, killed Mulik Rookn-ood-deen. After this he gained strength. It was then heard that the tribe of Meer Sudhs of Samanah had killed their Hakeem, looting his family, and sending his head to Mahomed Shah at Nuggurkot. Then Mahomed Shah, leaving that place, went to Samanah, and in the month of Rubee-ool-Awul he styled himself king there. The men of Meer Sadh, and the Zemindars of the country near the hills, did homage to him. Some of the Ameers and chief men of Delhi, leaving Aboo Bukur Shah, came to him, so much so, that he had collected 20,000 horsemen, with footmen out of number, when he left Samanah to go to Delhi. As he approached that city, his horsemen had increased to 50,000. On the 25th of Rubee-ool-Awul, 791 (A. D. 1389), he reached Jehan Nooma. On the 2nd of Jumadee-ool-Awul, in the streets of Pherozabad, the troops of Aboo Bukur met and fought with those of Mahomed Shah. On that day Bahadoor Khan, Mewatee, with many men, entering the city, gave great strength to Aboo Bukur, who the next day, having prepared everything for battle, fought with, and defeated Mahomed Shah, who, crossing the Jumna with 2,000 men, fled to the Doab. Again, in Shaban of the same year, he raised his standard, proposing to go to Delhi; he came and fought with Aboo Bukur, but being defeated, he again ran away.

"Until the fit time for doing anything comes, the assistance of friends is of no avail!"

Aboo Bukur pursued Mahomed Shah for 3 kos, and then returned to Delhi. Mahomed Shah went then to Chulpur, and getting together many men, in the month Rumzan of that same year, he wrote Firmans, which he sent to Lahore, Mooltan, and other large towns, directing the people to slay all who belonged to Pheroz Shah. Wherever these orders were received, many people were killed, much property was looted, and the world became wonderfully divided. In short, by seduction, he induced the Ameers to become enemies to Aboo Bukur, and they secretly corresponded with Mahomed Shah. Aboo Bukur, becoming as one without hands or feet, fled to Mewat. He reigned for one year and a half.

AN ACCOUNT OF SULTAN MAHOMED SHAH, THE SON OF SULTAN PHEROZ SHAH.

On the 16th of Rumzan, 792 (A. D. 1389), he became Sultan. The first thing he did was to turn out of the city all the attendants and slaves of Pheroz Shah, who had been his enemies. He killed many, proclaiming, that if any of them remained in the city, his blood would be upon his own neck. He entered the city with great state, taking much care of the country and property. When he had attained great power, it came across him that it was not fit to neglect Aboo Bukur, therefore he sent his youngest son, Hoomayoon Khan, with many Ameers, and a large force against him. When these got near Kotulah, where Aboo Bukur Shah remained, Bahadoor Khan Nahur, who was born in the house of Pheroz Shah (by whose assistance Aboo Bukur had collected many men), fell upon the troops of Hoomayoon by night, but Aboo Bukur, being defeated, retreated to the fort of Kotulah. When Sultan Mahomed Shah heard of this, he went there by forced marches, and surrounded the fort. Then Aboo Bukur Shah, being helpless, asked for pardon. Sultan Mahomed confined him in the fort of Mewat, where he died. Sultan Mahomed went to Delhi, then to Guzerat; from thence to Bengal, where he stayed a long time, punishing the evil doers and disturbers of the peace. He remained at Mahomedabad, a fort built in his time. After a time he fell sick, when Bahadoor Khan Nahur looted some villages near Delhi. The Sultan, hearing of this, though unwell, marched towards Mewat. When he drew near Kotulah, Bahadoor Khan came forth to meet him. He was defeated, and took refuge in Kotulah, but not having strength, he fled. The Sultan then returned to Mahomedabad, to see some works which he had in hand. His sickness increased, and on the 17th of Rubee-ool-Awul, 796 (A. D. 1393), he went to heaven. He reigned six years and seven months.

AN ACCOUNT OF SULTAN ULA-OOD-DEEN SIKUNDUR SHAH.

This was the centre son of Sultan Mahomed; his title was Hoomayoon. When Sultan Mahomed Shah died, he mourned three days for him. On the 19th of Rubee-ool-Awul, in that year, with the consent of the nobles and men of weight, he sat on the throne. He confirmed in their situations and salaries all who had been in office under Mahomed Shah. By chance, on the 5th of Jumadee-ool-Awul, he was taken ill and died.

"In this world, if there is a king's throne, what is it, oh my friend!
For no one is able to eat of his food, except his own portion!"

AN ACCOUNT OF SULTAN NASIR-OOD-DEEN MAHOMED SHAH.

This was the youngest son of Sultan Mahomed Shah. When Sultan Ula-ood-deen died, some of the nobles went away towards their Jageers, without asking permission to leave. When Khan Jehan, the chief minister of the late Sultan Mahomed Shah, heard of this, by argument he brought them back to the city. On the 20th of Jumadee-ool-Awul, 796 (A. D. 1393), by the exertions of the Ameers and influential men, Sultan Nasir-ood-deen ascended the throne, in the palace of Hoomayoon. He received the title of Sultan Nasir-ood-deen Mahomed Shah. He confirmed in their situations and salaries the chief minister, the nobles, and officials, the same as they had enjoyed under his father. He gave the title of Moogurub Khan to Moogurub Mulik, naming him as his heir. To Khan Jehan he gave the title of Sultanut Ushruf, giving into his keeping the country from Kanoge to Behar, and he dismissed him, attended by a large force. The government of all that country he left to him. Khan Jehan became very powerful there, getting all the Zemindars under his authority, and rebuilding forts which had been destroyed; and the Kings of Bengal, and other neighbouring chiefs, presented gifts and rarities to Mahomed Shah, as they had formerly been in the habit of giving to Pheroz Shah.

In that year the Sultan gave orders to Sarung Khan to take Daibulpoor, Mooltan, and Sind. At that time Shakha Khokur was creating disturbances at and about Lahore; upon hearing of which Sarung Khan went in that direction. As he drew near, Shakha Khokur went forth with many men, and at 12 koss from Lahore the two forces met and fought. By the kindness of God, the wind of victory struck the standards of Sarung Khan. Shakha Khokur, being defeated, fled to the hills of Jumoo. On the day following, Sarung Khan took possession of the fort of Lahore, and all it contained. He gave the title of Adil Khan to his brother Mulik Khundoo, and leaving him there, he himself marched upon Daibulpoor.

After this, in Shaban of the same year, 796 (A. D. 1393), Sultan Mahomed Shah, leaving Moogurub Khan, with men of trust, and a large force, at Delhi, went in the direction of Gwalior, on approaching which, Mulik Ula-ood-deen Dharwal, Moobaruk Khan the son of Mulik Rajoo, and Muloo the brother of Sarung Khan, were projecting some treachery. Suadut Khan, hearing of this, he seized and hung Mulik Ula-ood-deen and Moobaruk Khan. Muloo, being seized with fear on hearing of this, went to the Sultan, but seeing that he was angry, by soft artifice he withdrew, and leaving the army, returned to Delhi, where he made many enemies to the king. The Sultan and Suadut Khan came and surrounded the city, when there was daily fighting for three months. The agents of Moogurub Khan then by deceit induced the Sultan to leave Suadut Khan, and to enter the city. When Suadut Khan saw that his plans were destroyed, and that it would be difficult for him alone to take the place, the more so as it was the rainy season, he broke up from thence, and went to Pherozabad. On arriving there, with the concurrence of good men, in Rubee-ool-Awul, 797 (A. D. 1394), he brought Nusrut Shah, the son of Pheroz Khan, the son of Sultan Pheroz Shah, from Mewat, and put him on the throne at Pherozabad, with the title of Nasir-ood-deen Nusrut Shah.

The royal Ameers were annoyed at seeing Nusrut Shah so quickly placed on the throne: on this account they attacked Suadut Khan when he was unprepared. He, being unable to fight, made his escape, seeking refuge with Moogurub Khan, who seized and killed him. After this, the Ameers, with Nusrut Shah, viz. Mahomed Zufur Khan, Shubab-ood-deen Fuzl-ool-lah Beekhee, and the slaves of Pheroz Shah, being without remedy, paid fresh homage to him, and took much country.

Sultan Nasir-ood-deen Mahomed Shah was very much distressed at the perfidy of the Ameers and the army— he did not know what to do. There was constant fighting between the troops of the two parties. In the year 798 (A. D. 1395), enmity arose between Sarung Khan, who was over Daibulpoor and Mooltan, and Khizur Khan, the Hakeem of Mooltan, when the adherents of Mulik Bhittee, joining, gave strength to Sarung Khan, and he took Mooltan. In Rumzan 799 (A. D. 1396), he went to Delhi with a large force. The nobles, collecting their forces, marched forth to drive him back. In short, in the month of Mohurrum 800 (A. D. 1397), the two forces met, and Sarung Khan, being defeated, retreated to Mooltan. On account of the enmity of the two princes, the country had become divided, and without arrangement at that time. In the month Rubee-ool-Awul 800 (A. D. 1397), Meerza Peer Mahomed, the grandson of Ameer Taimoor Saheb Kiran, crossing the waters of the Punjab, surrounded the fort of Ooch. Mulik Ali, the Hakeem there on the part of Sarung Khan, held his post, fighting for one month, when Sarung Khan sent 4,000 horsemen to the rescue, with Mulik Taj-ood-deen. On hearing of this, the Meerza, leaving Ooch, marched to meet him. The Mulik was defeated, when Meerza at once advanced upon, and surrounded Mooltan. Sarung Khan fought him daily for six months, after which he asked for quarters, and surrendered. Having conquered Mooltan, Meerza Peer Mahomed remained some time in that country.

When, in Shuwal 800 (A. D. 1397), the royal Ameers heard of the doings and of the strength of the Meerza, they assembled at the tomb of Shaikh Kootb-ood-deen Ruktirjor Kakee, and entering into a compact amongst themselves, they became superior in strength to their king, being united amongst themselves. The people of Sind ceased attending to the orders of the Kings of Delhi, when Saheb Kiran, following his grandson Meerza Peer Mahomed, arrived at Mooltan in Sufur 801 (A. D. 1398), when he administered justice to all who had been confined by Peer Mahomed. After this, the Hakeems of Sind did not obey the orders of the Kings of Delhi— every one made himself strong on his own account, in the manner I now relate.

AN ACCOUNT OF THE RULES OF THE MEN OF SOOMRAH AND SUMMAH.

I have previously written that Sultan Mahomed Ghazee came from the seat of the Sultanut Ghuznee, and throwing the noose of subjection over the battlements of the fort of Mooltan, he captured it. After this he sent his agents to Sind, who occupied that country. After the death of Sultan Mahomed, the Sultanut descended to his offspring.

When the turn of government came to Ubdoor Rusheed, the son of Sultan Mahomed,— who, spreading the carpet of pleasure, his heart was occupied in festivals and things of delight,— he did not turn his mind to the matters of the state. On this account the people at many of the distant borders began to disobey orders, they took their heads from out of the ring of submission: in short, at that time men of Soomrah collected in great numbers near Thuree, and placed Soomrah the son of Chundur on the throne of the Sultanut of Sind. (The tribe of Soomrah had its name from this Soomrah.) He for a long time was the Sirdar of his tribe. He cleared away from the borders of his country all the thorns and refuse, the breeders of dissension, and the disobedient. Zemindar Sad lived in that country, in much power. Soomrah laid the foundation of a connexion with him, and married his daughter. He had a son born to him called Bhoongar, who sat on the throne of the hereditary Sultanut, on the death of Soomrah. During his time he extended his rule. At the latter end of his age he was taken ill, and he gave his life to the angel of death.

His son Doda, succeeding him, took the duties of king. For some years, with great power he managed the country, extending his power to Nusurpoor. He died in the prime of life, leaving a young son called Singhar, and a daughter named Thuree. This Thuree for some time conducted the duties of the government, having the Ryuts under her command. When Singhar grew up, he ascended the throne. He made good arrangements for the country and property; to such men as were powerful and disobedient he gave punishment. Throwing the bridle of the horse of his intentions towards Kutch, he took Nanik Nai from that country. Some years after, he travelled from this world to the other, leaving no children. His wife Humoon lived at, and issued her orders from, the fort of Duhkah. She sent her brothers to govern at Thoor and Thuree. A short time after this, some of the brethren of Doda, who had concealed themselves, came forth, and took out by the roots these brothers of Humoon. One of these, named Peethoo (a descendant of Doda), was joined by many men. Such as set up claims to the throne he destroyed. Ascending it himself, he reigned as long as he lived, and after his death Khaira ruled the country, doing so in a very proper manner; all his acts were approved of. Some years from this, the sun of his life went to the sunset of death. With the concurrence of the Ameers, Khufeef succeeded him, and sat on the throne of the kingdom. Having made good arrangements for the country in his hands, he, with heart at ease, went and remained at Tatta. During his government, the Ryuts, and all the other people of Sind were relieved from thieves, and disturbers of the peace; all were happy and contented. By chance, it one day came into his mind that it was not proper for him to be always merely sitting on the throne; that it was better to spend some time in the Shikargahs, the jungles, and plains, which had become green from rain, and where the animals were grazing happily. After this, having collected many men, he marched against the Beloochees, the Sodahs, and the Jharejas. On reaching their borders, Runmul Sodah, Ram Rai Jhareja, and Mehran

Belooch, being introduced by the Ameers, and other men of weight, came and made great offerings. Khufeef, presenting them with handsome presents in return, made them very happy; he then gave them their dismissal.

He proposed returning to Tatta the following morning, but at that time a Belooch came, complaining that the thieves of the tribe of Summah had looted his tribe, taking everything they possessed. On hearing this, Khufeef was much astonished; and at the instant, mounting, with those who were with him, he started, and quickly came against this tribe. He took all the property which had been robbed from the Beloochees, and those men who had disobeyed orders, and acted in this manner, he punished with severity. His arrangements were such in all the country under him, from Kutch to Nusurpoor, that in the whole of that space none during his reign disobeyed his orders; if they did so, he gave them to the sword. When he found that there were none to give trouble, he was at ease, and came to Tatta. In his time all the people, the sepoys, the Ameers, the Ryuts, &c. were very happy. He lived a long while at Tatta, till, from this world, he journeyed to the next world.

After the death of Khufeef, the people, the men of weight under government, and those out of employ, agreeing that it was proper, raised Doda, the son of Oomur, and the grandson of Peethoo, to the throne of the Sultanut, in his place. When all the affairs of the state were firm in his hands, Singhar, a Zemindar, came to pay his yearly taxes. He became acquainted with Doda. This had lasted some time, when one day he spoke of Kutch in the following terms in his presence; saying that he had heard that the Summah tribe had determined to come to Tatta to take it, and that he should be prepared for this. On hearing this, Doda, collecting forces out of number, marched to Kutch, and he severely twisted the ears of those people. Then a man of the Summah tribe, named Lakhuh, came as ambassador, bringing presents and Kutch horses, making offering of these, and asking pardon for their sins. Doda, with great kindness, gave him presents in money, a horse, and a Khilat, allowing him then to depart. From thence, with heart at rest, he came to Thuree, where he spent a long time. All the people and Ryuts were so completely under his hands, that without orders from him they did nothing. When at Thuree, Runmul Sodah came, and making his Salaam, urged as a petition, that in the time of Khufeef, the Jut Beloochees paid tribute; but that now it seemed, that they through ignorance had taken their heads from out of the noose of submission. He added, that having heard of this, he made him (Doda) acquainted with it; and that it seemed advisable that a force should be put under him, which he would take against, and thus, making them pay up their arrears of tribute from the days of Khufeef to the present time, he would bring it to him.

The reason of his speaking in this way was, that formerly a feud existed between him (Runmul) and the Jharejas, when a fight had taken place between the parties, in which great numbers of Runmul's men had been killed and wounded. So he told as above to Doda, to enable him to have his revenge upon them. Doda, being of a good heart, gave him encouragement, keeping him near him; he also sent to call the men of Jhareja. When his messengers got there, and told what Runmul had said, they came before them with their swords suspended from round their necks, making their Salaam, and declaring that they and all their families were the slaves of Doda, and that, if he ordered them all to be confined, they would not ask the reason why. Then, taking presents for Doda, they came to him in one week. His messengers, who accompanied them, having received good treatment at their hands, spoke in their favour. Doda said to Runmul: "These men, having great confidence, have sent only two of their tribe, and these have come to make their Salaam; you told me another story." Doda for some time detained Runmul, on the plea of its being the rainy season: but in Runmul's breast, that thorn pricked him; so one day, with great earnestness he insisted upon being allowed to depart, when Doda gave him his leave, and he went to his tribe. On getting there, he became rebellious. Seeing this, Ram Rai Jhareja and Mehran Belooch, quickly going to Doda, told him of this circumstance. It came into Doda's mind, that probably these men were doing what Runmul had done; therefore he determined in the first place to send two men to Runmul, who, ascertaining all the facts, might come and tell him. He despatched two men, at the time of whose arrival at the tribe, Runmul was absent, he having gone to the jungles to collect troops. His brethren did not pay the messengers any attention, speaking improperly before them. Runmul, hearing of the arrival of these, came and sat down with them in a friendly manner, but he shortly after spoke in an unbecoming way; when Doda's men said it was not right to talk in that way; that he had best cease collecting men, and go to Doda, when, if he had anything to complain of, he might do so to him: but however much they advised, it had no effect upon him, so Doda's people, rising, left him, and returning, told all the circumstances to Doda. He, hearing of this, collected many troops, and went against this people. Runmul, having also got together a large force, came out into the plain. The two parties met, and fought for six hours, at which time the men of both sides stood resolute. Many had fallen in that time of either party. Being exhausted, and night coming on, all the men sat down where they stood, spending the time in planning operations for the morrow. In the morning, the two forces recommenced fighting, when, by chance, an arrow struck Runmul in the throat, and his life went to hell. Great fear then took possession of his troops, because an army without a Sirdar is like a man without a head; so they turned their faces in the direction of flight, when Doda's men, pursuing them, slew great numbers, and looted extensively. The force being put to flight, Rai Sing and Jugmul came as ambassadors, bringing presents to Doda, and they obtained forgiveness of their faults. Doda after this went to Nusurpoor, the Zemindars, chief men, and Kazees of which place brought him presents, and Doda, accepting these, remained there some time, during which period Sahibuh the son of Runmul Sodah brought two fine handsome Kutchee horses as an offering, and paid his respects to him. He declared that his brethren had induced Runmul to turn his heart from, and become rebellious against him (Doda); so much so, that these men were even now disobedient, and that if a force went from the Sirkar, and punished them, they would not do so again, but would always bring presents. Doda, upon this, left Nusurpoor, and by forced marches came there; but after doing so, he discovered that the brethren of Runmul and others would not agree to have Sahibuh as their Sirdar, so he understood that it was on this account that he had brought him there. Doda then summoned all the tribe, telling them to agree to have Sahibuh as their chief, with all their hearts. By this order they agreed to do so, when Sahibuh presented Rs. 20,000 as a Nuzurana.

Doda, marching thence, came to Tatta. Remaining there, from thence he travelled to that other world.

On the death of Doda, his son Oomur, with the aid of the nobles, and other men of consequence, sat on the throne.

When his father's country came into his hands, he took to drinking wine, paying no attention to the country. On hearing this, the Summahs, the Sodahs, the Juts, and Beloochees, left off obeying his orders, becoming rebellious. When Moolah Hamed heard of this, he told Oomur of it, who, collecting a large force, went towards Kutch. On his approach, the Summahs, having collected many men, went out into the plain to meet him. There was fighting, in which the men of Summah were the strongest. Seeing this, and that his affairs would be ruined, Moolah Hamed called the Sirdars, to whom he gave presents, saying— "Tatta is far distant; money is scarce: if you fight well, and defeat the enemy, much property will come into our possession, which will be enough to enable us to return to Tatta." Hearing this, the spirits of the force were raised, and, making an attack on the enemy, they defeated them, when much plunder of every kind came into their hands. After this, the men of Summah, bringing Raja Jugunnath Todah (who had quitted his brethren in anger, and had come to Kutch) as their mediator, came to Oomur, making their Salaam, and bringing presents. Oomur, returning from thence quickly, went against the Sodahs, Juts, and Beloochees, all of whom, fearing the consequences, made their Salaam. He then, with confidence in his heart, went to Thuree, where he died.

At this time his son Doda was small; therefore the men of consequence put Chunur, the son of Oomur's brother, in his place. Chunur went out to make arrangements in his country. Having done this, and placed the troublesome on the edge of the sword, his heart being at ease, he sat down. At that time Doda attained puberty, so Chunur wished by some stratagem to get him into his hands, and to confine him; but hearing of this, Doda turned his face towards Ghuznee, and crossing the river, he came to a place, Dhuryachuh Naree Sung, close under Futtehpoor, where he saw a man coming along with a bundle of sticks for Hooka-snakes on his head. As this man drew near, all his entrails became visible to Doda. At this he was much astonished, so, calling the man to him, he lifted the bundle of pipes off his head, when nothing of the kind was to be seen: so, being greatly amazed, he put the bundle on the man's head again, when he beheld as before. He then knew that there must be some device in these sticks, and he purchased them, giving the man some money for them. Then, sitting down at the river's edge, he put the sticks one by one into the water. All went down with the stream, but one from amongst them went upwards against it: so, taking this one, he divided it at all the knots. He then put each knot into the water. All of these went down the stream, except one, in which the device was, and this one went up against the current; so taking this one, he kept it, and went to Ghuznee. At that time the king of that place, Sultan Mondood Shah, was ill from severe sickness, which was without cure; so, on his arrival there, Doda gave out that he was a doctor. Historians write that Sultan Mondood Shah's sickness was caused in this manner. One day he went to see a Shikargah under some hills, when by chance an animal started from before him. It was then the custom, that whoever an animal started in front of, he alone pursued it; so, in accordance with this custom, the Sultan rode after this animal alone for a long distance, but he did not kill it. From this exertion, great thirst and hunger came upon him; so, searching about, he found a stream of water near the foot of the hills. Having no cup or basin with him, being helpless, he put his mouth into the water, and drank; when, in doing so, he swallowed two small snakes, which went down into, and remained in his stomach. In two years these had grown large, and began causing him much pain. All the doctors of the country had physicked him, but none of them could make him well.

The Sultan was approaching to death, when at that time Doda arrived, saying he was a Hakeem, and that he had come from Sind to cure the king with his physic. The royal physicians, hearing this, laughed, saying: "What wisdom has this Sindee, that he should say he was able to give medicine to the king." One of the attendants told the king of the arrival of this Sindee, and how the royal doctors laughed at him. The Sultan, hearing of this, called and received him with distinction, saying "he had suffered from this sickness for a long time; that many Hakeems had given him medicine, but all without effect: now you have come, I am in hopes that I shall get well by your physic." Then Doda, stripping the Sultan, he placed that stick on his head, when he saw that two snakes were in his stomach. Then, removing the stick, he told the Sultan that he understood what was the matter with him, and that it was a very bad disease. He added that if he, the Sultan, would give him a written document, to the effect that if he died whilst under his care no blame should attach to him, that he would give him medicine. The Sultan at once wrote such a document, and putting his seal to it, gave it to Doda. Then Doda did not give the Sultan anything to eat for two days. On the third day, tying up his eyes, he placed the stick on his head, and having got two small fine iron hooks, he tied a silken line to them, and wrapping them up in bread, he gave one to the Sultan, who, having swallowed it, he, Doda, saw a snake take it. When he saw that it was well in the mouth of one of the snakes, he pulled it up, and brought it out; then again he did the same, and in like manner he took the other from out of the royal stomach. In about an hour the Sultan felt much relieved, so, untying his eyes, Doda showed him the two snakes, when, being very happy, the Sultan said: "Ask from me whatever you wish." Then Doda said: "I am a chief, but by his superior strength, Chunur has taken my father's country, and on this account I have come here; if the king will give me a force, I will take my revenge on him." On hearing this, the Sultan gave orders to collect a force, and when it was ready, he gave it to him. When this army approached Tatta, being unable to meet it, Chunur sat down in the fort, which, being surrounded on all sides by the royal troops, they took into their hands the implements for breaking down forts, and fighting commenced. For twelve days they fought together in this manner, after which the wind of victory struck the standards of the royal troops, and Chunur and many of his men were given to the sword. Those who escaped the sword ran away and dispersed. By taking this fort, much wealth and property fell into the hands of those people.

When Doda the son of Oomur sat on the throne of his father, this force returned to Ghuznee. He reigned many years, with strength and wisdom.

Afterwards, by this order, "Every life will drink the sherbet of death!" Doda drank the sherbet of mortality at the hands of the cup-bearer of death: he took the apparatus of his life to the living world.

After him, one named Urruh Mehl sat upon the throne of authority; but he was an oppressor, giving the people much trouble: so their hearts became separated from him, and they plotted to kill him. Previous to this, some of the Summah tribe, having come to Sind from Kutch, had remained there, becoming kindred with them.

The influential men of Urruh Mehl secretly paid homage to, and brought into the city, one of this tribe, named Jam Oonnur, who bore on his forehead the signs of goodness. This happened in the morning, when a body of men, going into Urruh Mehl's house, killed him, and placed his head over the gateway, when all the people, paying homage to Jam Oonnur, placed him on the throne of the Sultanut.

AN ACCOUNT OF JAM OONNUR, THE SON OF BABUNIYUH.

When Jam Oonnur had become king, with the sanction of the men of power, many people flocked to him. He at that time, with great numbers, went to take Sehwistan, getting near which, he prepared a plain for a battle-field, on which to fight with Mulik Rutun, the Hakeem there on the part of the King of the Toorks. Mulik Rutun came out of his fort to this field of battle with a well appointed, large force. The fire of battle commenced burning between the two armies, and this increasing, Jam Oonnur was defeated, but, by the assistance of his brethren, he again brought up many men, and recommenced fighting. At that time Mulik Rutun galloping his horse, the animal's head came to the ground, and he, losing his seat, fell: Jam Oonnur, with his sword, separated his head from the body; and he then took the fort of Sehwistan. At that time Mulik Pheroz, and Ali Shah Toork, were the Hakeems at Bukkur, on the part of the King of the Toorks. These, hearing of the above, wrote to Jam Oonnur, to the following effect:— "This presumption is not becoming in you: now prepare your implements of war, to fight with the troops of the king, and fix your foot firmly on the field of valour." This language operated on Jam Oonnur, who went away towards Thuree. At that time he was taken ill, and went to the country of futurity. He reigned three years and six months.

Some historians write as follows:—

When Jam Oonnur, having conquered Sehwistan, turned back, he was drinking wine one night, at a pleasant assembly, when news came that some rebellious men were coming against him. He gave orders to Gahuh, the son of Tumachee, who was his Vukeel, to go and repulse them. So taking a force, and going with speed, he came upon them; but in fighting, Gahuh, being in liquor, was taken prisoner, and confined. Jam Oonnur, amidst his pleasures, did not bear him in mind, on which account Gahuh became his enemy, and by some device liberating himself from his enemies, he turned his head from Jam Oonnur, and went to Bukkur, where he had an interview with Ali Shah Toork, who lived in the fort of Munson Numee, in old Bukkur; and this Ali Shah and Mulik Pheroz, collecting many men, came to Buhrampoor, killing Jam Oonnur in that fort. Mulik Pheroz remaining there as governor, Ali Shah returned to Bukkur. Three days after his return, some of Jam Oonnur's men, by stratagem, killed both Gahuh and Mulik Pheroz.

AN ACCOUNT OF JOONUH THE SON OF BABUNIYUH.

On the death of Jam Oonnur, the people of Summah, giving the Jamee title to Joonuh, placed him on the seat of their Sirdaree. He, intending to take the whole of Sind, sent his brethren and relatives, with great kindness, appointing them over different places; then, crossing the river at Tuluhtee, began beating, looting, and destroying all the Ryuts, towns, and villages, under Bukkur. The Hakeem of Bukkur fought two or three times desperately with those people, but the Toorks had not strength to meet the men of Summah; so, being helpless, they left Bukkur and went to Ooch. When Jam Joonuh heard of their flight, he quickly went to Bukkur, and made his arrangements. In short, for many years he reigned absolute, until Sultan Ula-ood-deen, appointing his brother Ulug Khan to Mooltan, he sent Taj-ood-deen Kafooree, and Tatar Khan, to expel him. Before these hostile forces arrived, Jam Joonuh had died of the quinsey, having reigned thirteen years.

When the Sultan's troops came to Bukkur, and had taken it, and also Sehwistan, at that time the chief Sirdars placed Jam Tumachee, the son of Jam Oonnur, on the throne. Then there was a battle between him and the troops of the Sultan, who, taking him prisoner, conveyed him and all his family to Delhi, where he remained in confinement. The tribe of Summah remained at Thuree; but the officials of Jam Oonnur, keeping the affairs of state in their hands, exerted themselves in every matter. After the death of Jam Tumachee, his son Jam Khair-ood-deen, who in infancy went to Delhi, came to Sind, and, sitting over the government, took possession of it. A short time after this, when Sultan Mahomed Shah, by the way of Guzerat, came to Sind, he called Jam Khair-ood-deen to come and make his Salaam; but he did not obey, because he had spent a long time confined in the state prison at Delhi. Sultan Mahomed Shah died near Tatta.

After his decease, by his will Sultan Pheroz Shah sat on the king's throne, and went to Delhi, Jam Khair-ood-deen following him as far as Sind in Sehwistan, from whence he turned back; but the fact of his having followed him remained in the heart of the Sultan. After Sultan Pheroz Shah left Sind, Jam Khair-ood-deen spread the carpet of justice, and exerted himself to make the Ryuts happy.

Historians have mentioned a rare action of this magnificent Jam— that one day, with his attendants, he went for exercise to the jungle. By chance, as he was going along, he saw in a hole the bones of men, so, pulling the bridle, he stopped his horse, and after looking for a minute at the decayed bones, he turned his head round and said— "Do you know what these bones say to me?" His attendants, bending down their heads, remained silent. Then said the Jam: "These are inspired people, and they want justice." The Jam then turned his attention to discovering the circumstances of those bones of the dead, and calling a very old man, in whose hands the land was, he asked him about them; when this old man told him that "Sixty years ago, a Kafila came here from Guzerat, when they were destroyed by a certain tribe, who took away their property, much of which is with them now." When the Jam heard this, he gave orders to collect that property; when such as was found being gathered together, he sent a man of trust with it to the ruler of Guzerat, desiring that it might be restored to the heirs of those who had been killed; and, in retaliation, he destroyed those by whom they had suffered.

Several years after this, he left this transitory world, and went to the world eternal.

AN ACCOUNT OF JAM BABUNIYUH, THE SON OF JAM KHAIR-OOD-DEEN.

After the death of his father, by the aid of the Ameers he sat upon the hereditary throne.

When Sultan Pheroz Shah, having settled Hindoostan and Guzerat, came to take Sind, Jam Babuniyuh, preparing a field of battle, stood up to fight. The Sultan remained there three months, but when the inundations, with bad winds, and many musquitoes came, he marched away, going to Puttun in Guzerat.

After the rains, having collected many men, he again returned, and fought. In short, in that battle Jam Babuniyuh was taken prisoner, and all the people and country of Sind came into the hands of Pheroz Shah. When the Sultan returned to Delhi, he took the Jam with him, who remained for a long time in his service, behaving very well; seeing which, the Sultan extended to him his royal kindness, and giving him a royal crown, he placed Sind in his hands again, allowing him to depart. So he came to Sind, over which he reigned absolute.

He reigned for fifteen years, when he travelled to the other world.

His brother Jam Tumachee, succeeding him, sat on the king's throne. He turned his attention to making arrangements for the country. He was the friend of leisure, spending his time in pleasure. He reigned thirteen years, dying of the plague.

After the death of Jam Tumachee, Jam Sulah-ood-deen sat upon the throne of authority. His first act was to put to rights the border, which had become out of order by the hands of bad men, who did not obey orders. For this purpose he took a force, and sharply pulled the ears of those vicious people. Having given to all such correction and admonition, he turned his face towards Kutch. Upon arriving there, much fighting ensued between him and those people; but in every battle the breeze of victory struck the standards of the Jam, and after this he returned from thence, accompanied by victory and plunder. He made the necessary arrangements for the Ryuts, and troops. He ruled for eleven years and some months, when he departed from this perishable world for the world everlasting.

AN ACCOUNT OF JAM NIZAM-OOD-DEEN, THE SON OF JAM SULAH-OOD-DEEN.

On ascending the throne of the Sultanut, after the decease of his father, with the concurrence of the Ameers, he released Mulik Sekunder, Kurun Buha-ood-deen, and Ameer, his uncles, who had been placed in confinement for correction, sending them to a distance; and then, leaving the affairs of state in the hands of the officials, he spent his time in pleasure and gaiety. He never paid any attention to any business relating to the country; so much so, that his uncles, having collected some men, came to the city, and began to plot his seizure and confinement, which the Jam hearing of, by the advice of some of his troops he left the city at midnight, and fled towards Guzerat. In the morning, when his flight became known to the uncles, they went in pursuit of him. The people, seeing this dissension, brought forth from his concealment Jam Ali Sher, who, with the concurrence of all the nobles, was placed on the throne. At this time Jam Nizam-ood-deen became a traveller on that road which leads to the country of life eternal. His uncles, oppressed with shame and loss, went to the jungles, and sat down there.

AN ACCOUNT OF JAM ALI SHER.

When Jam Ali Sher, with the assistance of the nobles, ascended the throne, he threw open to the world the gates of justice and liberality. He himself was virtuous, and a great warrior. He first of all turned his face to putting in order the affairs of the kingdom, making such arrangements as were necessary for the country of Sind. All the people were happy during his rule, and in sweet contentment passed their time. Some time afterwards, the Jam turned his heart towards pleasure, being in the habit of going out to take exercise during the moon-light nights. Mulik Sekunder and Kurun, the sons of Tumachee, and Futteh Khan, the son of Mulik Sekunder, who was in the jungle, hearing of the Jam's going about in this way without apprehension, marching by night, and concealing themselves by day, came to the city, where they induced some to join them. One Friday night, the 13th of the month, hearing that the Jam had gone with a few attendants to take air on the river, according to his custom, at midnight, as he was returning, some men with drawn swords were ready, intending to kill him. His followers did all in their power to dissuade these from their purpose; but they would not listen to them, and slew the Jam. Having done this, they at once went to the palace, where there arose much noise, and alarm; and all becoming aroused and alert, they were aware that affairs had passed from their hands; so, being helpless, they bent their heads before the orders of the opposite party.

Jam Ali Sher ruled Sind for seven years. After the martyrdom of Jam Ali Sher, the fraternity collecting, placed Jam Kurun on the throne of the Sirdaree.

He did not agree well with the Ameers, and the men of consequence of the city. In the early days of his reign, he planned to seize and kill some of these, and confine others. At that time he gave a large assembly, to which he invited all, when he caressed and spoke in a friendly way to them. The dinner came, when they all eat together, after which the Jam withdrew; when the slaves of those nobles, having placed themselves as instructed, met and cut him to pieces there. The originator of this, and of the death of Kurun, was Futteh Khan, the son of Sekunder, who, with the voice of the army and the Ryuts, ascended the throne.

Whilst he was on the throne, he gave strength to the rules of justice, and to the affairs of the kingdom in general. He was very wakeful in all matters of state.

At that time Meerza Peer Mahomed, the grandson of Huzrut Saheb Kiran Ameer Taimoor Goorgan, came towards Mooltan, which he took, and Ooch likewise. He remained there some time, when, by reason of not finding forage, many of the horses of the sepoys died. Thus many men of the Meerza's army became dismounted. On hearing of this, Saheb Kiran sent 30,000 horses from the royal stables to him. Meerza Peer Mahomed, becoming strong from this present, made a Chuppao upon the men of Bhittee and Ahun, who were stubborn and disobedient, when he gave to the winds of death these and all their families. Sending a messenger to Bukkur, he summoned to his presence all the men of consequence, all the eyes of that city. The agent of the King of Delhi, who was there, being unable to fight, fled by the way of Jaisulmere.

An inhabitant of Bukkur, named Syud Abdool Ghais, a man of devotion, integrity, and piety, having offered up prayers in the name of the Sirdar of the Prophets (Mahomed), and having besought his intercession, went to meet the Meerza Peer Mahomed.

It is written that one night Huzrut, the Sirdar of the Prophets (the blessing of God on him!) came to the Meerza in a dream, showing to him Syud Abdool Ghais, saying: "This is my descendant; open the road to give him honour and reverence, and shorten the hand of oppression on him." The Meerza awoke from his sleep, and was anxious to see him whom he had seen in his dream. Eleven days afterwards, Syud Abdool Ghais arrived, when Meerza Peer Mahomed was sitting in his place of audience, with the Ameers around him on either side, when, his sight falling upon the Syud, he recognised him. Rising, he instantly came to the front, and embraced him, placing him near himself with much honour and reverence. The Ameers then inquired of the Meerza the circumstances of this Syud, when he explained to them what he had seen in the dream. On that day he gave the Syud a horse and a present as an offering, granting him permission to return. The Meerza settled upon Syud Abdool Ghais, the Purguna of Alore.

After the arrival of Saheb Kiran Meerza, Peer Mahomed turned his face to capture Delhi. Many days passed by, and many kings of different castes sat on the throne of Delhi. At that time Mooltan went into the hands of the Lungahs, and the whole of the country of Sind was in the hands of the Kings of Sind. Jam Futteh Khan was celebrated for his valour; his courage was of great repute. He reigned for fifteen years and some months, when his days reached their latter end, and his life, leaving this perishable world, went to the world eternal.

AN ACCOUNT OF JAM TUGHLUG SHAH, THE SON OF SEKUNDER.

When Jam Futteh Khan placed his side on the bed of sickness, from the sensations which he felt he saw the face of death. Therefore, three days before he died, he seated his brother Tughlug on the throne of the Sirdaree, placing in his hands the reigns of the government, and giving him the title of Jam Tughlug Shah. On ascending the throne of the Sultanut, Jam Tughlug Shah sent his brothers to rule over Sehwistan, and the fort of Bukkur. He himself spent much of his time in hunting and exercise. The Beloochees near Bukkur beginning to cause disturbances, the Jam, taking a large force with him, went there, and having given the Beloochee Sirdars severe punishment, he turned back. He placed Thanas in each Purguna, to prevent disturbances. The length of his reign was twenty-six years, when he died a natural death.

AN ACCOUNT OF JAM SEKUNDER, THE SON OF JAM TUGHLUG SHAH.

When he sat in the place of his father, he was a young man. The Hakeems of Sehwistan and Bukkur, becoming powerful in their respective districts, ceased placing the orders of government on their heads, and began to quarrel with each other. Jam Sekunder, leaving Tatta, went towards Bukkur. He had got as far as Nusurpoor, when one named Moobaruk, who in the time of Jam Tughlug was the commander of 2,000 men, started up, and arriving at Tatta, proclaimed himself Jam Moobaruk, and seated himself on the throne of the government. But he had not the concurrence of the people of the city; on this account his rule did not extend beyond three days, inasmuch as the nobles of Tatta turned him out, and sent to call Jam Sekunder. When this news reached him, he made peaceable arrangements with those Hakeems, and returned to Tatta.

One year and a half after this, he took the apparatus of his life from the ways of this perishable world, to the ample house of eternity.

AN ACCOUNT OF JAM ROYDHUN.

On the 6th of Jumadee-ool-Awul, Hijree 858 (A. D. 1454), Jam Roydhun came forth.

In the time of Jam Tughlug, he lived in Kutch, with the men of which country he had become connected.

He placed near his person many of those men, such as were penetrating, whose hearts he pleased without limit, constantly making them presents of horses and things of value. These men, perceiving on the forehead of his acts the signs of rectitude, with all sincerity placed themselves in his hands.

When the news of the decease of Jam Sekunder reached him, taking many men, he went to Tatta, and collecting the men of that city, he said: "I have not come to take the country, but I have come to save the property of the Musulmans. I do not consider myself fit to be king; he whom you consider fit for the situation, make him king, and I will be the first of any to give him the hand of homage." Amongst those men there was no one fit to be king, so all of them agreeing, placed him on the throne of the kingdom. In the course of one year and a half, he pulled beneath his rule the whole of Sind, from the ocean to Kajur, Mullee, and Khoondee, the boundaries of Matheluh, and Oobawruh. After reigning eight years, the wind (idea) of ruling over the Sultanut entered the head of one of his least esteemed friends, Jam Sunjur, and other slight acquaintances consenting, joined him.

Jam Roydhun was drinking wine in private, when Jam Sunjur, putting some poison in a bottle, gave it into the hands of one of his attendants, three days after drinking which Jam Roydhun died. It is also written by some, that a man, a Fakeer, one of judgment, who was considered in those times as a saint at Tatta, was in the habit of constantly coming to the Jam, who always treated him with great respect, seating him on his own seat; and whatever this Fakeer said the Jam agreed to it.

One day, at an assembly, the Wuzeers and nobles said to the Jam— "Ask that Fakeer, to whom you give so much honour, what God is like, and what is his description." When the Jam heard this, he placed it in his heart. Four days afterwards, when this Durwish came to the assembly, the Jam did not pay him the usual attention. The Fakeer understood that there was something in this. The Jam then asked him: "What is God like, and what description does He bear?" The Fakeer replied: "The description of God is this, that three days hence He will destroy you by means of a horse 16 kos from this, and he will place Jam Sunjur on your seat." The third day after this, the Jam went to hunt, not bearing in mind what the Fakeer had said. By chance he galloped his horse, when he fell, and his foot remaining in the stirrup, at the distance of 16 kos from Tatta his life was given to God.

AN ACCOUNT OF JAM SUNJUR.

Jam Sunjur was a handsome young man. Many people went mad from seeing his face, who did his service without receiving any yearly salary. Historians also write, that previous to ascending the throne, Jam Sunjur was on friendly terms with a Fakeer of deep counsel. One night Jam Sunjur went to him, and after the meeting he said: "It is my wish to reign over Tatta, if only for eight days." This Fakeer replied— "You will be king for eight years." When Roydhun journeyed to that other world, the nobles assembled, placing Jam Sunjur on the throne, placing in his hands the reins of the affairs of state. He, having been thus seated on the throne, through the prayers of the Fakeer, all the Hakeems on the borders obeyed his orders without fighting with him.

During his reign over Sind, such habits and customs were introduced as had never before been known in that country. The sepoys and Ryuts in his time lived in great happiness, spending their time confortably. Jam Sunjur was much attached to men of piety, and learning, and to all Fakeers. On Friday he distributed much in charity to Fakeers and the poor. He gave certain salaries to those having just claims.

Historians have written, that before the reign of Jam Sunjur, the Hakeems gave very little to the men holding office under government. When Sunjur obtained the sovereignty, there was a Kazee at Bukkur, named Kazee Munroof, who had been made Kazee in the time of the former Hakeem, and he received but little pay. On account of the smallness of his pay, he was in the habit of taking something from the people by intimidation. This reached the ears of Jam Sunjur, who gave orders for this Kazee to be present.

When he came, the Jam said: "I hear that you take something from those who quarrel with each other." The Kazee said; "Yes, I do; and I also wish to take something from the witnesses, but these, having given their evidence, get away before I can ask them for anything." Hearing this, the Jam laughed; when the Kazee said— "I sit the whole day in the hall of justice; I have passed my life in this business, and my children are hungry morning and evening." Hearing this, the Jam gave him a valuable present, and settled his pay according to his expenses, giving orders throughout the kingdom, that the salaries of all the men in office were to be increased, that they might pass their time free from anxiety and care. When his reign had lasted eight years, his life went from this house full of sorrow.

AN ACCOUNT OF JAM NIZAM-OOD-DEEN, WHO WAS COMMONLY CALLED JAM NINDAH, THE SON OF BABUNIYUH.

On the 25th of Rubee-ool-Awul, 866 (A. D. 1461), after the death of Jam Sunjur, he sat on the throne of the Sultanut. When he was firm as king, he raised on high the standard of his strong predominance. It is said, that at the commencement of his manhood he sought after knowledge, spending much of his time in the college and cloister. His disposition was modest and happy; he was celebrated for his good, affectionate temper; he offered much prayer to God, doing great abstinence. His excellences are beyond what little I can write. At the commencement of the reign of Jam Nizam-ood-deen, he went with a large force to Bukkur, remaining there one year, taking out by the roots those who thieved and disturbed the country. He placed in the fort of Bukkur great stores of provision, and requisites of every kind, appointing over it the son of one of his slaves. The people on the border were so well under his authority, that travellers went along the roads without apprehension. Having made all these arrangements in the space of one year, he returned to Tatta with his heart at ease (about A. D. 1509). For a period of forty-eight years he reigned at Tatta with absolute power; in his kingdom, the men of piety and learning, and the Fakeers, spent their time in great happiness, and the sepoys and Ryuts were in comfortable circumstances.

Jam Nizam-ood-deen and Sultan Hoosain Lungah of Mooltan were contemporary friends. Between them there were many roads of esteem and friendship; they were always sending something to each other.

The Jam was in the habit of visiting the stable every week. He was in the habit of stroking the horses down the face with his hands, saying— "Oh my wealthy one! I do not want to mount you, unless to go against Kafirs, because on all sides the rulers are Musulmans; do you ask of God, that I may not go beyond the order of the laws of Mahomed, and that no one may come against me. God forbid that the blood of any Musulman should flow, so that I should have shame before God!"

During the time of his rule, Mahomedan rules attained so much life, that my understanding does not extend beyond them. The congregations of both great and small assembled in the Musjids; no one was willing to say his prayers alone. If any one was not present with the congregation, he repented, begging forgiveness for two or three days.

In the latter days of the reign of Jam Nizam-ood-deen, the forces of Shah Beg Urghoon, coming from Kandahar, fell upon many villages of Chundooha and Sideejuh. The Jam sent a large force to expel these Moguls, which arrived at Duruh-i-Kureeb, commonly known as Joolow Geer, where a battle was fought, in which the brother of Shah Beg was killed, and his forces being defeated, they turned the bridle of retreat towards Kandahar; and during the life of Jam Nizam-ood-deen they did not come back again.

The Jam spent much time in discoursing on knowledge, with the learned of those times.

In his time Moulana Julal-ood-deen Mahomed Dewanee, proposing to come from Shiraz to Sind, sent Meer Shums, and Meer Mooneen, both his disciples, to Tatta, to ask the Jam to give him a place to live in. The Jam fixed upon a very handsome residence for him, settling the requisites for his subsistence, sending by his two disciples much money for his road expenses. But before these came, Moulana had travelled to another world: Meer Shums and Meer Mooneen, recollecting the society of the Jam, returned back to Tatta.

Some time after this, Jam Nizam-ood-deen raised on high the banner of his departure to the world eternal.

After his death, much dissension arose in the condition of the people of Sind.

AN ACCOUNT OF JAM PHEROZ, THE SON OF JAM NIZAM-OOD-DEEN.

When Jam Nizam-ood-deen went along the road to the other world, his son Pheroz was of tender age.

The Jam Sulah-ood-deen, the son of the daughter of Jam Sunjur, and the relative of Jam Nizam-ood-deen, laid claim to the country, wishing that he might be placed on the king's throne. Durya Khan and Sarung Khan, who were the slaves of consequence of Jam Nizam-ood-deen, having great power and dignity, would not agree to this; and collecting all the men of authority, and the nobles of Tatta, they placed Jam Pheroz on the throne of the Sultanut, and Jam Sulah-ood-deen, who had proposed fighting, being hopeless, went to Guzerat, and petitioned Sultan Moozuffur, of that country. Sultan Moozuffur was married to the daughter of the uncle of Jam Saluh-ood-deen; on this account his heart turned to what he said.

When Jam Pheroz, having ascended the throne, had attained manhood, he spread the carpet of pleasure, spending much of his time in the Harem, and when he came forth, he associated with jesters and loose characters. On this account, during his time, the people of the Summah tribe, and the Khasuh Khails, were in the habit of committing great oppression on the citizens, and when Durya Khan forbade this, they treated him with scorn, so taking his leave, he went to his Jageer, Kahan.

At that time, Moulana Mukhdoom Abdool Azeez Abhuree, a narrator of the traditional sayings of Mahomed, with Moulana Aseer-ood-deen, and Moulana Mahomed, his two sons, each of them being learned, came to Kahan, where they remained some time, exerting themselves to benefit the people, and to spread knowledge. They came from Herat because Shah Ismael had ascended the throne, in the year 918 (A. D. 1512).

Moulana Abdool Azeez was collecting knowledge of all the sciences, and of things related. He had composed very good books on all kinds of knowledge. Amongst them was a commentary on the Mishkat (a book of the traditional sayings of Mahomed), and he had written marginal notes to many difficult works. He went to the other world at Kahan. His tomb is in the burying ground there, and it is visited by those people.

When Jam Pheroz spent his time in pleasure, the nobles turned their heads to ruining the country. The chiefs of the intelligence department sent a letter by a man to Jam Sulah-ood-deen, giving him the news that Jam Pheroz was debauched, and without knowledge; that Durya Khan, the support of the kingdom, had gone to Kahan, with accession; and that now was the time for him quickly to convey himself there. Jam Sulah-ood-deen showed this letter to the Sultan, who placed a large force under his orders, giving him leave to go to Tatta, when, marching by forced marches, he crossed the river at Tatta, and arrived there. The men of Jam Pheroz, being all abroad, took him out by another road, and Jam Sulah-ood-deen mounted the throne in Tatta. He imprisoned all the slaves of Jam Pheroz, making them show his property.

The mother of Jam Pheroz took him to Durya Khan, at Kahan, when the Jam, weeping, said he had discontinued his former evil habits. Durya Khan, recollecting the former kindness of the Jam, collected a large body of men, and when the troops of Bukkur and Sehwistan had united, they came under the standard of Jam Pheroz. Many Beloochees, and men of other tribes, also joined him.

Durya Khan then turned his face towards Jam Sulah-ood-deen, to expel him. Jam Sulah-ood-deen proposed sending the fighting elephants and troops with Hajee Wuzeer, to fight, so he remained in the city, and sent forth the Hajee. When the troops of the two parties met, the fire of battle was set on light between them. Many men were killed. At length the troops of Durya Khan, being defeated, retreated, when, from the field of battle, the Hajee sent a letter to Jam Sulah-ood-deen, writing as follows: "The breeze of victory has struck your banner; make your mind easy." When Durya Khan retreated, the time was not propitious for the Hajee to follow him.

By chance, that Kosid, who bore this letter of the Hajee, fell into the hands of some of Durya Khan's men, who took him to their chief, who, quickly investigating the meaning, wrote another letter, as if from the Hajee, to the following effect: "Defeat has come upon our army; the enemy are very strong: do you take your family, and depart from Tatta. By no means make delay; our next meeting will be at Chachgan." When this letter arrived, it was the 9th day of Rumzan (fast), in the evening, and Jam Sulah-ood-deen, without even breaking his fast, crossed the river. In short, his condition was that of defeat. He reigned eight months. When Jam Sulah-ood-deen was met by Hajee Wuzeer, the latter reproached him, saying— "Why did you run away?" Then the Jam showed him his letter. The Hajee said— "This is not my writing"; and they afterwards discovered that it was a trick of Durya Khan's, so they became much dejected: but when a thing has passed from the hand, there is no use of repentence.

Durya Khan pursued the Jam for many marches, and bringing Jam Pheroz to Tatta on the day of the Eed Fitur, they said prayers. After this Jam Pheroz ruled for many years, until the year 926 (A. D. 1520), when Shah Beg Urghoon came to take Sind, the circumstances of whose battles I will relate in their place.

I have not seen any book in which the account of the Soomrahs and Summahs is well explained, therefore I have written their summary. If any one knows more, he must add it to this.

END OF CHAPTER II.

CHAPTER III.

AN ACCOUNT OF THE REIGN OF THE URGHOONEEYUHS; OF THE TIMES OF THEIR GOVERNMENT; OF THEIR WARS; AND AN ABRIDGED HISTORY OF AMEER ZOONOON URGHOON.

Meer Zoonoon was the son of Meer Husun Busree. He was famed for his valour amongst his tribe. He was in the ranks of the servants of Meerza Aboo Suneed. During the time of battle, his gallantry was apparent to all. On this account, the eyes of the Meerza were always on him, and he received so many kinds of valuable presents from his master, that his fellows were filled with jealousy against him. In this manner, his rank rose above that of all his brethren. After the battle of Kura Bagh, he went to his father at Herat, where he remained some time in the service of Sultan Yadgar Meerza. From thence he went to Samarkand, where the light of the sun of the kindness of Sultan Ahmed Meerza struck the side of his condition, and he stayed there two or three years. After this, on account of the wars between the Ameers of Turkhanee and those of Urghoonee, he returned to Khorasan, when he came under the eye of kindness of Sultan Hoosain Meerza, who placed him over the countries of Ghore and Dawur. At this time the Huzarah and Nukduree tribes in those borders were very powerful. In the year 884 (A. D. 1479), Ameer Zoonoon, taking a small force, went there, where for three or four years he was constantly fighting with those people; but by the good fortune of the king, he was the conqueror in all these fights, and he brought that country under his authority. The men of Huzarah and Nukduree, seeing his valour, bent their heads beneath his orders, and they did not commit such acts again. Sultan Hoosain Meerza approved of his arrangements, and placed all the affairs of Kandahar, Furat, and Ghore in his hands. By this means Ameer Zoonoon became very powerful, and he took under his authority Shawl, Mustoong, and the countries adjacent to them.

AN ACCOUNT OF HOW THE FRIENDSHIP EXISTED BETWEEN MEER ZOONOON URGHOON, AND BUDEEN-OOZ-ZUMAN MEERZA, THE SON OF SULTAN HOOSAIN SHAH.

It has been previously mentioned that the king looked upon Meer Zoonoon with the eye of kindness, giving him a Khilat and a standard, and placing him over Kandahar, Gurmsere, and Dawur. Three years afterwards, Meer Zoonoon collected together many of the men of Huzarah, Nukduree, Kubchag, and of the Moguls of Kandahar. When the news of this reached the ears of the king, he sent a royal Firman to call Meer Zoonoon, who without delay arrived at the foot of the throne, placing there offerings of great value. He also gave to the princes and men of consequence about court, according to their degree, various rarities. Therefore all the people loosened their tongues in praise of him, deeming him a wisher of happiness to the king. Yet, with all this, the king had not confidence in him. Meer Zoonoon was a wise man, and, following the track of knowledge, he determined in his own mind to effect his business through Budeen-ooz-Zuman Meerza, whom Meer Zoonoon was in the habit of visiting when he was alone, and he daily presented him with something fresh and new. One night, Meer Zoonoon said to him: "I perceive, from the manner of the king, that he will not now allow me to depart; it is therefore better that I give my people their leave, that they may go home." The Meerza, hearing this, gave him great praise. After Meer Zoonoon had remained there a year or upwards, one night, at a private assembly, in the presence of the king, they were talking of various matters, when his royal highness himself said: "What do you think of Meer Zoonoon being a well-wisher of happiness towards me?" Upon this, the people at that party became thoughtful. Meerza Budeen-ooz-Zuman said: "No Ameer agrees to take the government of Kandahar; and if any go there, in the space of two or three years they die through some disease or some quarrel: it would be better to give Meer Zoonoon his dismissal, for this would not be in vain, for two reasons— for Meer Zoonoon, on going there, will be either obedient or rebellious; if he is rebellious, it will not be fruitless, for two reasons— for he will either die of the disease of that country, and, if he does not die, he will not escape from our hands."

The king approved of this, saying: "The bridle of the choice of this matter is in your hands." Meerza Budeen-ooz-Zuman took security from Meer Zoonoon.

The king then gave Meer Zoonoon a handsome Khilat, a horse with saddle and bridle, and all the requisites for a force, such as a Nugarah, and a standard, and he directed the officers of state to furnish him with a Firman, with the royal titles affixed.

Meer Zoonoon gave a written engagement to the Meerza, to the effect that "when the king's Firman arrives, I will attend without delay."

Meer Zoonoon, seeing the kindness of the Meerza, sent a man to Kandahar to call his son Shah Beg, who, with Abdoor Rahman Urghoon, Zeenuk Turkhan, Janfur Urghoon, and Meer Fazil Kookooltash, and 200 horsemen, quickly came to Khorasan. By the arrival of Shah Beg and these others, the king, the Meerza, and all the government officials, gained confidence.

On account of Meer Zoonoon's going to Kandahar, Meer Zoonoon remained a long time with the king, when the princes, Ameers, and Wuzeer, exerting themselves in his favour, represented to his highness that the borders of Kandahar were much disturbed; that if it was so ordered, Meer Zoonoon would go there, and put matters right. The king ordered that Zoonoon himself should go to Kandahar, leaving his son and nobles there. On hearing this, Meer Zoonoon, abandoning all his property, horses, tents, &c. went quickly to Kandahar, taking with him his son and all his nobles. Two or three days after this event, the king issued orders for Meer Zoonoon to remain until the first days of spring, and that he might then depart for Kandahar. The attendants went to his house, and seeing that only his property was there, they came to his royal highness, telling him the circumstance of his departure. Hearing this, the king said: "Zoonoon having left in this manner, I shall not see him again." The princes and Meers said: "Why should he not come? all his horses, camels, tents, and property are here." His royal highness replied: "This is the stratagem of his cleverness: he has made game of me, and gone away." And so it was.

The king then wrote a kind Firman, which he sent by a trusty attendant, named Sarban Ali, who, going with great speed, met Meer Zoonoon as he was marching out of Furat, when he delivered the Firman to him. Meer Zoonoon, advancing to the front, took this with great humility, and reading its contents, he was much pleased. He apologized to Sarban Ali, saying: "I am two marches from home, I will have a meeting with my children, and, having filled my stomach with everything, I will then accompany you to the king." When he got to Kandahar, he did Sarban Ali much honour, givin ghim large sums of money. One day he was in a tent with his two sons Shah Beg and Mahomed Mokeem, and his brother Meer Sultan Ali, when he called Sarban Ali. After speaking on various subjects, Meer Zoonoon said to him: "I think that if I went to the king, he would not allow me to return again: tell me the truth." Sarban Ali, who had experienced a great deal of kindness at his hands, replied as his heart desired. Then Meer Zoonoon, presenting him with a handsome Khilat, a horse with gold caparisons, and much money, he gave him his leave. When Sarban Ali reached the king, he told him all the circumstances, giving him the letter which he had brought from Meer Zoonoon. The king was distressed at this; but it is no use to be sorry for that which has left our hands.

AN ACCOUNT OF THE GOING OF MEERZA BUDEEN-OOZ-ZUMAN, OF KANDAHAR.

By reason of the change of temper of the king, Meerza Budeen-ooz-Zuman becoming displeased, and being hopeless from his brothers, turned the bridle of his intention to go to Gurmsere and Kandahar. Before he arrived, Meer Zoonoon, and his son Shah Beg, went in front to meet him, being most humble and submissive. They endeavoured to meet his wishes as much as they could, saying they were ready to do all in their power for him. Then Meerza Budeen-ooz-Zuman was married to the innocent daughter of Meer Zoonoon. On this account he was happy, passing his time agreeably, and great friendship sprung up between him and Meer Zoonoon and his sons. At that time Ameer Shaikh Ali Tighaee, who was the private tutor of Meerza Budeen-ooz-Zuman, fell under suspicion, and was imprisoned. It was in this way:— One day Meer Zoonoon went to make the circuit of a certain tomb at Dawur, when a slave, coming in front of him, as if with a petition, struck him with a knife. The attendants immediately cut him to pieces, as they knew that he had done this at the instigation of Shaikh Ali, whom Meer Zoonoon and his sons intended to kill; but he fled to Meerza Budeen-ooz-Zuman, whose house was surrounded by the Urghooneeyuhs, asking for him to be given up to them. The Meerza told them to depart, saying he would send him to them; but they would not agree to this. At length, having sworn great oaths that they would not kill him, he delivered him up to them.

Meer Zoonoon was again satisfied with Meerza Budeen-ooz-Zuman, doing him service as before. Shaikh Ali Tighaee remained confined for a long time in the fort of Gurmsere: he was then liberated, and told to go where he pleased. He went to Sultan Hoosain, where he got service. In the days when Meerza Budeen-ooz-Zuman was at Dawur, he heard of his son Mahomed Momin having been killed.

A NARRATIVE OF THE IMPRISONMENT AND KILLING OF MAHOMED MOMIN MEERZA, THE SON OF MEERZA BUDEEN-OOZ-ZUMAN.

Mahomed Momin was a prince of as great beauty as the sun. At the commencement of his manhood, the young tree of his life fell by the sharp breeze of death. This is an abstract of the statement.

When, being displeased with his father Sultan Hoosain, Meerza Budeen-ooz-Zuman turned the bridle of his intentions towards Kandahar, Mahomed Momin Meerza was at Asterabad. On his father departing for Kandahar, he sent word to his son, that he had better accompany him. The prince replied that "it is not proper in you to turn your face from the house of the Sultanut, and to go beneath the shade of servants." Hearing this, Budeen-ooz-Zuman greatly praised his son's wisdom, and sending to him some of his most trusty men, he warned him, that his uncles were seeking his death, that he must not be deceived by what they said; that if his grandfather called him, he should obey the summons, and go to him, but that if any came against him without the orders of his grandfather, he should oppose them.

Moozuffur Hoosain Meerza approached Asterabad, hearing of which Mahomed Momin wished to go and meet him, and, having made over the country to him, to depart himself for some other place. At that time a letter reached him from his father, filled in this way:— "On no account loosen the bridle of your strength from your hands. Collect your sepoys, and place your foot on the battle-field." Upon this, Mahomed Momin, having assembled his forces, went forth from Asterabad, turning his horse's bridle in the direction of battle. At that time Moozuffur, with a large army, also came to the plain of battle, where the beating of Nugarahs and the blowing of horns commenced on both sides. In the twinkling of an eye, arrows and bullets fell like rain, and brave men of both sides, mixing together, fought in such a manner, that it appeared as if the signs of the last day had arrived. Mahomed Momin threw many of the valiant men of the opposite side to the ground of death; but at that time, from the displeasure of heaven, the girths of the saddle of his horse broke, and he fell from the saddle to the earth. At that moment a sepoy, one of the enemy, ran to slay him, when Meerza Moozuffur Hoosain, seeing this, he himself reached the spot before him, and clasping his nephew in his arms, he kissed him, and taking him with him, he went to Asterabad, where he put silver chains upon him. After some days, Moozuffur Hoosain sent Mahomed Momin to Herat, in charge of the brother of his mother (maternal uncle), Ameer Mahomed Burnodug Burlas. In the month of Sufur 903 (A. D. 1497) he arrived there, and placing him in the fort as a prisoner, he turned his face towards the king, whom he found, or in whose presence he arrived, on the banks of the Ab Moorghan, when he made known to him the above circumstances. At that time Khodaijuh Begee Begum, the mother of Moozuffur Hoosain, was present, and it came into her mind that the destruction of Mahomed Momin would give immortality to her son; so the intent of her heart was in this way— to cast this young tree of the king's garden to the ground by the hot wind of severity; so she associated herself with Khwaja Nizam-ool-Moolk, who at that time held in his hands all the king's country and property. One night, when the king had been drinking deeply of wine, she got his order to kill the prince; and having obtained this, she quickly sent upon this errand

Yar Ali Bukshee, and Abdool Wahid, a Chobdar, with ten other men of trust. The following day the king, recollecting his orders of the previous night, sent a swift courier after these, writing a Firman to them: "By no means cause harm to the cooler of my eyes!" But those bad men, by the direction of the Begum, had gone with great haste, arriving at the place where Mahomed Momin was confined. The prince, on their coming, arose, asking after their health; when those of bad fortune, not thinking of the future, killed this youth, who had not his equal in the whole kingdom. They went that night towards the banks of the Ab Moorghan, but had only proceeded a short way, when the courier, with the Firman which was to preserve the prince, overtook them. But fate had done its business; and except lamenting, there was nothing else to be done. In the morning, Ameer Sarban Joonaid, who was in the city, collected many men to place the winding-sheet, and to give him burial, placing him in the large college of Herat.

When the news of the martyrdom of his excellent son reached Meerza Budeen-ooz-Zuman, he was much grieved, and, with the intention of avenging him, he gave orders to collect troops.

AN ACCOUNT OF THE MARCH OF SULTAN HOOSAIN TOWARDS KANDAHAR, AND OF HIS TURNING BACK WHEN ON THE ROAD.

When the news reached the Sultan that Meerza Budeen-ooz-Zuman, with Meer Zoonoon, and many troops, which he had collected, was coming to take revenge for Mahomed Momin on the field of battle, he unfurled the banner of his intention to march in the direction of Gurmsere and Kandahar. Meerza Budeen-ooz-Zuman and Zoonoon, hearing of the king's coming, issued orders to all the Ryuts of Furat, Dawur, and Kandahar, to convey all their grain and articles of subsistence to the forts, and when much produce of those countries was gathered together, they placed men of strength over it. Meer Zoonoon went and sat down in the fort of Pishing, which he had previously made so strong that an insect could not get into it. Budeen-ooz-Zuman, and Meer Sultan Ali (the brother of Zoonoon), occupied other forts. Shah Beg remained in the Hissar at Kandahar. Meerza Mahomed Mokeem went to the fort of Dawur. They made an agreement, that if the king fell upon Pishing, Budeen-ooz-Zuman was to attack him from the rear, and if he first fell upon the Meerza, Zoonoon was to act in this manner. The king, having passed through the country of Furat, entered that of Dawur, when his army was much distressed for want of grain, and his sepoys were on the point of going over to Meer Zoonoon. When the king heard that there was much grain in the fort of Beest, which was held by Abdoor Rahman Urghoon, and that it would fall to him without much trouble, therefore the king cast the shadow of his standard around that fort, when, great alarm entering the breast of Abdoor Rahman, before placing his hand on his weapons, he placed his head on the foot of the king. If Abdoor Rahman had performed the work of a Kiledar for two or three days, the king's army must have dispersed from hunger; because, after this victory, they had but little grain, and their hunger was as before. The king, thinking it best to return from that place, he returned back towards Herat.

AN ACCOUNT OF THE EXPEDITION OF MEERZA BUDEEN-OOZ-ZUMAN, ACCOMPANIED BY SHAH BEG URGHOON, AGAINST MEERZA SULTAN HOOSAIN.

Sultan Hoosain Meerza was spending the early days of spring in pleasure at Alung Musheen, and his troops had gone to their homes, a few of the nobles of the army remaining near the king. Intelligence of this reached Budeen-ooz-Zuman, and Shah Beg the son of Meer Zoonoon, at Gurmsere. These, perceiving that their time had arrived, determined to march quickly against the king with three or four thousand horse, so that the news of their movement should not reach him. With this intention, they mounted their horses, and without an hour's repose on the road, on the fifth or sixth day they arrived near Subzwar; when Fureedoon Hoosain Meerza, the son of Sultan Hoosain Meerza, hearing of this, strengthened the fort, and sent successive runners to the king, conveying the news of this matter to him. On this reaching Alung Musheen, the nobles fell into the ocean of agitation, for the want of soldiers. The Sultan sent one of the men of consequence about him to Herat, with orders to strengthen the fort, and to tell Ameer Ali Sher to prepare everything there, and that when he should receive the royal Firman to that effect, he was to send him troops. The king had ditches dug to save his sepoys, and threw out advanced parties, the men of which brought word that the enemy was not stationary, but that he was coming on like wind and water.

Without doubt, if Budeen-ooz-Zuman and Shah Beg had fallen on the royal troops that night, in the same manner in which they had hitherto advanced, they would have taken the ball of victory from before the king, and their affairs would have been according to their desires; but from the strength of the fortune of Sultan Hoosain, they were not able to arrive, and they went to sleep near Esfuraiyan. In the morning, when the royal forces began to appear like the stars, bodies joining the king's camp, Budeen-ooz-Zuman and Shah Beg awoke, and, thinking as before, they advanced against the king's army. When the two forces came in sight of each other, the Nugarahs were beaten, and the clamour of the troops began to arise on both sides. Budeen-ooz-Zuman and Shah Beg, with their men all in one body, came on, and set on light the fire of battle. They fought very well with the royal troops, when, at the latter end of the battle, the king himself came upon the field on his marching throne. At the time of the shining forth of the sun of the Sultan, the sepoys of Budeen-ooz-Zuman, as the stars set, so they turned their faces in flight. Budeen-ooz-Zuman went in the direction of Gore, Shah Beg towards Dawur.

The king, having conquered, was happy, and turning his face towards Herat, he gave praise to God.

This occurred in Shaban 903 (A. D. 1497).

AN ACCOUNT OF THE PEACE-MAKING BETWEEN SULTAN HOOSAIN AND BUDEEN-OOZ-ZUMAN.

When Budeen-ooz-Zuman left Kandahar with Shah Beg to go to Alung Musheen, Meer Zoonoon was in the Gore country. On this account Budeen-ooz-Zuman, not having effected his wishes against the king's troops, turned the bridle of his horse in that direction, when, Zoonoon going in front to meet him, gave thanks to God that he had arrived alive. To take revenge for this calamity, he sent men to collect the troops at Kandahar, Dawur, and Gore. In a short time, a large force of the Urghoon tribe of the Huzarahs, the Tukdurees, the Kubchags, &c. had assembled under the shadow of the standards of Budeen-ooz-Zuman and Zoonoon, and they were fully prepared for war. When this news reached the king, in the opinion that he would again twist the ears of Budeen-ooz-Zuman, he left Alung Musheen, going towards Herat. At that time Shaikh Julal-ood-deen, Aboo Suneed Pooranee, and Moulana Mahomed Soorkh, came to the king from Budeen-ooz-Zuman and Zoonoon, to make the strong roots of peace. The king was outwardly not willing to make peace, but inwardly he placed the happiness of his son before his mind.

The explanation of this abstract is this:— One or two days prior to the former battle, this excellent king had sent Shaikh-ool-Islam, Sail-ood-deen, Ahmed Tuftazanee, Shaikh Julal-ood-deen, Aboo Suneed Pooranee, and Syud Ghuyas-ood-deen Mahomed Sudur, towards Gurmsere, to give advice to Budeen-ooz-Zuman, and to bring him from the jungle of enmity to the road of peace. When these three arrived near Furat, they heard that Budeen-ooz-Zuman was coming quickly with a force against his father's head; then Shaikh Julal-ood-deen and Syud Ghuyas-ood-deen had an interview with Budeen-ooz-Zuman and Meer Zoonoon, when Shaikh Julal-ood-deen spoke on the subject of peace to the prince, who replied, that if the king in his kindness would give him sufficient country for the subsistence of himself and his followers, he would follow the road of obedience to his orders, and place the saddle of submission upon his shoulders; but that otherwise he would not do so. The Shaikh and the Syud, receiving their dismissal, came to the king, telling him what his son had said. Again, after the battle, these two men, with Ameer Shaikh Ali Tighaee, went to Budeen-ooz-Zuman, and having conferred with him on the matter of peace, they returned to the king, representing to him that Meerza Budeen-ooz-Zuman wished to hold, as formerly, the government of Seestan and Tumachee, and that then he would not again be at enmity. The king did not agree to this, and leaving Alung Musheen, he marched towards Herat. After this, the people knew that the Sultan was going to fight against Budeen-ooz-Zuman and Zoonoon. At that time Ameer Ali Sher came to the king from Herat, and as he made his Salaam he received honour from his highness, whom he urged to be pleased with Budeen-ooz-Zuman, speaking in favour of reconciliation; when the Firman was written, placing Seestan and Furat in the hands of Budeen-ooz-Zuman, and Shaikh Ali Tighaee took this Firman to him at Gore, when he proceeded from Gore to Seestan. This occurred in the latter days of Sufur 903 (A. D. 1497).

AN ACCOUNT OF THE RAISING OF THE STANDARD OF DEPARTURE BY MEERZA BUDEEN-OOZ-ZUMAN SHAH-ZADAH, TO TAKE HERAT.

When Sultan Hoosain Shah turned the bridle of his intention towards Asterabad, Budeen-ooz-Zuman came from Seestan, and Meer Zoonoon from Dawur, to the Sailaf of Gore; and intending to attack Khorasan, they collected the men of Huzarah, the Nukdurees, and the Kubchags. After consultation, with an innumerable host, they marched against Herat. All the Sultan's nobles' cattle that they found in the grazing district they took, and pushed on towards Herat. This news, preceding them, reached Herat, when Ameer Nizam-ood-deen, Ali Sher, and the other nobles in that renowned city, fell into the ocean of anxiety: they strengthened the towers and parapets, and bringing the men of Bulookat into the fort, appointed them to remain there. When Budeen-ooz-Zuman came to the town of Admeeyah, Meer Zoonoon marched in advance. Some of the men of Bulookat had remained at Baghat, who, seeing Meer Zoonoon with his large force, those who had the power, from consideration, brought presents before him, saying they did not advise his advancing any further, because Mahomed Moosoom Meerza had come from Chichuktoo, Mahomed Walee from Aundghas, Meerza Abdoola, the son-in-law of Abdool Bayee Meerza, Meer Baba Ali, and the sons of Khwaja Ufzul, with numerous and well appointed bodies of horse; that they were assembled near Baghat, looking for his approach. Hearing this, Meer Zoonoon retreated a little, and wrote word of the circumstance to Budeen-ooz-Zuman, who came up and joined him at Bukluk. Both of them were sitting in one tent when some from the advanced parties came in, saying that many men appeared coming from Baghat. Meer Zoonoon, upon this, mounted with his Urghoons, and turned his face to fight. The forces met near Alung Musheen, when the brave men of either side, drawing their swords, fell upon each other, fighting in such a manner that the dust from the field of the battle ascended to the heavens. At that time, the light of the predominance of the crescent of the victorious banner of Budeen-ooz-Zuman Meerza fell upon the scene of action. The men of Herat, seeing this, their hands stopped from their work, their hearts left their places. First of all, Abdoola Meerza and Ameer Baba Ali fled; after these Mahomed Moosoom Meerza and Mahomed Walee. Budeen-ooz-Zuman did not approve of entering the city, and turned his face in the direction of the royal army. Those who fled from the battle ran to the fort, the gates of which they shut, giving into the hands of trusty men the towers and defences. Budeen-ooz-Zuman and Zoonoon, with victory, returned to, and encamped at, Alung Musheen. Some days after, they went to Pooli Malan. They did not wish to fight against the city of Herat; their desire was that the men of that place should give it up to them of their own accord. On this account, Ameer Ali Sher spoke with great kindness, and gave encouragement to the people of the town, ordering his troops not to fight. In this way forty days went, when news arrived that the king had left Asterabad, and that he was approaching. Upon this, Ameer Ali Sher sent many successive letters to the prince, forbidding his fighting against his father, and requesting him to leave Pooli Malan, and go to some other place, so that he might not meet him, and that the fire of battle should not be again ignited.

The prince, approving of this advice, marched from Pooli Malan to Pooli Salan; from thence he returned the bridle of his intention to go to Ab Moorghan.

AN ACCOUNT OF BUDEEN-OOZ-ZUMAN MEERZA OBTAINING THE SULTANUT OF BALKH, AND OF THE RETURN OF MEER ZOONOON AND SHAH BEG TO KANDAHAR.

When Budeen-ooz-Zuman, leaving the vicinity of Herat, went to Ab Moorghan, many of the men of Badghees and Chichuktoo went beneath the shadow of his standard, and Shah Beg, coming from Kandahar, joined him. In short, a very large force was collected. The prince sent some men to Purindah Beg Bukshee, the Governor of Muru, desiring him to evacuate the fort; but he would not listen to this. So Shah Beg, taking the Tukdurees, and the Huzarahs, marched against it, and with such arms as they had, they went against this fort. Purindah fought from morning till midday, when, his strength failing, Shah Beg took the fort of Muru, and making prisoner of the Bukshee, sent him to the prince, who, forgiving his fault, liberated him. At that time the king arrived at Herat, when he heard the prince had a very large and duly prepared army, at which his highness was much agitated, because at that time, from the constant harassing work at Asterabad, his men and horses had become thin and weakly, and without some rest they could not fight against Budeen-ooz-Zuman and Meer Zoonoon. The king asked counsel from Moogurub-ool-Huzrutee Sultan (the minister with his titles), and they determined to conciliate the prince. They sent Moolana Fuseeh-ood-deen Asterabadee to Ab Moorghan, to arrange this matter. Moulana Saheb, meeting Budeen-ooz-Zuman and Zoonoon, communicated to them what he had to say, inviting the prince towards the kindness of his father. The prince, looking at the rights of his parent, agreed to make peace, and after many men had come and gone between them, it was settled to give to Budeen-ooz-Zuman the Sultanut of Balkh, and its dependencies; and that in that country the name of the prince should follow that of the king. The prince, after this, left to go to Balkh. On the road, Khwaja Shuhab-ood-deen Abdoola Murwareed overtaking him, delivered the Firman of the Sultanut of Balkh to him. After his arrival there, Budeen-ooz-Zuman bestowed great honour and distinction upoor Meer Zoonoon and Shah Beg, and then gave them leave to depart for Kandahar. He gave Seestan to Ameer Sultan Ali, the brother of Meer Zoonoon.

In short, Meer Zoonoon and Shah Beg, raising the banner of government, arrived at Kandahar.

AN ACCOUNT OF IBN-I-HOOSAIN MEERZA GOING TO SEESTAN; OF THE MARCH OF MEER ZOONOON TO THE ASSISTANCE OF HIS BROTHER; AND OF THE BATTLE BETWEEN THE PARTIES.

In the year 908 (A. D. 1502), Hajun Boordee, and Khoda Kolee, Kotwal of the fort of Lush, became rebellious to Meer Sultan Ali Urghoon; and wishing the happiness of the king, they sent a petition to his highness, to the effect that if one of the princes threw the preponderance of his shadow over that country, as a matter of course Seestan would be conquered without difficulty. The king then sent Ibn-i-Hoosain with 10,000 horse, and he arriving at, looted the borders, raising the standard of his residence at Oog. When this news reached Meer Zoonoon, he, on hearing it, marched with his son Shah Beg against him, and he got over the road very quickly. One morning, when Ibn-i-Hoosain was asleep, and his troops here and there, Meer Zoonoon drew near Oog. The Meerza, hearing of this, with 300 horsemen who were ready, went to meet him. Meer Fazil Kookooltash, and his uncle Magil Atkuh, were the leaders of the advance of the Urghoons. They formed their line in front of Ibn-i-Hoosain. The men of both sides quickly took in their hands their swords, bows and arrows, and spears. Things were in this state, when Meer Zoonoon, with many men of Turkhan and Urghoon, came up on one side, and Shah Beg, with the Yukkuhs, Tukdurees, and Huzarahs, on the other; and in rear of these Bagur Urghoon, and Beg Ali the son of Meer Sultan Ali Urghoon. These quickly came on the field of action; thus Ibn-i-Hoosain became surrounded. In this condition the Meerza fought for one hour, when, receiving a spear wound from Meer Fazil Kookooltash, he turned the bridle of flight towards Herat, and Meer Zoonoon forbad pursuit of him. After this victory, Meer Zoonoon went to Seestan, and met his brother Meer Sultan Ali. In 909 (A. D. 1503) he returned to Kandahar.

AN ACCOUNT OF THE CAPTURE OF KABOOL BY MAHOMED MOKEEM, THE SON OF MEER ZOONOON, AND OTHER INCIDENTS.

Stability and perpetuity are peculiar to the inscrutable essence of God!— To make migration from this bad world belongs to men, who are the inhahitants of one quarter of it!

In the year 907 (A. D. 1501), Meerza Ulug Beg, the son of Sultan Aboo Suneed Meerza, found the mercy of God in Kabool. His son Meerza Abd-oo-Ruzag became ruler there, and sat on the throne of his father; but on account of the youth of this prince, enmity arose amongst the Ameers, and Shere Ruzm Zukkuh took into his hands all the affairs, large and small. At that time Ameer Yoosoob, and Mahomed Kasim Beg, Ameer Yoonoos Ali, and some other nobles, having left the city, were watching a favourable time. In short, on the day of the Eed-i-Koorban, in the morning, when Shere Ruzm was drinking conjee, these entered Kabool with 300 armed men, and drawing their swords of enmity, they cut the roots of his life.

On this account, much destruction came upon the men of Kabool. Intelligence of this reached Mahomed Mokeem, the younger son of Meer Zoonoon, at Gurmsere, who, in the last day of 907 (A. D. 1501), collecting the Huzarahs and the Nukdurees, placed the intention of taking Kabool before his mind, and he went in that direction. Meerza Abd-oo-Ruzag, being unable to fight, fled; and Mahomed Mokeem, taking the country, married the daughter of Meerza Ulug Beg. News of this reached Budeen-ooz-Zuman and Zoonoon, when they were on the banks of Ab Umweeyuh. They were pleased at it, but their anxiety exceeded their joy; and Meer Zoonoon from thence wrote a letter to his son to terrify him, saying: "This business of yours is not good; it is not good, because you have done that which you ought not to have done: now it is necessary that you are not careless of yourself, and do not place the Ameers of Kabool near you." Then Mahomed Mokeem dismissed from Kabool many of the people who had always been connected with the state, placing near himself his own people; and he ruled Kabool.

After this, at the commencement of 910 (A. D. 1504), Huzrut Zaheer-oos-Sultanut Wulkhitafut Mahomed Babur Badshah, returning from Samarkand, took the road to Kabool, and passing very quickly over the intervening space, he shed honour around this city, fortunate by the sacredness of his "blessed feet." Mahomed Mokeem, not having strength to go out to fight the army of Mahomed Babur Badshah, sat down in the fort. After Kabool had been surrounded some time, the men of Ooloos and Eemag were inclined to make their Salaam to the victorious Babur, and the men of the city were also well wishers to the king. Mahomed Mokeem, being unable to remain, wrote to him for quarter, requesting leave to come to him to deliver up the keys of the fort. Huzrut Badshah Mahomed Bahadoor consented to this, and he took oath that when Mokeem opened the gates he would show him such kindness as he might merit.

Then Mahomed Mokeem, being an expectant of the kindness of the king, came forth from Kabool, and found the virtue of kissing the royal carpet; and he made suitable offerings to the king.

Huzrut Babur, agreeably to his promise, showered upon him royal kindness, and then gave him leave to go to his country.

AN ACCOUNT OF THE MARTYRDOM OF MEER ZOONOON URGHOON.

The moon of the month Mohurrum 913 (A. D. 1507) had appeared, when Mahomed Khan Shaibanee Oozbuk, with forces out of number, like ants or locusts, crossing the Goorg, turned his intention towards taking Khorasan. At this the royal family of Sultan Hoosain Meerza became greatly alarmed. Budeen-ooz-Zuman sent a courier to Meer Zoonoon, showing the circumstance to him. Meer Zoonoon consulted with those of his family who were near him, all of whom had different opinions. At length, Zoonoon said: "It is necessary that I should go, for my manhood does not give me leave to sit quiet. I do not expect that I shall return, because the army of the Oozbuks is very formidable and strong, and it appears that the rule of the family of Sultan Hoosain turns its face towards declination." In short, Meer Zoonoon, taking with him the troops of Urghoon, departed to join Budeen-ooz-Zuman. He had only gone two or three marches, when he received the news that his daughter Chochuk Begum had given her life to God at Herat. Although deeply distressed at this, he opened the tongue of thanks to God, that on the approach of these troublesome times he had become free from anxiety on that side.

At that time he sent a messenger to Shah Beg, telling him to proceed to the seat of government, Herat, taking with him the innocent ladies of the family, to give to those their food, and to remove their garments of affliction; adding that after this he was to return quickly to Kandahar. He ordered Mahomed Mokeem to hold Dawur, Ameer Sultan Ali to stay in Seestan, and Ameer Janfur Urghoon, Abdool Ali Turkhan, and others, to remain at Kandahar. He impressed upon all these to place great care and watchfulness before their minds, and not to be careless. Meer Zoonoon then quickly marching on, joined Budeen-ooz-Zuman, whose hand he had the honour to kiss. All the princes and nobles took council with Zoonoon; but they were aware that the deliberations of man could not be a shield to the arrow of the fate of God, when it should be the desire of the perpetual Master of the earth that the kingdom of Khorasan should go into the hands of Mahomed Khan Shaibanee, and that the end of the reign of the family of Sultan Hoosain should arrive; that there would be no avail in assembling the troops of the cities, and that there was no advantage in asking the aid of the deliberations of the nobles. At that time the sepoys of the Oozbuks and Mawuranunhur, had passed the waters of Umweeyuh, when the princes and nobles of Khorasan fell into the sea of care, and again commenced consulting with each other. Meer Zoonoon, from his natural valour, thought it best to fight; Ameer Mahomed Burnodug Burlas deemed it best that they should remain in the fort at Herat. Before the minds of all were united upon one of these two opinions, one morning, the signs of the close approach of the army of Mahomed Khan became as apparent as the misfortunes of heaven, and the royal troops of Mahomed Khan, the Burangurs and the Juwangurs, all prepared, came upon the field of battle.

The princes, turning their attention to drawing up their troops, formed them in a line upon the places for fighting. On both sides the clamour of the brave, the beating Nugarahs, and the shouts of the horsemen, reached above the planet in the seventh heaven. Meer Zoonoon, with the tigers of the jungle of battle, fell upon the enemy, and by the striking of the swords of the design of the crocodile, numbers of the enemy who trod the path of valour were thrown into the waters of mortality. In this manner he several times fell upon them. But the forces of the Oozbuks were double those of Khorasan; they followed each other like the waves of the ocean: therefore the two could not be won in fight. In short, the princes lost all heart in fighting with them, and they turned the bridles of their intention towards the jungles of flight; and all the bodies of their troops, with great dispersion, fled towards Khorasan. Zoonoon fixed his foot on the battle-field, assaulted the enemy on the right and left; from the strokes of his sword the dust on the plain of battle had become red from the blood of the bravest of the enemy. He behaved with the greatest courage, till at length the Oozbuks, coming on all sides of that noble ruler on the field of battle, he, receiving many wounds, fell from his horse. The enemy wished to take him alive, to convey him to Mahomed Khan, but Meer Zoonoon did not give his body up to inactivity, but remained fighting until he died.

AN ACCOUNT OF SOME OF THE CIRCUMSTANCES OF SHAH BEG, AND MAHOMED MOKEEM, URGHOONS.

After the death of Meer Zoonoon, these two brothers united at Kandahar, performing properly all the forms of lamentation. At this assembly Mahomed Mokeem, with all the Sirdars and troops, agreed to accept Shah Beg for the Sirdaree. On that day, in the afternoon, Shah Beg ordered the Nobuts and Nugarahs to be beaten as formerly, and he confirmed in their situations all who held office under Meer Zoonoon. He did not oppose any, therefore all were happy to remain in his service. Shah Beg had given the ornaments of knowledge and respect to the commencement of his manhood. He found a great share of wisdom, always associating with men of learning. When Mahomed Khan had taken Khorasan, he went to Furat. From thence, proposing to take Kandahar, he turned the bridle of his intention that way. When he reached Gurmsere, Shah Beg and Mahomed Mokeem sent ambassadors to him, saying they would obey his orders; the sermon and coinage were altered to the name of Mahomed Khan Shaibanee; and they proposed receiving the honour of making their Salaam to him.

Mahomed Khan, being pleased with them, returned to Khorasan, sending three horses, a handsome Khilat, and a tent, in charge of Abool Hadee and Khwaja Taimoor Tash. Shah Beg hearing of the approach of these, thought, by two coming, that it would be for two matters: either that they were to make a treaty, or else that they wished to see the extent of the city and his troops. At that time he sent men in all directions to collect his people, and taking many men, he went forth in front to meet them. He remained with them three days outside the city, and having pleased them, gave them their leave.

During 913 (A. D. 1507), Mahomed Babur Badshah, raising on high the standard of departure to take Kandahar and Dawur, left Kabool and Ghuznee with many victorious troops. Shah Beg and Mahomed Mokeem went out to meet, and fought with him on a field of battle. After many men had been slain, the breeze of victory struck the tassels of the banners of Mahomed Babur, and Shah Beg and his brother fled. All the countries of Kandahar and Dawur came into the hands of Babur, who took all the treasure which Zoonoon had collected with so much labour, dividing it amongst his soldiery. Appointing his brother Sultan Nasir-ood-deen Meerza Governor of Kandahar, he himself returned to Kabool, taking with him Mah Begum, the daughter of Mahomed Mokeem. Some months after this, Shah Beg and his brother, with a numerous force, full of bravery, came upon Kandahar, freeing that country from Nasir-ood-deen, who retreated to Kabool. Shah Beg and Mahomed Mokeem turned their hearts to putting to rights the arrangements of the country.

At that time the angel of death came upon Mahomed Mokeem, who passed from this to that world. Afterwards Mahomed Babur married Mah Begum to Kasim Kokuh, agreeably to the rules and forms of Mahomed. After a space of time, she bore a daughter, to whom was given the name of Naheed Begum. Kasim Kokuh was afterwards killed, fighting against the Oozbuks.

AN ACCOUNT OF SHAH BEG GOING TO TAKE SEEBEE, AND OF THE FLIGHT OF THE DESCENDANTS OF PEER WULLEE BURDAS.

When Shah Beg came to Shawul from Kandahar (Kunudhar), Meer Fazil Kookooltash and Abdool Ali Turkhan went to meet him, taking and showing to him for service many tribes of the neighbourhood, to the Sirdars of which Shah Beg gave encouragement, and they became expectants of his kindness; but the tribes were afraid of the army, not knowing where it was going. At length, they discovered it was going against Seebee, and by degrees this news reached the descendants of Sultan Peer Wullee, who governed in that country, upon which they sent some of their confidential men with presents to Shah Beg, assuring him that they were his most sincere well-wishers. After some time they were allowed to return, Shah Beg remaining at Shawul, to make arrangements. He spread the carpet of consultation before his nobles, all of whom were of opinion that it was best to go against Seebee; and Shah Beg thought so too, because in the year 915 (A. D. 1509), Shah Ismael had taken Khorasan, and Sultan Babur was at Kabool, and between these the door of warfare was constantly open; and if in this dissension Kandahar should pass from their hands, where should they go to? So Shah Beg sent a body of troops from Shawul towards Seebee, and following these, he by successive marches arrived there, and took the fort. Of the men who were in it, some made their Salaam, others, who had houses there, fled to Futehpoor. After this, Shah Beg sent Meer Fureed Urghoon and others to Kandahar; he himself went towards Futehpoor, 50 kos from Seebee, in the direction of Sind, now deserted, but the fort and houses still remain. When the descendants of Peer Wullee heard of this, they advanced to give him battle with 1,000 horse and two or three thousand men of the Dowlutshaees, the Burgudaees, the Koozpaees, the Noorghaees, Beloochees, and other castes. In the battle, Shah Beg was victorious. Some of the enemy were slain, the rest fled to Sind. Shah Beg, after making the needful arrangements, returned to Seebee, where he stayed some time, giving orders to build a house and to make gardens. He built another fort, placing in it some of his veterans, and he himself then returned to Kandahar. After his return, he went to take exercise in Dawur, and towards Gurmsere, giving encouragement to the inhabitants of all the places he visited. On arriving at Dawur, the mother of Mah Begum, named Beebee Zureefuh, placing a coarse black woollen cloth round her neck, stood before the door of his house, and on Shah Beg's arrival, she placed her hands on the hem of his garment, saying: "Mah Begum is the memorial of your brother; it is necessary that by some means or other you bring her back." On hearing this, a fresh burn of the affliction of separation fell upon the heart of Shah Beg, who, towards the recovery of Mah Begum, consulted secretly with those behind the curtain. Fatima Sultan Begum and Khanuzud Begum, the two wives of Shah Beg, advised that Dowlut Kutuh, who was a slave girl in the Harem of Mahomed Mokeem, should be sent to Kabool, and that by some device she should meet Mah Begum, and bring the news; that after this, a party of their trusty near relations should go, and secretly taking her out of Kabool, and proceeding by the road through the Huzarah country, bring her to Kandahar. Shah Beg, approving of this advice, married Dowlut Kutuh to Dowlut Khan, and sent her to Kabool. By great ingenuity she got into Mah Begum's house, passing herself off as one unknown; but when there was no one else present, she spoke that which was in her heart. But Mah Begum would not agree, fearing for her life, because she had been taken away by Babur Shah, saying: "God forbid!— but after my arrival at Kandahar, my relations, for the sake of their reputations, may destroy me." To remove this dread, Dowlut Kutuh was constantly taking oaths of weight before her, when she at last agreed to escape secretly.

Dowlut Kutuh conveyed this news to Shah Beg, who, on hearing it, was very happy. He sent Baba Meerkai Sarban, Dowlut Khan, and others to Kabool. These, going through Huzarah, took more men from thence, and arriving at Kabool, they put up outside the town. In two or three days, having rested their cattle, and having shod their horses with reversed shoes, they were all ready to depart. One day Mah Begum went to the bath in the afternoon; at sunset she left it, and with Dowlut Kutuh she joined her friends. But she did not bring her daughter Naheed Begum, then a year and a half old. After joining her friends, she remembered her child, and was much afflicted; but these thought it a great blessing that she herself had come, and at once mounted, taking her with them. They marched that entire night, halting in the afternoon of the following day to eat food. After going another night and day, they got over the path of fear, and arrived in the Huzarah country. Here they stopped some days to refresh, and then proceeded to Kandahar. Shah Beg came to the door to meet her, showing great kindness to her, and taking her in his arms, he carried her into the house. He gave horses and Khilats to those who attended her, making them all happy. One year after the death of Kasim Kokuh, Mah Begum was married to Shah Hoosain.

AN ACCOUNT OF SOME OF THE CIRCUMSTANCES OF SHAH BEG.

When Shah Ismael in 917 (A. D. 1511), took Khorasan, the star of his sovereignty shone forth brightly. He killed Mahomed Khan Shaibanee Oozbuk, after which he attained great strength. Those who were near, and those who were far away, when they heard of his army, they all feared. At that time Dermish Khan, coming towards Furat and Seestan, raised the standard of his authority on high. Shah Beg, on hearing this, was alarmed, and took counsel with his friends, saying: "I am fallen between two kings such as fire and water: on one side is Shah Ismael, on the other Babur Shah." His friends in their wisdom settled that he should go to Shah Ismael, through the introduction of Dermish Khan; and that it was necessary to make friends with Babur Badshah. So he sent Kazee Abool Hoosain with many presents to Kabool, declaring that he was the very great friend of the king, and he himself, through Dermish Khan, went to Shah Ismael, who was very kind to him, excusing him from bowing his head, and ordering him to make his Salaam in the manner of Chughtiyuh, bending the knees.

Shah Beg remained in attendance a long time, the king promising that he should have leave to depart on the first day of spring. Dermish Khan was sent to the fort of Ekhtiyar-ood-deen, when the flatterers turned the temper of the king from Shah Beg by evil words. As the spring drew near, on the plea of some pretended business, Ismael withdrew his face from Shah Beg, and confined him in the fort of Zufur. His attendants, being helpless, some remained secretly there, others went to Kandahar. When Shah Ismael went to remain at Irag, Mehtur Soonbool, a slave of Shah Beg's, went to Zufur, setting up a sweetmeat shop underneath where his master was confined. Through his sweetmeats he became acquainted with all the prisoners, and sometimes he ventured inside, when by signs he understood what Shah Beg wanted, and it was arranged between them, that twelve of his trusty men should come, and taking him from thence, convey him to Kandahar. Mehtur Soonbool told these men to come, and then he cooked some sweet-meat, with which he mixed intoxicating things, which he gave according to custom to the door-keepers, who, after eating it, loosened the bridle of alertness from their hands. After this, the twelve men came to the slave's shop, and he, taking two of them, went to the to wer where Shah Beg was kept, and with a rope they lowered him down; but the rope being short, he let go, and fell to the earth, when, on account of the irons on his legs, he fell on his face instead of on his feet, breaking one of his teeth. He then mounted a horse, and after marching all that night and the next day, he by some means got another horse. In this manner he arrived where there was no fear. The keepers of the prison, on coming to their senses, made great search, but not being successful, with great vexation they returned back again.

AN ACCOUNT OF MAHOMED BABUR BADSHAH GOING AGAINST KANDAHAR.

When Babur Badshah heard of the imprisonment of Shah Beg, he determined to take Kandahar; but from many impediments which existed in the direction of the towns of Mawrauh, Unur, and Budukshan, he could not bring forth that which was on his breast. But when he had put his heart at ease with respect to those, with a very large force, he raised on high the standard of march against Kandahar. Shah Beg collected in the fort all the necessary articles of subsistence that he could find, and making up his mind to hold and fight the city, he repaired the towers and defences, placing men of trust over these. He sent spies into the royal army, to discover and let him know daily fresh news as to their condition, strength, &c. When these arrived there, and saw the army, they sent word that the king, with a large force, and great munitions of war, had turned his face that way. Shah Beg, with much valour, declared it as his opinion that they ought to go out to fight on the plain; and he consulted with his friends on this, all of whom decided that it was necessary for them once to try their strength on the battle-field, where, if God showed the face of victory in the looking-glass of their desire, it would be as they wished; if not, they could return to the fort and fight there. But, as Babur Badshah drew near, he became indisposed, so much so that his sepoys' hearts left their places, and their hands let go their work. Shah Beg, hearing of this, sent a valuable present to the king by influential men of the city, laying the foundation of peace between them. Babur sent a horse and a Khilat to him, and then, turning his face, he took his army back to Kabool.

Shah Beg went to Seebee, remaining in that country some time, telling his nobles that "Babur Badshah had come this time to see the road to Kandahar: it is probable that he will again raise on high the banner of march against it next year; for until he has turned me out of my place, he will not find repose." To confirm this, he advanced two proofs, one of which was, that "Mahomed Mokeem having done that which he ought not to have done, that thorn rankled in his (Babur's) heart. On this account he took away Mokeem's daughter: he also thinks that if he does not take Kandahar, the Urghoons (God forbid!) may again do as Mokeem did. The other proof is, that the king has many princes, who have not strength to fight the Oozbuks and Kuzulbashees, but they are strong enough to war against me: on this account, some day they will take Kandahar; so it is necessary for me to be alert, and careful on all sides."

In the early days of the cold season, he sent 1,000 horsemen from Seebee towards Sind. These looted the villages of Kahan and Baghbanan in the month Zilkut 921 (A. D. 1515). Mukhdoom Janfur, who was one of the well known men of learning of Sind, says that he heard from Meerza Eesa Turkhan, that in this expedition 1,000 camels belonging to the wells of the gardens fell into the hands of that force. From this the produce and cultivation of that country may be understood. This force remained a week in the vicinity of those places.

During that year, as Shah Beg had foretold, Babur Badshah came upon, and surrounded Kandahar. He commenced digging mines, on account of a famine that season. This siege caused very great distress to the citizens. In short, peace was made. In the early days of the month Peer, on account of fever attacking his troops, Babur was forced to return to Kabool. During this year, Shah Hoosain, being displeased with his father, left Kandahar, going to Babur Badshah, who received him with the eye of kindness. He stayed two years near the king, during which period Babur was constantly saying that he had not come for service, but to learn the customs of kings from him.

In 922 (A. D. 1516), before the collections of tribute in grain were made, the standard of march of Babur Badshah arrived at Kandahar, when he encircled it. By his coming at that time, Shah Beg became much distressed, so he sent Shaikh Aboo Suneed Pooranee to make terms of peace, upon which Khwaja Abdool Uzeen came into the city, when a treaty was written, to the effect that in the following year Shah Beg should deliver up the city to Babur Badshah, who returned to Kabool after this was settled.

Shah Beg then strengthened Shawul, and he remained there and at Seebee. In 923 (A. D. 1517), agreeably to the treaty, he sent the keys of the royal palace and fort of Kandahar to the king, who much approved of this conduct. Shah Beg passed the next two years in Shawul and Seebee, with great difficulty: one season his sepoys had nothing to eat but carrots and turnips. At length, being helpless, he turned his face towards looting Sind, and a second time his troops came to the fort of Machee, and to the country of Chandooka. During that year, Durya Khan, who was called the son of Jam Nindah, the ruler of Tatta, taking a large force, arrived near Seebee. At this time Shah Beg was not present, having gone on an expedition against Seestan. There was much fighting between the Moguls (of Seebee) and the Sindees, in which Aboo Mahomed Meerza drank the sherbet of martyrdom. Rozee Beg, and the few men of the Urghoons and Huzarahs who were there, did very good service, and the Sindees went back to Tatta again.

In that year Jam Nindah, taking the articles of his being, went to the world of everlasting life, and Jam Pheroz sat in his place; and this I have mentioned before.

During the life-time of Jam Nindah the men of Dowlutshaee and Noorghaee, coming to Tatta, went into his presence. Rai Beg Urghoon, with some followers, also came there, because he had spilt blood with his hand; to these the Jam assigned a quarter to live in, called Mogulwara. Meer Kasim Rubkee also came in secret, and stopped some time in Tatta, and having made himself acquainted with all its circumstances, he went back to Shah Beg, to whom he gave temptation to go and take it, and on what he said Shah Beg prepared a force for that purpose, in the latter days of that year. Historians say, that when he began to collect men at Futehpoor, great numbers joined him; that from thence he sent a large body under Beg Albee Meerza and other Sirdars, to Shawul, to protect his family and the fort; he left Sultan Mahomed at Seebee, and placed some men in Futehpoor and Gunjabah. He placed under Meer Fazil Kookooltash 40,200 brave men, sending him in advance towards Tatta, he himself following.

When Shah Beg halted at Baghbanan, the head men came and paid their respects to him. It was the wish of Shah Beg that all the people should come of their own accord and obey him, but these would not do so; then he marched upon Tatta by the way of Goondee, and by successive marches he arrived on the bank of the Khanwah (canal), 3 kos to the north of Tatta, where he halted. Shah Beg remained some days, considering how to cross the canal, where one day a poor man was seen coming over on foot. He was seized by the men on chokee (guard), and through intimidation he agreed to show the way, and Abdoor Rahman Dowlutshaee, putting his horse into the water, followed him, and after having crossed over he came back again, and gave the news to Shah Beg. On the 11th Mohurrum, 926 (A. D. 1509), leaving many to take care of his camp, he himself put his horse into the canal, his army following him. In short, the whole crossed over, and arrived near Tatta. Durya Khan, leaving Jam Pheroz in the city, went forth to the fight, with many men. The battle began between the two armies, and they fought to such an extent, that it cannot be described by the pen. At length victory came to Shah Beg, and Jam Pheroz, turning his face in the direction of flight, crossed over the river to the other side. Durya Khan, after being made prisoner, was slain with the men of Summah.

Shah Beg gave Tatta up to plunder till the 20th Mohurrum, his troops throwing the dust of villany on the heads of the inhabitants.

It is true that "when a strong king enters a town it becomes desolate!" (Koran.)

Shah Beg seized and confined many of the families of the men of note of the city, for he was angry. His anger ceased through the exertions of Kazee Kazin, who was the Kazee of the town, in this manner:— His family was confined, and he, like one out of his senses, went about the streets seeking, as if looking for something he had lost. In this condition he wrote a letter, in which he showed forth the unhappy state of the people. This was given to Shah Beg by Hafiz Mahomed Shureef Emam. On reading it, Shah Beg's heart was affected; he gave orders to have it promulgated by tom-tom, that none of his men were to lay hands on the citizens, and taking an arrow from his quiver, he gave it to Kazee Kazin, and sending a man with him, directed that such people as he should point out were to be made over to him.

Previous to this, Jam Pheroz, with a small body of followers, went to the village of Perar, where he sat under great affliction, for his family, and that of Nizam-ood-deen, remained in Tatta, and he knew that his affairs could only be improved by his attendance on Shah Beg. So he sent a well-spoken man to him, by whom he conveyed a most humble verbal message: "My degree is so small, that I could not fight with one of your sepoys. This business, which has come to this result, has been brought about by fear for my life, and by the instigation of others: if the water of your kindness and forgiveness washes off the dust of my faults, I will place the ring of submission to your orders in my ear, and, as long as I live, my foot shall not swerve from the pathway of obedience to you; and when your honorable troops shall leave, and encamp outside the city of Tatta, I will come to your presence, and give light to my eyes, which are clear-eyed by the dust of your doorway." Shah Beg, with great kindness, which was in his original nature, at this humility, pitied him greatly: to those who came from him he gave Khilats, sending messages full of kindness. Then Jam Pheroz, with his brethren, came to the water side at Perar, and suspending his sword from his neck, he made humble submission. Shah Beg directed Ula-ood-deen, the son of Moobaruk Khan, to permit the families of Jam Pheroz and his relations to go to him. In the latter end of Sufur, Shah Beg left Tatta. At his first encampment, Jam Pheroz sent him many acceptable presents, and, through the introduction of the nobles, he attained the honour of kissing the hand of Shah Beg, and, in his presence, the Jam much lamented what he had done. Shah Beg gave him a large sum of money in a present, and also the Khilat which Sultan Hoosain had conferred upon Meer Zoonoon; on receiving which, Pheroz became very happy. He also gave to him all the chief buildings in Tatta, desiring him to go there, and take his people to their homes.

Shah Beg then held consultation with his chiefs, proposing— "Sind is a large country; many men will be required to take care of it— a few cannot do so; it seems proper to make one-half of it over to Jam Pheroz, and to leave the rest under our men of trust." It came into the wisdom of the council, that it would be preferable to make over to the Jam the country from Lukee, near Sehwan, to Tatta, and that the country above Lukee should remain in the hands of his (Shah Beg's) slaves. After settling the treaty, Shah Beg, by successive marches, arrived at Sehwistan, the men of which, before his arrival, had gone off to Tuluhtee, where numbers were collected— among them, many of the tribes of Shuhta, and Sodah, all of whom had agreed that they would not withdraw the hand from war as long as they lived. Shah Beg took the fort of Sehwan. He then sent Kazee Kazin to the sons of Durya Khan, to try and induce them to leave the jungle of enmity, and to bend their heads in the path of submission. When he came to these, they would not agree to what he said. Shah Beg then came, and halted opposite to Tuluhtee, and three days after, a man, coming from thence, showed him the strength of the enemy, saying Mahomed Khan and Mutun Khan (the sons of Durya Khan) proposed coming to his presence, but that Mukhdoom Bulal, the chief priest of that country, had prevented them from doing so, instigating them to fight. This was in this manner— when Shah Beg conquered Tatta, he placed a fine on this priest.

Shah Beg that night collected boats, and in the morning Meer Fazil Kookooltash crossed the river by these, and the Urghoons, the Turkhans, and the whole army. At breakfast time Shah Beg followed them. All the men of Tuluhtee came forth from their fort, Runmul and Todah, Sodah, being in advance. Meer Fazil, with the vanguard, began the attack, breaking the enemy's force; and when Shah Beg came up, the battle was taken to the gates of the fort, and his men, falling upon the enemy with great impetuosity, many of the Summahs were killed. Some, throwing themselves into the river, drank the water of the occan of death; some fled to Sehwistan. Shah Beg remained three days in Tuluhtee, giving to the winds of death the harvest of the lives of those men. In this battle the Sodahs fought well, fixing their feet of valour on the battle-field. Most of them were slain.

AN ACCOUNT OF SHAH BEG SENDING HIS SON SHAH HOOSAIN FROM SHAWUL AND SEEBEE TO EXPEL JAM SULAH-OOD-DEEN.

When Shah Beg, having conquered Tatta, gave the government of that country to Jam Pheroz, and returned towards Seebee and Shawul, and when those men of the Jam's who through fear had fled were now again collected near him, at that time Jam Sulah-ood-deen (who formerly hoisted on high the standard of war against Jam Pheroz, after the death of his father, and who for some short time ruled over Tatta, and was defeated by the stratagem of Durya Khan, and went to Guzerat) again turning the desire of government on his head, with 10,000 horsemen (composed of the three sects of Jharejas, Sodahs, and Kungurs) turned his face towards Sind. Shah Beg had left in Tatta Meer Aleek Urghoon, Sultan Mahomed Beg Lar, with others, to give confidence to Pheroz, who, hearing of this, wrote a letter to Shah Beg, which they sent by a Kosid. The Jam also sent with much despatch Ula-ood-deen the son of Moobaruk Khan, saying he needed aid. When this news came, Shah Beg called his nobles, asking their advice. They said it was best that he should send his son Shah Hoosain with a good force, and that he should arrive quickly to the help of Jam Pheroz. On the 14th Mohurrum, 927 (A. D. 1521), Meerza Shah Hoosain left Shawul, and in twenty days he got over the road, and arrived at Tatta, and Shah Beg sent other troops and supplies after him. When the news of the arrival of Shah Hoosain reached Sulah-ood-deen, he retreated, and going to Joon, halted there. Jam Pheroz left the city, and went out to meet Shah Hoosain, bringing him presents; and having an interview with him, Shah Hoosain, according to what his father had told him, showed much kindness and distinction to the Jam. These two, collecting as many men as they could, marched against Sulah-ood-deen, and when they had got some marches, he also got ready, sending his son Haibut Khan, the son-in-law of Sultan Moozuffur Guzeratee, in advance. Meerza Shah Hoosain had in front Meerza Eesa Turkhan, and others, and the fight commenced. The Mogul sepoys stoutly fixed the foot of bravery on the plain of battle, slaying numbers of the men of Jam Sulah-ood-deen, and Shah Hoosain, coming up, broke his army. The son of Sulah-ood-deen fell, hearing which his father, with many men, fell upon the forces of Shah Hoosain, fighting gallantly; but at length he also was killed, and then those who escaped the sword fled to Guzerat.

Meerza Shah Hoosain, the conqueror, remained three days on the field of action. He then turned back with Jam Pheroz.

In the month of Rubee-oos-Sanee, Shah Beg, coming with all the families to Baghbanan, wrote a Firman to Shah Hoosain, calling him and all the nobles. With Shah Beg were some of his relatives, and taking these alone, he went against the men of Machee (those who were disobedient), all of whom he killed, looting their property, cattle, &c. and razing their houses and fort to the ground.

AN ACCOUNT OF SHAH BEG'S SOJOURN AT BAGHBANAN, AND OF HIS GOING FROM THENCE TO SEHWISTAN.

When Shah Beg was in Baghbanan, Meerza Shah Hoosain came with victory: his father embraced him with great affection, showing him every kindness. He also directed kindness to the chiefs of the army. He remained there some time after the arrival of Shah Hoosain, that he and the troops might have repose. Then, leaving him there, he himself, with the chief Sirdars, and a large force, and having the principal men of Baghbanan with him, went to Sehwistan. Having inspected the fort at Sehwan, he placed a Thana there, under some of his men of experience, directing that all the tribute paid in kind should be collected in it. He told the Sirdars remaining there to build houses for themselves, dividing such as were there among them. He then returned to Baghbanan. From thence he strengthened the bridle of his intention to go to Bukkur. At that time Kazee Kazin came: he received a large present in money from Shah Beg. On his first march from Baghbanan, men from Jam Pheroz arrived, bringing petitions from him: they placed in front of Shah Beg offerings of a horse and presents sent by their master. Shah Beg, giving them Khilats and presents in return, gave them leave to depart, giving them a letter for the Jam, writing as follows: "It is my intention to take the country of Guzerat. When it shall come into my hands, I will certainly leave Sind in your possession, as before." He then went towards Bukkur.

AN ACCOUNT OF THE DESTRUCTION OF THE PEOPLE OF THE TRIBE OF DHAREJA.

When Shah Beg arrived at Chandooka, which is 30 kos west of Bukkur, Sultan Mahomed Khan, the son of Meer Fazil Kookooltash, sent Baba Chochuk Ulkuh to his father, telling him all the circumstances of the country under him (Bukkur). Meer Fazil made this known to Shah Beg, who gave him leave to depart, with 200 horse. So leaving Chandooka, he crossed the river opposite to it. To all the head men of the villages who came to him he gave great encouragement, taking them with him. When he got to Bhiryaloe, Sultan Mahomed proposed going to meet his father, but he, hearing of this, sent word to his son: "On no account put your foot outside the fort; act like a brave man, get into your hands all your enemies, and imprison them in Bukkur." When Sultan Mahomed Khan was placed in authority over Bukkur, the Soduts (Syuds) became surety for him, and Shah Beg directed that the chief men of the Dharejas should live in the fort; but these, from want of wisdom, broke these orders, and withdrew, and, opening the gate of war, they wished to annoy Mahomed, exerting themselves to get him out of the fort. They ceased paying tribute, and when Mahomed's men went to them, they were treated with indignity, and sent back again. Collecting many men, they prepared a field of battle near Loree (Roree). At that time Sultan was twelve years of age, and being young and hasty, he wished to go against them; but the Syuds forbade this, and would not permit him to go to fight, giving him encouragement and confidence. The Dharejas twice made great efforts to cross the water to take him, but the Soduts, finding this, stood up to fight, manning the towers and gateways; but the Dharejas did not agree to fight with them.

Meer Fazil arriving near Bukkur, Lalee Muhur, the head man of the Zemindars, with his brethren, came to pay his respects: he received honour. The head men of the Dharejas, being helpless, also came in to him, to such an extent, that on reaching Bukkur there were forty-seven of these with him. Sultan Mahomed received honour by kissing his father's foot, telling him his grievances, in revenge for which he (Meer Fazil) slew twenty-seven of the Dharejas. When Shah Beg heard that Meer Fazil had reached Bukkur, he quickly started, and halted on the plain near Sukkur. Sultan Mahomed had an interview with him, kissing his feet, and receiving great kindness from him. Kazee Kazin, who, previous to Mahomed coming, had spoken to Shah Beg, now arrived, bringing some of the town's-people with him. Sultan Mahomed told Shah Beg of the conduct of the Dharejas, on hearing which he turned his face towards Kazee, who said: "This country of Sind becomes inundated, and from the waters many thorns arise: to root these out, it is necessary that you take an axe in your hand." On hearing this, Shah Beg gave orders for the destruction of the Dharejas, and Mahomed, going to the town, in that night he struck the necks of those people, casting them out from a tower which was called Khoonee Burj (the bloody tower). The following morning, taking the Syuds with him, he went to Shah Beg, obtaining an audience for them, speaking to him favourably of their good will. Shah Beg, on hearing this, addressed them kindly, asking after their families, and giving them honour. When the assembly broke up, he called Mahomed on one side, asking him about these Syuds. He repeated what he had said, adding that although well-wishers, still it was not proper that so many of one caste should remain in the fort. Shah Beg laughed at this, saying he had given a good recommendation for them. He then sent word to these Sodats by Humza Beg, that the Moguls had all brought their families with them, and that these must be placed in the fort; that it was necessary, therefore, that all the Syuds should go and live in one or two of the largest houses, and that all the other buildings must be given up to them. The Syuds did not see fit to remain in the fort, making it known to Shah Beg that they would leave it, to which he agreed, giving them ground in Roree to build upon.

The Syuds are inhabitants there to this very day.

After this, Shah Beg went into the fort, and was pleased on seeing it. He distributed the houses amongst his chiefs and soldiers. He then measured out the fort, and dividing it into separate parts, he allotted these over to his nobles, that they might each build from hand to hand (quickly). These, breaking down the fort of Alore, which was formerly the seat of government, brought the burned bricks from thence. They also pulled down many houses of the Toorks and Summahs, which were about, and with these materials they built the fortifications of the fort of Bukkur. When the foundation of this fort was about to be dug, Shah Beg said to Shah Hoosain: "Those two hills which are to the south are against this fort: first of all we must care for them, and then put our hands to building this." In about an hour afterwards, having thought upon it, he remarked: "It is best to build the fortifications of this fort at once, in the first place, for the river being on all four sides of it, it is not necessary to have much fear for those hills, because the king who is powerful to take this fort, he will not surround it, and the king and chiefs who are defeated will do nothing." In short, after some time, the works of the fort reached their end, and he arranged that Shah Hoosain and himself should live in the citadel. He also gave room there to a few of his nobles, such as Meer Fazil and his sister, Sultan Beejah, Mulik Mahomed Kokuh, Meer Mahomed Savhan, and Sultan Mahomed Mohurdar.

Those fortifications are standing at the time of writing this book, 1009 (A. D. 1600).

One year afterwards, when Shah Beg had put his heart at rest regarding this fort, and by his arrangements with the Ryuts, he turned his attention to punishing those Beloochees who would not take their hands out of dissension, and he determined that the fire of their discord must be quenched by the water of the sword. He saw the face of this business in the looking-glass of deliberation in this manner: to place in every village of these Beloochees bodies of his tried men, who should stay there some time; that a certain period should be fixed upon, when at one and the same time those bodies of men should destroy each of those villages.

In short, as he proposed, he sent these troops to every village of these Beloochees, and going there, these waited for the appointed time: when it arrived, all taking their swords in their hands, they brought the affairs of these people to an end. In these encounters, forty-two villagers were killed and wounded.

In the beginning of the cold season of 928 (A. D. 1522), leaving Payundah Mahomed Turkhan as Governor of Bukkur, Shah Beg, with a very large force, marched to take Guzerat. At every halting-place he punished the disturbers of the peace on both sides of the river, clearing the country of them. He then arrived at Chandooka, where Meer Fazil became sick from fever, so, obtaining leave to return, he went back to Bukkur, and Baba Ahmed, his son, also had permission to accompany, and attend upon him. Shah Beg, seeing the sickness of Meer Fazil, became very sorrowful: in this affliction he became aware that Meer Fazil had heard— "Oh my quiet people, return to your God with pleasure!" (Koran); and that he had joined the people of Paradise. Shah Beg and Shah Hoosain, on this account, became much dejected; and that night Sultan Mahomed Khan, and all the near relatives of Meer Fazil, had leave given to them, and these, in the hope of finding him alive, went with great haste, arriving at Bukkur the next morning, when they found that he had left this world, so, putting on the winding-sheet, they placed him in his grave. On the third day, Shah Beg came with haste, performing all the customs of mourning, taking off the clothes of affliction from the members of the family, saying: "The death of Meer Fazil shows me the road to death, I shall follow him!" The people of the assembly, hearing this, begged for mercy, saying— "May you live!" He went from thence to the Harem, to the attendants of which he said the same. These exclaimed as the others had done, saying— "What words are you bringing upon your tongue?" In short, Shah Beg, with Shah Hoosain, and all the Ameers, having done everything that was necessary, marched away, and punishing those on either bank who were troublesome, he set his heart at ease, and by the way of Tatta he went to take Guzerat. By successive marches he arrived at Akhum, from whence, sending to call Jam Pheroz, he remained there some time.

AN ACCOUNT OF THE DEPARTURE OF SHAH BEG FROM THIS WORLD, IN WHICH THERE IS TROUBLE.

The decree— "Upon every one death will come!" (Koran) is approaching all; and the decree— "All that breathe are the drinkers of the sherbet of death!" (Koran) is coming down on each.

When Shah Beg had set his mind at ease with respect to the affairs of Bukkur and Sehwistan, he proposed to take Guzerat. After leaving Bukkur, the news reached him that Babur Badshah had arrived at Bheeruh, and Khooshab, and that he intended to take Hindoostan. Shah Beg, on hearing this, said to those at the assembly: "Babur Badshah will not even permit me to remain in Sind. Some day he will take this country from me, or from my descendants: it is fit for me to go away to some other place." When this care fell upon him, some disease was bad within him: such medicines as were given made no impression upon him, and he made the journey to that world before reaching Guzerat. It is written, that when near death, he called Hafiz Mahomed Shureef, saying to him— "Read a chapter of the Yaseen." When Hafiz came to "It is not proper for me that I should not read prayers to Him who created me, to whom we all shall go," Shah Beg became revived, saying— "Oh special reader of the Koran, read that over again!" Hafiz did so, and when he came to "Said it would be good if my people knew what kindness God shows to me," he (Shah Beg) made over his life to God. This occurred on the 22nd of Shaban, 928 (A. D. 1522). On that night the Ameers and all the men of consequence agreed to obey the orders of Meerza Shah Hoosain, as they had those of his father. Shah Hoosain and his friends performed all the customs of mourning, and took his corpse to Bukkur. Three years afterwards his coffin was taken to Mecca, where it was placed in the Monulla, and a tomb was built over him. After the death of Shah Beg, the news arrived, that on hearing of it Jam Pheroz was very happy, beating Nugarahs. When Shah Hoosain heard this, great perspiration of enmity came upon him, and the fire of anger became lighted in his body. The Ameers did not think it right to go to Guzerat then, and the standard of taking Jam Pheroz out by the roots, and of conquering Tatta, was raised on high.

A SHORT ACCOUNT OF SOME OF THE CIRCUMSTANCES OF SHAH BEG.

At the commencement of his youth, Shah Beg went into the presence of Khwaja Abdoola, saying he was a humble man, and he repented before him. At that time he brought perfection to himself, spending much of his time in prayers to God. When he was with his father at Herat, he always attended the assemblies of the learned, and he was in the habit of calling these to his house twice a week. The results of his good sense were "An Explanation of Kaffeeyuh"; "Marginal Notes to the Commentary of Mutalim"; also "Marginal Notes to the Commentary of the Furayuz of Meer Syud Shureef"; and he also wrote notes to other books.

SOME ACCOUNT OF THE WONDERS OF SEEBEE.

One of the wonders of the country of Seebee is, that to the north of it is seen a cupola, which is called, in Sindee tongue, Maree, or Gurhee, and when any one goes there, it disapprears from the sight. One time Sultan Mahomed Bukree, taking two or three thousand people, went all over those hills, but he could not see anything of it; he did not find this cupola. It is said that it is a talisman, made by former people, and that beneath it there is treasure. A Durwish once went there, when he found something: after that, on the strength of this many people went there; but none of these found anything. The fort of Seebee is upon a small hill, the stones on which are all round; and as much as the earth is dug, such round stones are found. In Kore Zumeen, which is a part of Seebee, the cotton plants are as large as Bheree trees, and the men there, getting on horseback, pluck the cotton. On each of these plants there are always one or two hundred snakes, which are knocked off by sticks, when the cotton is gathered: if a person is bitten by one of these, the part is pricked at the time with the point of a knife, and the blood drawn out, and he generally recovers. A small river near Seebee ran over brimstone: if any one drank the water, he became sick— many have died of this sickness; but it did not affect the inhabitants, because it had become habitual to them. Sultan Mahomed every year sent people to try this water, and the greater part of them always died. In the time of Khilafut Punahee, a great flood of waters came, and taking this brimstone out by the roots, washed it away; from which time the sickness has been less. The water of this river runs 50 kos beyond Seebee, collecting at Saroh, where it is taken away for the fields; that which is in excess flows into the lake of Munchoor, which is near Sehwan. On the banks of that lake there are many snakes, the bite of which few survive. The men about there wear very long, wide drawers, to defend themselves.

I went there, and saw the men irrigating their fields; and as I was going along, I saw snakes at every step of my horse. I wished to dismount, but for fear of these I did not do so, going off to a distance in the plain for that purpose. In the country of Seebee, there were formerly many forts, and much cultivation; but all has now become deserted. The hot winds blow there. The country between Seebee, Dehra, and Kushmoor is called Bargan, the horses of which are not inferior to those of Irag: when a foal is born, they place it upon gravel, upon which it walks for one year, and its hoofs become like stone; so much so, that it is not necessary to shoe, and these go amongst the hills without shoes.

A tribe remains at Chauttr, called Kuheree. The reason of their having this name is this: Kuheer is the name of a tree, on one of which one of their ancestors mounted, and striking it with his whip, it moved like a horse: in this manner the name Kuheree originated. Near Gunjabah, which is part of Seebee, there is a place where water comes forth, and with this, fishes; much ground is occupied by this water. Amongst the hills at Gunjabah there is one very high and perpendicular: from this hangs an iron cage, in which, it is said, there is something— the hand cannot reach it: if any one, by getting to the top from the other side, tries to get hold of it, it goes far from him, and if one attempts to get up to it from below, it rises, or goes to one side, the earth underneath appearing to recede far away. Seebee and Gunjabah are in this way: the hills of Sitore and the river Ab Kuseedah (drawn water) from Seebee and Gunjabah run to the river Sind. All this country is desert. The road to Kandahar lays over this Rhunn, which is 100 kos in length from the river to Seebee, and it is 60 kos in breadth. For four months in the days of the sun, the hot winds prevail here.

AN ACCOUNT OF THE WONDERS OF KANDAHAR.

At 10 kos to the west of Kandahar there is a village called Bekhnahee, near which there is a hill, in which there is a cavern, with running water on all sides. Bats, like rats, are very numerous here: a room has been cut out of the rock, and other rooms appear to those who go forward; but it is so dark that no one can go without lights, and when these are taken, these bats come upon you, and the lights, in such nnmbers, that it is very difficult for a person to proceed. They say there is talisman there, and a revolving wheel, around which there are bricks of gold; also that Baba Husan Abdool went there, and throwing a hide upon the wheel, he went forward, and brought out one gold brick. I will presently relate the circumstances of Baba Husan.

Another curiosity is, that by the order of Babur Badshah, at a hill called Seepoozah, the rock was cut, and a recess made, which he called Peshtag. It is a very lofty recess: for nine years eighty stone-cutters were employed, and then they finished the work. Certainly it is a spot to delight the eyes, close over the Urghoondab, with many fields and gardens about. On this account, during the spring, many go there; but the recess is very high up, on which account no one goes there, being afraid of falling. In the inscription in this recess are written the names of Mahomed Babur Badshah, Meerza Kamran, Meerza Uskuree, Meerza Hundal, and that these were all men of good spirit, &c. But Hoomayoon Badshah, not being of the kings there, his name was not written, and of all his country Kandahar alone appeared. When I went there, seeing that the names of Hoomayoon and Ukbar Shah, and their countries, were not mentioned, and this when thousands of countries like Kabool and Kandahar were in the hands of their slaves, it came into my heart to write the names of their countries and cities. For this purpose, I called from Bukkur good writers and stone-cutters, who wrote the names of Hoomayoon Badshah, and Huzrut Shahun Shah Ukbar, and also of their countries and cities, from Bengal to Luheree Bunder (Tatta), and from Kabool and Ghuznee to the south. In four years this was finished, and it certainly was well executed, so that many went to see it. Near the hill in which this recess is, there is a cavern, the end of which God only knows. This is the cavern from whence, it is said, Baba Husun brought the brick of gold. The distance between these is seven or eight kos. On the hills near Kandahar, Mookhtisuh is found, which saves from the poisonous bite of a snake, and from other poisons. This is not found anywhere except on these hills. On the top of one of these hills there is a fire-temple. This building is made of sun-burnt bricks, each of which is 2 guz square, and 1 span thick. It is there now, not in the least decayed. In Kandahar there was formerly sickness every year, when Shah Tuhmasp ordered Sultan Hoosain, who was governor there, to plant canes on the banks of such rivers in the vicinity whose waters the inhabitants used for drinking and other purposes. He did as he was directed; after which the yearly sickness abated much, but in some seasons it broke out worse than before. Many people die from passing blood, which also comes from the mouth, nose, and ears. In the time of Khilafut Punachee Ukbar Shah, when I went to Kandahar as governor in the year 1007 (A. D. 1598), 200 men, horse and foot, of the Thana, died of this disease.

The men of Huzarah in Kandahar are not in the habit of wearing clothes coloured red, blue, &c.; they are plain men, wishing only for simple cloth and shoes.

About Kandahar there are many graves of the workers of miracles. Amongst these is that of Shah Musnood Abdal. On the hill side (at the base of which is this grave) vines, apple trees, quince trees, pomegranates, and many other fruits grow of their own accord: there are many springs of water running there. Such as this is only to be found at Kandahar, nowhere else. Shah Musnood planted a vine there, which remains still. Near this hill there is a tract of land called Tunbeel, where the melons and water-melons are particularly fine; they are watered from Kareezes. Wherever these are sown, half of the fruit, more or less, have insects in them, the fruit becoming on that side as hard as a stone; but this is not the case with those grown at Tunbeel.

Another grave is that of Baba Husun Abdool, of the true family of the Syuds of Subzwar.

At the beginning of his life he had an inclination towards God. He made a journey to Mecca, performing the pilgrimage to both that shrine and Medina, remaining there some time. He came to Subzwar in the time of Shah Rookh Badshah, who placed great faith in him. On this account he took him with him on his journey to Hindoostan, and when he returned Baba Husun remained at Lungur of Kandahar. When there, he said to his disciples: "From this earth the smell of friendship comes to me!" He remained there all his days, dying there. His grave is on high ground, beneath which is the Urghoondab, with many villages; and on Fridays the men and women, the little and big, the good and the bad, all flock there on pilgrimage: but few remain in the city on that day— all go there. It certainly is a delightful situation, and those who come from other parts say there is no place like it.

His (Baba Husun's) miracles are many; from amongst them these are a few— I have related how he went into the cave, bringing out the gold brick:—

In front of the door of his tomb there is a temple of a conical shape, made of stone, but the stones are not cut, and each weighs 5 Kandahar maunds; there is not any plaster or mud between them. They say this was his cloister, and that with one disciple he built it in one night. The stones are so joined, that water does not pass between them; and yet, what is most extraordinary, the sky is to be seen between through the crevices. On the peak of the hill, on the base of which stands this tomb, there is a temple built by Baba Husun Abdool. All who see it say it is one of his miracles, because there is no way for a man to get there, and it must have been most difficult to convey materials for building there.

Syud Meer Hoosain Zunjeer Rai is also of the true family of Subzwar; there are nineteen generations between him and Imam Moosa Kazim. His mother was the sister of Baba Husun Abdool. When Baba Husun returned to Subzwar from his journey to Mecca, he married his sister Fatima Beebee to Syud Uain-ood-deen, who was of the chief family of the Syuds of Subzwar. It is said, that nineteen years after this marriage Meer Hoosain Zunjeer was born, and that at the age of seven years he disappeared from the sight of his friends, who ran about in every direction, but they could not find him. On this account great sorrow came upon his parents. After seven years all at once he came to their door, crying out. When this reached their ears, with great happiness they ran out, and cured their eyes of the tears of separation. They asked him why he had left them: he replied that the Musulmen Genii, at the desire of his maternal uncle, Baba Husun, had carried him away to him in Hindoostan, where he had remained one year with him, when he gave him leave to depart, and the Genii brought him back to a priest's monastery, where he stayed six years, finding inclination to learn the traditions of Mahomed, and the ordinances of God. After his return home, he followed the path of the jungle of theology of the Soofees: he chose to go about, wandering, gathering from each harvest (of their travels) one ear of corn; from every corner (of inquiry) he found bread. When the fire of the love of God commenced burning in his breast, he began to seek a perfect priest: in this search he came to his uncle Baba Husun.

It is said that one forenoon Meer Syud Hoosain was coming to visit Baba Husun at Lungur, who became lost in rapture, saying to his disciples: "I perceive the scent of a man from whose coming the eye of my heart will receive light; do you go in front to meet him." These Fakeers had gone but a short way, when they met Syud Hoosain, whom they brought to Baba Husun, who embraced him, kissing his face and head, and seating him in his own place. Hearing of the arrival of Syud Hoosain, all the priests of Kandahar came to visit him; many were collected to see him. Then Baba Husun said to him: "Oh son! many good people have come to see you; it is necessary that you give them something to eat." Meer Syud Hoosain arose, and placing a vessel on the fire, he put into it five seers (Khandaharee) of meat, and ten seers of flour, which began to cook. When it was done, Baba Husun said— "Are you able to fill the bellies of the Fakeers with this?" Syud Meer Hoosain said he could, and he got up.

Many men of truth state that from this vessel he took out 150 dishes filled; that the stomachs of all were satisfied, and the vessel remained full as before.

It is also said that he was one day standing on the road near Lungur; when a man with a loaded camel passed by, going towards the town. The Syud asked him what there was upon the camel. The man, in fear that he would beg something of him, replied "stones." The Syud exclaimed— "It will be so." When the man got to his house, and unloaded the camel in his enclosure, he opened the load, and found that it had become stone; so he took it up, taking it to Syud Hoosain, excusing himself, and placing these stones at his doorway. These stones were placed over his grave by his disciples, and they are there to this day. His praise is beyond what I can write: I have left all, having written but a little.

AN ACCOUNT OF SYUD MAHOMED, CALLED SYUD SHERE KULUNDUR.

Syud Mahomed was the son of Meer Syud Hoosain Zunjeer Rai. From infancy he ran in the direction of the ways of abstinence; he brought himself to a very high degree. He spread the carpet of the ways of God, to show them to the people. He quenched the thirst of the jungle of desire from the fountain of the knowledge of God. His miracles are beyond the geometrician of knowledge, who cannot encompass them. I mention a few of them.

This is the reason why he is called Syud Shere Kulundur, because he changed his appearance to that of a tiger, in this way:—

When his miracles became well known, the men of Kandahar, Bulookat, and Huzarah, became his disciples, giving him offerings and presents. At that time one Syud Kushnuh spoke against him before Meer Zoonoon, who became so angry with him, that he sent a man to call him. Meer Syud Mahomed, coming from Uskulchuk, met Meer Zoonoon in the Jamin Musjid on Friday. On going away, Meer Zoonoon ordered him to be confined. Those who received this order placed him in an empty house, where many took care of his safety. Meer Zoonoon, on reaching home, became vexed at having acted as he had done, and sent trays of food to him. When the bearer of these reached the house, they found a tiger, which was rolling on a woollen cloth, seeing which they came to Zoonoon, telling him. He said they were afraid, and sent two of his attendants. These going, saw the same, and returning, told Zoonoon; who then, taking his children, went there, and saw it with his own eyes. He then begged for forgiveness of his fault, and was very submissive, when this tiger changed its appearance, and Zoonoon gave him leave to depart.

It is said that Sultan Ali Korjee, who was also called Lug Dug, was opposed to Syud Mahomed. One day, for the sake of examining his miracles, he went to the Syud, sitting down like one without respect, when the Syud looked towards him with earnestness, upon which Sultan Ali arose, tearing his clothes. He shaved his beard and head, going about naked for some days. His sister Beejuh Junnut and her husband went to the Syud, asking his forgiveness of Sultan Ali, when he gave them the water which remained after performing his ablutions previous to prayer, for him to drink. On drinking this, he became as before, and a disciple of his. As long as he lived he brought firewood on his head for his kitchen. Sultan Ali says, that one very cold night Meer Syud Shere went out for exercise with his disciple; that he slept an hour, when he had a dream. Awaking at the time, he told Sultan Ali that such had happened to him, and to take off his clothes. Meer Syud then placed a cloth around him, and breaking the ice on the water, he went into the canal. At this time, says Sultan, "I was shivering all over, when the Syud said to me—'What, are you cold? Come and behold the secrets of the men of God!' So I arose, and went to him, when I found the water so warm, that my body ceased to shiver, and getting out, I did not find it cold." One day, this Syud went to the village of Sofaidruwan, where the air was warm. Khwaja Shuhub-ood-deen Sofaidruwanee, who was one of his disciples, says that on account of the heat he went forward to meet him, requesting him to come to his garden for an hour: the Syud, agreeing to what he said, Khwaja went in advance, to prepare a place for him near a water reservoir. He says: "On account of the smallness of the doorway, I proposed tying his horse under a tree outside; when I saw him entering on horseback. At this I was much astonished. How had he come in on his horse, through so small a gateway? The Syud said— 'It is nothing at all; there is no occasion for surprise!' I offered to bring him any fruit that he might choose. (I had, previously to his arrival, in the morning selected, and placed in a corner, two baskets full of fruit, to send to the ministers.) The Syud said— 'Oh Shuhub-ood-deen, bring to me those two baskets of fruit which you picked in the morning to send somewhere, and send others there!' Much wonder came upon me, and in just faith I kissed his hands and feet." Meer Syud Shere came from Dawur to the village of Sarbangilla, where his disciples went into the houses of the Ryuts, wishing to remain there till the afternoon. These not allowing them to do so, it was made known to the Syud, who said: "Go from out of this village, for it will burn." When they had gone outside, this village was burned. He found death during the days of Washoora 933 (A. D. 1526). His tomb is at Uskulchuk, 10 kos to the west of Kandahar, the people of which and Dawur make pilgrimage to it, bringing offerings and presents for his descendants, giving goats and ewes for the kitchen; and all Fakeers and travellers receive food there. The people of Kandahar, Huzarah, and Bulookat, are his disciples. The entrance to his tomb is never empty; it is always filled with people.

AN ACCOUNT OF KHWAJA MULIK.

His tomb is on the bank of the Urghoondab; it is a spot to ravish the heart. The inhabitants of Kandahar call it Peer Wulayut. The Ryuts at the time of cultivation agree to give a share of the produce to his descendants, and when the crops are gathered, they take this share to them: if, at the time of sowing, they do not agree to give this share, some misfortune comes upon their crops.

AN ACCOUNT OF KHWAJA ALI NAITAZ.

He was a master of miracles; his tomb is at Kundkan. This is why he is called Naitaz:—

One day, riding on a reed (Nai), he visited some person, to whom he said— "Give barley to my horse." Thinking he was joking, this person threw the reed into his granary. In the morning, he found that all his grain was gone, and that horse-dung was there.

AN ACCOUNT OF KHWAJA ALI NAISHAPOOREE.

He was a great friend of God's. His miracles are numerous. One day, many men of consequence were going to see him, some on foot, some on horseback. Hearing of their coming, he mounted a wall, on which he went forward to meet them, on the road. That wall remains to the present day.

AN ACCOUNT OF KHWAJA WAIYOOB UNSAREE, WHO WAS THE BROTHER OF KHWAJA ABDOOLA UNSAREE.

On Mondays many people collect at his tomb, which is on the base of the hill of Ukkuh. It is customary to burn lights there on Sunday nights, when there are always 220 torches burning.

AN ACCOUNT OF THE SITTING ON THE THRONE OF THE KINGDOM OF MEERZA SHAH HOOSAIN; AND OF THE READING THE NAME OF BABUR BADSHAH IN THE SERMON.

When Shah Hoosain ascended the throne of his father at Nusurpoor, the Syuds, Kazees, and the chiefs, represented to him that it was right to have his name read in the sermon. Shah Hoosain said it was not proper for him to do so, as long as any of the descendants of Saheb Kiran were remaining, and the name of Babur Badshah was read. After the days of Eed, Shah Hoosain went towards Tatta. Jam Pheroz, hearing of this, sent presents by Hafiz Rustreed Khoosh Nuwees, and others, to him, showing forth his extreme submission, saying how much he was afflicted; but these ambassadors, in private, said that this was all outward show; that inwardly he was different, and ready for war. Shah Hoosain sent these men back, marching himself in that direction by the stages. When the Jam heard of his approach with a large force, being unable to fight, he made up his mind to run away, and shortly afterwards he left the city, and crossed over the river to the other side. Meerza Shah Hoosain ordered his troops to cross the river, and to enter the city. When they were doing so, Manik Wuzeer and Shaikh Ibrahim, the son-in-law of the Jam, came on the waters with many boats full of men, with guns, and bows and arrows, to oppose the passage; but numbers of Shah Hoosain's brave men going against, fought with them, sending them all by the way of the river to annihilation. Jam Pheroz then fled to Kutch, where he collected many men.

AN ACCOUNT OF THE COMING OF JAM PHEROZ TO CHACHGAN, AND OF THE VICTORY OF SHAH HOOSAIN OVER HIM.

When Jam Pheroz, having got together some 50,000 men, horse and foot came to Chachgan to fight, all the people in Tatta became much alarmed. Meer Mahomed Miskeen Turkhan, and other nobles, went to Shah Hoosain, telling him of these circumstances. He sent these back, appointing them to take care of Tatta, going himself to expel the enemy. Crossing the river, he made successive marches, and getting near the foe, he put his troops in order, and advanced against them. When the two armies came in sight of each other, the men of Jam Pheroz dismounted from their horses, and taking off their Pugrees from their heads, they tied themselves one to another by the corners of their waist-sheets. It is the custom of this Sind, that when the people make up their minds to die, they get off their horses, bare their heads, and tie themselves to one another with the ends of their sheets.

Shah Hoosain, seeing this, gave the congratulations of victory to his Sirdars, directing all his men to take their bows and arrows in their hands. He himself dismounted from his horse, and having performed the previous ablutions, said his prayers, making supplication for victory. The arrow of his prayer struck the target of consent. He then mounted his horse, and all his troops, drawing their swords, rushed upon the enemy. The fight lasted from morning till evening: 20,000 of the foe were slain. Jam Pheroz, with ill fortune, went to Guzerat, remaining there till he took his life to Paradise. Meerza Shah Hoosain remained three days on the field of battle, and such property as was found was divided amongst his soldiery. He showed great kindness to his Ameers.

From thence he returned to Tatta, with victory, remaining in Tughlugabad. Six months afterwards he left to go to Bukkur, by the way of Halakhundee. When he arrived opposite Sehwistan, the Sirdars then brought presents, offering their congratulations on his victory. The Arbabs and Zemindars of that country also came, and having offered their congratulations, they received permission to return. The men of Suhtuh and Doorbeluh also arrived to make their Salaam. This last place he gave to Meer Furookh, and hunting on the way, he arrived at Baburloe, which is 3 kos from Bukkur, where the nobles and men of consequence, coming in front, met him. He spoke with great kindness to the men of Bukkur, making them presents. During this year Shaikh Meeruk Pooranee came from Kandahar to Sind. The following year Shah Kootb-ood-deen, a descendant of Shah Tuyub, arrived at Bukkur from Herat. He had an interview with Meerza Shah Hoosain.

AN ACCOUNT OF BABA AHMED BEING SENT BY SHAH HOOSAIN TO PUNISH THE DUHURS AND MACHEES.

In the beginning of 928 (A. D. 1521), Shah Hoosain heard that the Duhurs and Machees of Oobawruh and Bhittee Wahun were always fighting with the Muhurs and other Ryuts of Matheluh. Upon this, he directed Baba Ahmed, the son of Meer Fazil Kookooltash, to take a force to punish them. Preparing his troops, he made forays upon Oobawruhabad and Bhittee Wahun, looting both places. He then returned to the fort of Matheluh. The Duhurs then said to the Beloochees in the fort of Sewraee: "The Moguls have come upon us, taking our cattle and property; if you do not stretch forth your hands upon them, this will always be their road." These Beloochees, then, collecting their men, went against the Muhurs; hearing of which, Baba Ahmed went in pursuit of, and came up to them close to Oobawruh, where a battle took place, in which the Beloochees were defeated, many of them fell, and some Duhurs being taken prisoners, were confined. Shah Hoosain afterwards sent another force as far as Koodhee and Darawur, who punished the Beloochees severely.

As Baba Ahmed was returning, he killed and confined many Machees of Oobawruh, severely twisting the ears of these last. This tribe then gave him a present, and one of their daughters; and having put that country to rights, he left some men there, and returned to Bukkur. During the inundations, the camels belonging to Shah Hoosain were sent to Matheluh to feed under Mahomed Furash, and the Duhurs and Muhurs were called upon to tend them. The Beloochees of Sewraee, and the Juts of Darawur and Futehpoor, hearing of this, assembled and looted the whole of them. The news of this reached Bukkur, when Baba Ahmed started with 300 horsemen. He reached Darawur with great speed, killing many of the people, and recovering the camels. When he arrived near Bhittee Wahun, the Beloochees of Sewraee and the Duhurs took possession of his road; there was a severe fight between them, when Baba was severely wounded. He withdrew from the field, and had nearly reached Matheluh, when he fell from his horse, and the bird of his life flew away from his body. When Abdool Futeh, the son of Meer Fazil, heard of the death of his brother, he was greatly afflicted, and dejected. He received permission from Shah Hoosain to go there, and he sent with him Meer Kasim Kubuk Posh, who was his father-in-law, that he might not rush headlong on the enemy. Abdool Futeh arrived, and sent the body of his brother to Bukkur; he himself waited there for an opportunity of revenge. One day he found this, falling upon Rahman Duhur's host, many of whom he slew, pursuing them as far as Mow, dispersing the whole. Men then came between them, and peace was made, the border of Sind being extended to Bhittee Wahun, where Abdool Futeh remained some time. He placed near himself Meer Mahomed Kootee, the son of Baba Ahmed. One day the news reached him there, that the cattle of Oobawruh had been looted: he at once girded on his weapons, and went forth. At that time the hot winds were blowing, which entered his nature, so much so, that by the time he got home he was dead.

After these two deaths, in the year 930 (A. D. 1523), Shah Hoosain summoned all his Ameers to Bukkur, when he gave them orders to prepare every requisite for two years, to go against Mooltan.

SOME MENTION OF BABUR BADSHAH GOING TO HINDOOSTAN; ALSO OF THE MARRIAGE OF MEERZA SHAH HOOSAIN WITH GOOLBURG BEGUM; AND AN ACCOUNT OF THE CIRCUMSTANCES OF THE KINGS OF MOOLTAN.

When Shah Hoosain had strengthened his intention of going to Mooltan, he wished in the first place to make arrangements with the men of Urghoon, Tukduree, and Huzarah, who had brought their families, and lived at Seebee.

In one week, with 1,000 horse, he arrived at Seebee, the fort of which he repaired and strengthened, placing it in the hands of twenty men; and then, with his mind at ease, he returned by the road of Luhree and Chauttr, looting the Rindhs and the Mugsees on the way, taking many of them prisoners, all of whom he released after having made strict arrangements with them. Their Sirdars he took with him to Bukkur.

When Shah Hoosain heard that Babur Badshah was going against Hindoostan, he sent ambassadors to him with valuable presents. He also wrote a petition to him.

At the time when Shah Hoosain went (as formerly related) to Babur Badshah, he made the friendship of, and was betrothed in the relationship of son-in-law to, Meer Khuteefuh, who was the minister and Dewan Begee of Babur Badshah, who approved of the proposed connection. To renew this engagement, he sent Shah Sultan, the grandmother of Abdool Bakee, of the family of Syud Janfur, to Babur, to make this known to him. Huzrut Babur becoming the cause of the union, Goolburg Begum, the daughter of Meer Kateefuh, was given in marriage to Meerza Shah Hoosain, being sent with her younger brother, Hoosain-ood-deen Meeruk, to Bukkur, where Shah Hoosain received her into his house, giving to Hoosain-ood-deen the Purguna of Baghbanan for his expenses during his stay. Shah Hoosain then proposed going towards Mooltan. Babur Badshah gave in marriage to Mohib Ali Khan, the son of Meer Khateefuh, Nasheed Begum, the daughter of Mah Begum, whom I have previously mentioned as having been left behind in Kabool when her mother secretly fled from thence. This was brought about to strengthen the friendship on both sides.

It will not be secret that the conquest of Mooltan was effected by Mahomed the son of Kasim Sukafee, in the time of Hujjaj the son of Yoosoof. After this, it was again taken from the Tupihls by Sultan Mahomed Ghazee, and it remained a long time in the hands of his descendants. When the rule of the Kings of Ghuznee had reached its limit, Mooltan went into the hands of the Kiranutuh. From these, again, it was wrested by Sultan Munz-ood-deen Mahomed Sham, and it remained under the Kings of Delhi till 800 (A. D. 1397), from which time, there being dissension amongst these, the Hakeem became rebellious, and it passed away from Delhi.

After this various men ruled over that country, such as Shaikh Yoosoof for two years, Sultan Kootb-ood-deen for thirty-four years, then his son Sultan Hoosain for twenty-seven years; Sultan Mahomed for some months; after him Sultan Hoosain.

When Sultan Ula-ood-deen, the son of Mahomed Shah, the son of Pheroz Shah, the son of Moobaruk Shah, the son of Khizur Khan, became King of Delhi, troubles arose in the affairs of that state, and in the country of Hindoostan there became many kings.

On account of the oppression of the Moguls, Mooltan became without any ruler: throughout that country, with the great and humble, there was much faith in the family of Shaikh Buha-ood-deen Zukreeya. On this account all the good and weighty men assembling, placed at the head of the state Shaikh Yoosoof, who was the superintendent of the Monarkees of Shaikh Buha-ood-deen Zukreeya, and his name was read in the sermon in the pulpits of Mooltan, Ooch, and other cities. He turned his attention to put in order the affairs of the kingdom. In the first place, he increased the forces, he brought the hearts of the Zemindars beneath his orders, and he gave ornament to the matters of the state and country. One day, by chance Rai Suheeruh, the Sirdar of the Lungahs, and who lived at Ripree, sent this message to Shaikh Yoosoof:— "My father and grandfather formerly placed faith in your family: now there is much dissension in the kingdom of Delhi; so much so, that Mulik Boohlool Lodhee has taken it, reading his own name in the sermon: if at this time you will take into your service some of the Lungahs, I will be your servant, and in such duty and business as you may show to me, I will not excuse myself from giving my life. To show you my faith I now send to you my daughter, and I accept you as my son-in-law." The Shaikh, hearing this, was very happy, and married his daughter. Rai Suheeruh occasionally came to Mooltan to visit his child, bringing handsome rarities for Shaikh Yoosoof, who did not fix upon any place of residence for him in the city, but was in the habit of encamping outside, and leaving his people there, he went in alone. One time, assembling all his people, he went there, with the intention of seizing Shaikh Yoosoof, and of becoming king himself. When he got near the city, he sent word to the Shaikh, that on this occasion he had brought all the men of Lungah that he might inspect them, and give service to such as were fit. Shaikh Yoosoof, being free from suspicion of treachery, with carelessness treated him with attention, and Rai Suheeruh showed him his horses and men. At night, leaving his men outside, he came into the city, attended by one servant, whom he told to bring a kid, which he was to kill in secret, and bring the blood to him in a cup. The slave did as he was ordered, and Rai Suheeruh drank the blood. In an hour afterwards he began crying out that he had pains in the stomach. His cries increasing every minute, at midnight the Vukeels of Yoosoof, who were in attendance upon him, went and called their master to come and hear his last will. On his arrival Rai Suheeruh vomited blood in the presence of all, and explaining his last wishes, he cried the more, requesting that his relations and servants might be called to forgive him. The Vukeels, seeing his state, did not prevent these from coming. When many of his men had entered the fort, he lifted his hand from the bed of false sickness, sending men of trust to the four gates, to be alert, and not to allow admittance to the men of Shaikh Yoosoof. He himself went to the private sleeping apartments of the Shaikh, and seizing him, turned him out of the fort, and he went towards Delhi.

Rai Suheeruh, styling himself Sultan Kootb-ood-deen, had his name read in the sermon.

AN ACCOUNT OF MEERZA SHAH HOOSAIN TURNING HIS FACE TOWARDS MOOLTAN.

In the year 931 (A. D. 1524) Shah Hoosain, marching towards Mooltan, passed over the intervening space, and arrived near Sewraee. He then gave the orders to plunder; so his troops looted, and wherever they found an enemy they put him to the sword. The Beloochees, hearing of this, fled to Ooch: some few went to the fort of Sewraee, where they determined to fight. This was the strongest fort in all that country. Shah Hoosain encamped near a tank, and Sultan Mahomed Bukree, galloping to the front, towards the fort, commenced fighting with those men who were near, and outside of it. At that time he had with him eighty men. I have myself heard, from the tongue of Sultan Mahomed himself, that in this battle of Sewraee thirty men fell to his sword alone, and that his men behaved most bravely, slaying two hundred of the enemy.

When the Beloochees saw this, they fled from the fort. In the morning, when Shah Hoosain heard of it, he gave credit and praise to Sultan Mahomed, but calling him in private, he struck him three times with a stick, rebuking him, saying: "This bad gallop of yours, and your going in advance, was not good." The next day he marched, coming near Sewraee, the destruction of which he ordered; and in seven days it was level with the ground. He went from thence to Mow, encamping at a tank near it.

Shaikh Roo-ool-lah, the son of Shaikh Himad Koraishee, a great Musulman saint, came to visit Meerza Shah Hoosain, saying in his presence, that the men of Mow were very weak, and had no heart to fight. Shah Hoosain ordered Meerza Mahomed Miskeen Turkhan to take some men and go into the fort, and see what was in it in the way of provisions, and not to raise the hand of violence against any Lungahs and Beloochees whom he might find there. He went as directed, and he did not touch these; but he seized and sent bound to Shah Hoosain all the other men whom he found there. Shah Hoosain remained outside till the third day, when he entered the fort, making pilgrimage to the tombs of many saints there. He arranged with the Shaikhs of the place, that if any of his men passed to and fro, they were not to annoy them, and that they were not to admit amongst them any of his enemies. Shaikh Roo-ool-lah afterwards requested him to forgive the faults of Rahman Dahur. Shah Hoosain replied that Sultan Mahomed Khan knew him, as two of his brothers had died through the opposition of him and his people. At length, seeing advantage, he called him, and Rahman presented himself with his sword suspended from around his neck. Sultan Mahomed Khan forgave him the blood of his brothers, and after this Rahman said he would give the daughter of his brother in marriage to him, which was agreed to. So he presented to him the sister of Jan Jeewun Dahur.

Mohib Ali Turkhan, with 500 horse, was appointed to lead the van in the march from Mow, and Shah Hoosain, following him, encamped near the border of Lar. Here one called Bunduh Dahur, who was the bravest of all the men in Mooltan, came to Shah Hoosain, who gave him a Khilat and a present. He then made him over to the care of Sultan Mahomed Khan. From thence he marched to go to Ooch.

AN ACCOUNT OF MEERZA SHAH HOOSAIN FIGHTING WITH THE LUNGAHS AT OOCH.

On the morning of the following day, Shah Hoosain mounted his horse, and marched, with the expectation of a battle. He exerted himself in arranging his troops, putting all in their proper positions. He placed in command of the right Mahomed Miskeen Turkhan, and Meerza Eesa; over the left he put Meer Furookh, and Meer Abeek Urghoon; he gave charge of the advance to Sultan Mahomed Khan, Meer Mahomed Sarban, and Meer Aboo Mooslin.

The descendants of Rai Suheeruh, the Beloochees, and all the sepoys of Mooltan, advanced to meet him, placing the men of Nahur in their front. The forces of Mooltan were double in number to those of Shah Hoosain.

When the two forces came in front of each other, the Moguls began to light the fire of battle, and the Lungahs and Beloochees raised their hands to shoot their arrows. At that time Shah Hoosain fell upon, and put the enemy to flight. In that attack numbers of them were slain. Boohlool, a descendant of Rai Suheeruh, and many others, were taken prisoners, all of whom Shah Hoosain ordered to be given to the sword. From the field of battle Shah Hoosain advanced, coming in sight of Ooch. He broke down the gate of the fort, and commenced fighting. The Lungahs, standing on the walls, threw arrows and stones. The Moguls, then, raising on bamboos the heads of their Sirdars, showed them to the garrison, on seeing which fear seized them, and they fled, casting themselves down from the walls and bastions, seeking a way to save themselves, but such as fell into the hands of their enemies were slain, agreeably to the orders of Shah Hoosain, and the people of the city were looted by the Moguls. Then Junab Zain-ool-ula-bideen Bookaree and others went to Shah Hoosain, telling him of what was going on in the city. He gave orders to his attendants, that from that time there was to be no violence offered to any one, that such as had been taken prisoners were to be released, and that the heads of those who disobeyed their orders were to be raised on high on bamboos. He directed the fort and chief buildings in Ooch to be destroyed, and placing the timber of these latter on boats, he sent it to Bukkur.

When the news of the strength of Meerza Shah Hoosain, and of his capturing Ooch, reached Sultan Mahomed Lungah, the King of Mooltan, he sent men, through his country, to collect the Beloochees, the Juts, the Rindhs, the Dodaees, the Koraees, the Chandeeyuhs, and all fighting men. In the space of one month he had assembled 80,000 men, horse and foot, in Mooltan. With this large force, Sultan Mahomed Lungah, with great arrogance, went forth from Mooltan towards the field of action, intending to fight. Shah Hoosain, hearing of his collecting troops, encamped on the Ghara, looking for his approach. Sultan Mahomed spent one month near his city, putting his materials for war in order. Having prepared this, he marched from thence with greater pride than before: he did not know that "The Creator of fate makes His decrees behind the curtain." Certainly no one has gathered the flower of fortune from the garden of the unkindness of heaven until the thorn of the non-obtainment of his desires has pricked the foot of his heart: what man has drank one sip of good fortune in the pleasure-house of this world, without finding the sickness of bad fortune? The produce of this is: Shaikh Soojan Bookaree, the son-in-law of Sultan Hoosain, held in his hands all the affairs of the state. On some account he became treacherous with the attendants and slaves of Sultan Mahomed, who, on hearing of this, became very wrath. These, seeing that their lives depended on his death, girded their loins to kill him, and forgetting his kindness, gave him very potent poison, which was in the treasure chest for some one else, and he, drinking half a cup of this, became so intoxicated, that his eyes did not again see the face of wakefulness. When the mother of Sultan Mahomed heard of this, she said in her heart that it was right for her to remain there, and to get all the troops to her side. This was kept secret for two or three days, when it became known, and all the Beloochees and Lungahs assembling, placed Sultan Hoosain, the son of Sultan Mahomed, on the throne of the kingdom; and they did not find any other medicine save to make peace. In short, they placed between them as mediator Mahomed Shaikh Buha-ood-deen, which honorable Shaikh had an interview with Shaikh Hoosain on the Ghara. The Meerza received him with great distinction, bowing before him, and showing him much veneration; and on what the Shaikh said, he agreed to make peace. He wrote a treaty to this effect:— "The boundary of the country of Mooltan is the water of the Ghara: from this day no ruler of Mooltan is to go beyond that limit." He then gave the Shaikh his dismissal, presenting him with nine horses, a string of camels, with some ready money, and he returned full of happiness. Shah Hoosain gave orders for another fort to be built with great expedition at Ooch, which was done as directed, and that building is standing at this time. After this, leaving men of trust there, he prepared to return. At that time Ikbal Khan, the servant of Sultan Mahomed, came and made his Salaam to him, saying he wished him happiness. Shah Hoosain showed him kindness, agreeing to meet his wishes.

AN ACCOUNT OF MEERZA SHAH HOOSAIN GOING TO TAKE THE FORT OF DILAWUR, AND AGAINST GHAZEE KHAN.

Ooch having been taken by the Meerza, Ikbal Khan came to him, saying that there was much treasure buried in Dilawur; that the wealth collected by many kings was concealed there. Shah Hoosain wrote a letter to Ghazee Khan, saying: "Now I have come to the country of Ooch, it is proper for you that you and all your people, putting the rings of obedience to me in your ears, present yourselves before me without any delay."

But Ghazee Khan wrapped his foot in the sheet of independence, and gaining support from the strength of his fort, he did not go to him. The result of this was as follows.

On the morning of Friday the 1st of Rujub, the Meerza issued orders, that it was necessary for the troops to provide themselves with grain and water for one month's consumption. This being prepared, he turned the bridle of his departure in the direction of Dilawur. Soonbool Khan, with horsemen, gunners, and footmen, and slaves, got there in advance, and making places for his tents about the fort, he distributed batteries. He took a great deal of labour in surrounding and attacking the place.

Certainly this fort is such, that its walls are equal in height to Alexander's wall, and it is built in such a desert, that the eyes of the birds of the air, on account of there not being one drop of water in that desert, always look towards the clouds of heaven.

These men, working hard, made there a hundred wells in that desert in three days, and there was an abundance of water. On the fourth day, Shah Hoosain arrived, and surrounding the fort, made it his centre. He commenced doing everything that was necessary to take it, and there was fighting on both sides. After some days had passed in this manner, agitation came upon the hearts of the garrison; from no place did aid arrive, and many days had been passed in fighting, and this still continued. Their distress for food was so great that a boiled skin was not to be had, though wished for a hundred times. Soonbool Khan, having made mines on two sides, blew up the town in front of a gate. The garrison, seeing the face of death, began to throw shells and fireballs. When the battle was raging very fiercely, the brave men, losing their heads, ascended the towers, killing and wounding numbers of the garrison; making prisoners those who escaped from the sword. Having taken the fort, Shah Hoosain placed men of trust over the treasure, and the following morning he divided much money amongst his sepoys; and placing his own share in the treasury, he turned his bridle in the direction of Ooch and Bukkur. He arrived at Bukkur in fifteen days, and getting there, he was very happy.

AN ACCOUNT OF MEERZA SHAH HOOSAIN GOING AGAINST AND CAPTURING MOOLTAN, AND OF THE MASSACRE OF THE INHABITANTS.

In the latter days of 932 (A. D. 1526), on account of the death of Sultan Mahomed Lungah, quarrels and dissensions arose amongst the Ameer and his relations. Every one strengthened himself in his own place, and all took themselves away from listening to the orders of others. At that time Sultan Hoosain was young, and in the hands of Shaikh Soojan Bookaree, and the ladies of Lungah: he was unable to do anything. On this account, much discord, violence, taking away other men's wives, &c. arose. Seeing this, the influential men amongst the Zemindars wished for some other ruler. At that time Lungur Khan went to Shah Hoosain, describing to him the state of the country.

The Meerza had previously considered how he could throw the noose of conquest over the parapets of Mooltan; and on hearing what Lungur Khan said, his wishes on this subject were strengthened.

Having made up his mind to march against it, he sent Mahomed Miskeen Turkhan in advance.

The Lungahs, hearing of the approach of the Urghoons, after deliberation, sent Shaikh Ismael Koraishee to make peace. He arrived at Mow, where he had an interview with Shah Hoosain, who showed him all the honour and reverence he could, giving him money for his entertainment. The Shaikh spoke to strengthen the root of peace, but no benefit arose from this. He then said to Lungur Khan: "My relations are at Tatta; send me there." Lungur mentioned this to the Meerza, who complied with the request, and the Shaikh obtained leave to proceed to Sind, and a village near Tatta was given to him in Jageer. From thence Shah Hoosain proceeded towards Mooltan. When his forces drew near, much anxiety fell upon the men of Lungah, all of whom betook themselves inside the fort. At that time Lungur Khan, who was with the Urghoons looting Thuttee Khulwan, brought much grain, cattle, and other things to the army. Mooltan was surrounded, and fighting commenced on both sides. The king sent one of his brothers to Shah Hoosain, with Shaikh Soojan, saying that he would obey orders. Meerza received him with much kindness, saying— "Tell your brother to come out of the fort to visit me, to agree to obey my orders, and I will show him every kindness. I will then leave the fort in his hands, and turn the bridle of my intentions to return back." These, returning, told what had passed; but the Lungahs, with much pride, would not leave the fort, and they deliberated how to get rid of their enemies. They lighted the fire of war by throwing open the gates, and taking in their hands their bows and arrows, and swords. They fought very well, killing some of the Urghoons. Thus the fire of anger became ignited in Shah Hoosain: he pitched his tent to the eastward of the fort, opposite the Shams gate, erecting batteries around the city. From both sides the fire of battle blazed, and the arrows and bullets began to fall like rain. There was fighting daily. During this time, grain became very scarce in the city, so much so, that one maund (Mooltan weight) of it was priced at 100 Tunkahs, and one cow the same; in this manner things were sold. Many men eat the hides of cattle, which were not fit to eat, and if the flesh of dogs and cats fell into their hands, they looked upon it as the meat of kids. Shaikh Soojan Bookaree had placed Jaduh

Mahehee in command over 3,000 foot soldiers, (Kusbatees, fighting men of the town,) who were the garrison. This man of ill-fortune, without consideration, entered those houses where he even suspected there was grain, looting them. On account of this conduct, the poor people raised their hands in supplication: "Change is good, however it comes upon us!" They prayed for the decline of the rule of the Lungahs.

In short, the men of Mooltan strengthened themselves for death, casting themselves from the walls into the ditch below. Shah Hoosain, hearing of this distress on account of hunger, forbade the destruction of those who acted in this manner.

By reason of the scarcity of supplies, the Ameers of Mooltan prohibited any from eating to the full; they ordered the people to subsist themselves upon the water in which grain was cooked. When they had been besieged for one year, they became close upon death—the knife had reached the bone. On the 11th of Jumadee-oos-Sanee, in the year 933 Hijree (A. D. 1526), the brave men of the Urghoon army emptied many of the bodies of their enemies of life, by the blows of their arrows, and in the morning, putting forth great strength, they broke down the Loharee gate, and gained an entrance into the city. The hands of plunder being then drawn forth from the sleeves of violence, commenced looting and massacreing.

All the inhabitants of the town from the age of seven to that of seventy were confined, and such occurrences befell the Mooltanees, that it reminded them of the last day: they secreted themselves in the monasteries of their most sacred saints.

Ten or twelve days after the place had been given up to plunder, Mohib Ali Turkhan, taking some men with him, went to these monasteries of the saints, looting the people, and setting fire to the buildings. The blood of many was spilt in these. Numbers of the Lungahs and Mooltanees were destroyed in that general slaughter. In the plunder, many precious jewels, and money not to be counted, fell into the hands of the Moguls. After this, the fire of anger was cooled in Meerza Shah Hoosain: he showed pity to those who had escaped, giving orders to take up the bodies of the dead from the streets, and to bury them in pits, and from that time none of his men were allowed to lift their hands against them. Mukhdoom Shaikh Buha-ood-deen brought Sultan Hoosain and his sister to Shah Hoosain, who made them both over to the care of Mahomed Miskeen Turkhan, who married the lady, taking her brother into his bosom, as if he had been his own son.

Two months after the conquest of this city, intending to return to Bukkur, Shah Hoosain placed as governors over Mooltan, Dost Meer Akhoor, and Shums-ood-deen Nakhwanee, with 200 horsemen, 100 topechees (men with fire-arms,) and 200 footmen. He fined Shaikh Soojan Bookaree, and the slaves of consequence of Sultan Mahomed Lungah, taking from them all the money they possessed. He then turned towards Bukkur, where, after his arrival, a petition arrived from the Ameers of Tatta, with these contents: "Khungar has the intention to bring a force against Tatta." On receiving this news, the Meerza marched to go there. Dost Meer Akhoor and Shums-ood-deen, who were left at Mooltan, remained there nearly eleven months, when Lungur Khan, separating himself, went away to the presence of Mahomed Babur Badshah, who received him with honour.

After this, Shah Hoosain wrote a petition to Babur Badshah, making Mooltan over to him as a present, and Dost Meer Akhoor and his companions came to Bukkur. Babur Badshah placed Mooltan in the hands of Mahomed Kamran.

AN ACCOUNT OF SHAH HOOSAIN'S WAR WITH KHUNGAR, IN THE DIRECTION OF KUTCH.

I have before mentioned, that at the time when Shah Hoosain had returned to Bukkur, a petition came from the Ameers of Tatta, saying that Khungar was preparing to come against them. Shah Hoosain immediately went in that direction with expedition. On arriving near it, ambassadors came to him from Khungar, saying: "My relation Ameer Amravee was formerly slain in your quarrels: my people collected to take their revenge, but you had gone to take Mooltan, and I preserved your reputation in not coming upon your families at that time. Now it is necessary for you to make peace, and to give me a portion of Sind; if not I will make war with you." Meerza Shah Hoosain replied: "There is no other language for me except war. The plain which I coloured with the blood of Ameer Amravee still retains the mark of the blood of him, and before your arrival, I am coming there." Shah Hoosain, leaving some troops at Tatta to protect the families, marched against Khungar. Having passed the intermediate space, he came near Kutch, where the failure of grain came upon his army, from which his people became much distressed. Shah Hoosain and all his chiefs agreed that it was advisable for them to attack Khungar from four directions, and that whoever by chance first felt him, those who were near should come to his assistance. The first of these bodies directed upon the enemy was that of Sultan Mahomed Khan Bukree; the second was that of Meer Furookh; in the centre was Shah Hoosain himself; and with the fourth were Meerza Eesa and Meer Abeek. Khungar only received news of Shah Hoosain alone coming with a weak force, so he marched with 10,000 men, horse and foot, in his direction. By chance, marching along, the noise of the beating of Nugarahs reached the ears of Sultan Mahomed, who said to his men: "The noise of the Nugarah comes to my ears." All expressed their wonder at such being heard in the jungle. He then again heard the noise, and sent some people to the top of a hill, to look about, and bring the news. These brought word that Khungar was moving with a large force towards Shah Hoosain. The Meerza, having heard of the approach of the enemy towards him, marched quickly with his troops to meet him. In the mean time Sultan Mahomed, having come across, arrived in front of Khungar. He then sent a stirrup-holder to Shah Hoosain, saying: "Do not advance from where you are; God willing, I will not allow him to come upon you." He also sent a Kosid to Meer Furookh, to come up quick. When Khungar's forces came in sight of their foes, they dismounted from their horses, forming lines, and taking their shields and spears in their hands, tied themselves to each other by the ends of their waistcloths. Sultan Mahomed directed the brave men with him to take nothing in their hands but their bows and arrows. In this manner there was good fighting for two or three hours. Khungar's two leading lines became food for the eagles of the brave men of Sultan Mahomed like pigeons; the remainder of his troops placed their faces in the direction of flight, and those, running away, came upon Meer Furookh, who made grass of them with his sabres. The troops remained there that night; the next morning the whole went forth to plunder the villages and country, making many prisoners, and numbers of horses, cattle of all sorts, and property of various kinds, fell into the hands of the sepoys. Shah Hoosain, returning with victory, arrived at Tatta.

AN ACCOUNT OF HOOMAYOON BADSHAH GOING AGAINST GUZERAT, AND OF THE MARCH OF MEERZA SHAH HOOSAIN IN THAT DIRECTION, AGREEABLY TO HIS ORDERS.

In the year 942 (A. D. 1535), Hoomayoon Badshah, taking numerous forces from Delhi (especially against Infidels), marched upon Chittore, near which were made fixed places for the royal tents. At that time Sultan Bahadoor Guzeratee wrote a petition to the Badshah in behalf of the Raja of Chittore, showing forth his sincerity; but at the latter end of this, some harsh words appeared; seeing which, the heart of the king was offended, and he turned the bridle of the intention of his horse towards warring with Sultan Bahadoor in Guzerat, and getting over the country, he arrived there, looting and killing as he went. On this account Sultan Bahadoor went to a bunder.

During Hoomayoon's progress, he wrote a Firman to Meerza Shah Hoosain, telling him to preserve the ways of friendship, to turn his face in that direction, and to halt near Puttun, from whence he was to write a petition to him, when he must do as he might be ordered. Shah Hoosain, with a very large force, marched from Nusurpoor by the way of Radhunpoor, on Puttun. Khizur Khan, who was the Hakeem in the fort there, on the part of Sultan Bahadoor, retired within his fortress; seeing which, the Ryuts drove their flocks and herds to a distance. Sultan Mahomed, taking 500 horse, proceeding in advance, arrived at 7 kos from Puttun, where he halted, sending Jan Ali back to Shah Hoosain. He also sent Jonaid and Joonuh, Dharejas, to Khizur Khan in the fort, saying: "Shah Hoosain has come with a vast force; it is better for you to go and make your fort over to him, and remove your families wherever you please." Khizur Khan sent back word, that Sultan Bahadoor was alive at Gurnal (Joonagur), and that he did not see how it was necessary for him to give up the fort of Puttun to the Moguls of Sind. These two then went to the mother of Khizur Khan, telling her what Sultan Mahomed had said, adding that they did not think it proper for them to return without taking some present from her to him. The mother of Khizur Khan said— "What is your advice?" These replied that it was fitting for her to send one lakh of Ferozshahees for the entertainment of Shah Hoosain, and thirty thousand for Sultan Mahomed; and, if you will give this, we will take away the army. In short, she sent one lakh and thirty thousand Ferozshahees by her men of trust.

The following morning Shah Hoosain arrived at some high ground near Puttun, when Sultan Mahomed came to him, requesting permission to proceed in advance. Shah Hoosain replied that it was preferable to send some one to the king, to acquaint him of their arrival there, and that we will go wherever he orders us. He sent an Urzee by Abdool Koodoos to the king. At that time men arrived, bringing presents from Khizur Khan to him. He remained there fifteen days, in which time Sultan Mahomed went to Mahomedabad, plundering the country, when much money and valuable property fell into the hands of the sepoys. Meer Furookh at that time represented to Shah Hoosain that "When the royal orders arrived for us to go and encamp with his highness' army, there will be no other medicine for us but to do so, and it is not proper for us to go there, because the Badshah gives much money to his troops from the wealth of Guzerat, and there is much valuable property with the Chughtteeyuh Ameers. If our Urghoons and Turkhans see this, they will not remain with us, many men will go away. It is better that we turn the bridle of our intentions back to Sind. This was approved of by the Meerzas and all the chiefs, and determining to abide by it, he sent an Urzee to the king by Meerza Kasim Beg, saying: "I came here with a large force; now I have received a petition from the Ameers of Tatta and Bukkur, who tell me that the Kulumtees and Guttooees (Zemindars) having assembled, men are looting the country, and much discord has arisen; for this reason my return there is necessary." Hoomayoon was plundering the country, and twenty days previous to his arrival at Ahmedabad Shah Hoosain had turned back from Puttun. This was in the early days of 945 (A. D. 1538).

He returned to Tatta by Radhunpoor, looting and slaying the Jharejas and Sodahs as he passed.

AN ACCOUNT OF BADSHAH HOOMAYOON (THE SON OF BABUR BADSHAH) GOING TO SIND, AND OF MEERZA SHAH HOOSAIN'S ENMITY WITH HIM.

When, in the year 947 (A. D. 1540), Shere Khan Afghan, commonly called Fureed, the son of Husun Afghan, became rebellious in the eastern countries, on the 10th of Mohurrum of that year, Hoomayoon marched against him. There were two or three battles between them on the river Joosa. In short, the royal army was defeated, when the king turned the bridle of his intentions towards Juwunpoor, whence with expedition he went to Agra. In the previous year (946), Shah Hoosain sent Meer Abeek Urghoon to Badshah Hoomayoon, offering his congratulations on the conquest of Guzerat and Bengal; he also sent Meer Khoosh Mahomed Urghoon with a similar message to Meerza Kamran on his conquest of Kandahar, and the destruction of Answar Khan. Both of these were good sepoys, men of wisdom and council. When Meer Abeek presented himself to the king, seeing his carelessness and pride, he understood that the foreign sepoys in a short time would write in their hearts the words of mutiny. Without asking the permission of the king, he left his army, conveying himself with great diligence to Shah Hoosain, who, on hearing of his arrival, became anxious. When Meer Abeek had an interview with him, he asked what had occurred; he replied: "I found the king in such disorder, that in a short time the rebellious people will find strength against him; underneath him there will be roads of discord; and I have come to give this news, that you may be on the alert." Shah Hoosain several times summoned his nobles to the assembly, to deliberate with them. At that time the news of the defeat of Hoomayoon arrived, when all gave great credit to the wisdom of Meer Abeek, praising him much. It was decided upon to leave the country, and destroy the cultivation from Ooch to Bukkur on both sides of the river.

When the news of the flight of the king was confirmed, he erected buildings in four gardens at Baburloe, and placing in these all the requisites, with munitions of war, he caused all the country and towns about Bukkur to be entirely deserted. In the minds of Shah Hoosain and his people it became fixed that the king would come to Sind, because Meerza Kamran and Meerza Uskuree had left the paths of friendship towards him. When, on the 1st Rubee-ool- Awul, 947 (A. D. 1540), the king arrived at Lahore, all his brethren and nobles were collected there, but these had not gained knowledge, though they had seen what had occurred; and they did not bind the girdle of truth around the loins of spirit; so much so, that one day Khwaja Kodawund Mahomed, Meer Abdool Buga, and other men of consequence in the kingdom, assembled together, and wrote a bond of friendship between themselves, to which all those Ameers put their signatures as witnesses. When this bond was perfect, they collected to deliberate, but their language was not from their hearts: on this account the assembly broke up, and the matter on which they were deliberating was unfinished.

In the latter days of Jumadee-oos-Sanee 947, Hoomayoon Badshah, Meerza Mahomed Kamran, Mahomed Humdal Meerza, with other princes and nobles, and all the army, crossed the river at Lahore, and Shere Khan drew near that city. The Afghans stretched forth the hand of violence against the Moguls wherever they found them, looting and destroying their families and property; for this reason the whole of the Moguls, having joined Hoomayoon, went towards Kabool. When they reached the Chunab, Mahomed Kamran Meerza, and Mahomed Uskuree Meerza, with Khwaja Kodawund Mahomed and Khwaja Abdool Huk, without the permission of the king, turned their faces towards Kabool. The king, being helpless, went in the direction of Bheruh, when Mahomed Sultan Meerza, and Ulug Meerza, &c. also separating themselves from the king, joined Mahomed Kamran Meerza. Hoomayoon, seeing the enmity of his brethren, on the 1st of Rujub of that year, turned the bridle of his intentions towards Sind. In the last days of Shaban, the royal army arrived at Ooch, near which lived Bukshoo Lungah, to whom the king sent by Beg Mahomed Bukawul, and Kochuk Beg, a handsome Khilat and Firman, granting to him the title of Khan Juhanee, and presenting him with a standard and Nugarah. On this account he sent to the Badshah many boats full of grain, but he did not take the fortune of an interview with the king. Hoomayoon, with his nobles, and some of his forces, proceeded towards Sind, and the places for the tents of his troops were made about Roree. He himself, with much happiness, went to reside in the gardens (Char Bagh) of Baburloe, which have no fellows in verdure and elegance. Previous to this Sultan Mahomed had cleared all the country about, strengthened the fort of Bukkur, underneath which he had collected and secured all the boats. When the royal army came to Roree, the king sent a Firman to Sultan Mahomed to this effect: "You must come and find fortune by kissing the royal threshold, and deliver up the fort to the king's sepoys." He replied: "I am the servant of Meerza Shah Hoosain; until he comes to the royal presence, my going there would not be in accordance with the rules of eating salt, and without the order of Meerza Shah Hoosain, it is not proper that I should give up this fort." The king held him excused. Grain beginning to become scarce in the imperial camp, Mehtur Ushruf, the Meer Bazar, went to Sultan Mahomed, informing him of this circumstance, who then sent 500 kurwas of grain for the army, and something for the consumption of the king, who approved of this attention.

In those days Hoomayoon sent Ameer Tahir Sudur and Lumundur Beg, who were in his confidence, to Meerza Shah Hoosain at Tatta, writing and pointing out the strength of his good will towards him, and bringing to his recollection his sincerity to Babur Badshah. On their arrival, Shah Hoosain received them with much honour and distinction. He determined in his heart, that as the king had come in this direction, it was proper for him to make over, for the expenses of the royal family, the country from Halah Kundee to Batorah,* on the opposite side of the river, and that after arrangements were made, it would be proper for him to present himself to Hoomayoon Badshah. He also proposed to himself, after the settlement of affairs, and his visit to the king, to take a force to conquer Guzerat, and then to return back again. Having arranged matters in this way in his own mind, he sent Shaikh Meeruk Pooranee and Meerza Kasim Tighaee with valuable presents to the king. These received honour by making their Salaams to his royal highness near Bukkur, representing to him the good faith of Shah Hoosain, and delivering his petition. Its contents were these:— "The country of Bukkur affords small produce; the territory of Chachgan is superior to all in cultivation: it is proper for the kingdom (king) to turn the bridle of intention that way, and to take possession of it, as there the sepoys and animals will experience no distress, and I shall be in the vicinity of the king. Wealth and fortune are my friends by your coming to this country: in a short time, removing suspicion from my breast, I will gather fortune by kissing your stirrup." Badshah

Hoomayoon in the first instance gave orders to write to Shah Hoosain, to inform him that he will act as he suggested; but afterwards, in private, the ministers petitioned him in opposition to what Shah Hoosain had written, saying: "What is the meaning of this, that he mentions the names of towns and villages? If he was at heart the well-wisher of the king, why does he not make over forts as a present, that we may leave in them our families, and go to conquer Guzerat? Does he not see that Shere Khan, our enemy, is sitting over our heads at Lahore? That which he proposes is distant from rectitude and concord." Hoomayoon, after this, turned his face towards surrounding Bukkur, on hearing the news of which, Shah Hoosain remarked: "My heart is at ease with respect to Bukkur, because the king will not quit the gardens at Baburloe, the givers of contentment to the heart, and of happiness to the brain, to sit down before and conquer it himself, and nothing will be done by those nobles whom he may send to besiege it." Prior to this, Sultan Mahomed, leaving Meerza Janee Turkhan, and other chiefs of confidence, in charge of Bukkur, had proceeded to Sehwistan, causing that part of the country to be deserted, as the others had been collecting all the grain and other things together under cover of the fort there. About that time the remainder of the royal troops having come from Matheluh, arrived at Roree on the 28th of Ramzan, 947 (A. D. 1540), encamping near the hills there. Such of the Dharejas and Soofyanees, who had remained outside about the country, came and received honour, by bowing their heads in the presence of the king. On Friday he went to the college of Meerzaee; the day following he returned to the gardens, by the light of the sun of his countenance upon which, jealousy was caused to Paradise.

The king highly approving of those gardens and their buildings, all his Harem and his nobles resided there, and in the vicinity. Meerza Yadgar Nasir remained in the college at Roree, between which and Baburloe there are about 3 kos. In this space all the royal forces were encamped. We hear from men of weight, that these numbered two lakhs of men. On Friday Hoomayoon went to the Musjid, saying the prayers of the day there. His name was read in the discourse in the Musjid. On that day a poet in that assembly presented to the king this Kytah, by which gift he found much honour:—

"When the impression (on coin) upon its heart wrote the name of Hoomayoon, the sun, for friendship of him, filled the face of the impression with gold.
"That pulpit which from the naming of his titles receives ornament,
"On the top of that pulpit, Jupiter scatters pearls!"

From the presence of the royal army, and other circumstances, grain became very dear in the cold season of that year about Bukkur, so much so, that the people gave up their lives in the search for bread; hearing of which, the king gave much money from the treasury to his sepoys. One thin bread (Chupatee) cost 1 Miskal, *i. e.* 4 Mashas and 3½ Ruttees, or about 6 annas. When grain had become so scarce as not to be procured in the Lushkur, Hoomayoon sent Meerza Hindal towards Pattur, he himself remaining at Char Bagh for five or six months, because he thought the Shah Hoosain would come and make his salaam, and do that service which it was proper for him to do, since he had in the first instance pursued the path of submission. But the Urghoon nobles who were about Shah Hoosain, did not allow him to go near the king, turning him away from the road to friendship; and seeking the ways of deliberation, they found that the arrangement of their affairs laid in enmity to the king, so they pursued that road which leads to war. Hoomayoon, leaving Baburloe, went to Durbelah. After remaining there some time he proceeded to Pattur, when he married Humeeduh Banoo Begum, the daughter of Shaikh Ali Ukbar Jamee, one of the Meerza Hindal's Sirdars. She was equal to Bilkees (the Queen of Sheba). When all the grain and supplies were consumed, the king again turned the bridle of his intention towards Bukkur. From not obtaining grain, much distress fell upon the troops. After this Meerza Hindal, leaving the king, went towards Kandahar. At the instigation of his Hakeem there, Kurachuh Khan, he wrote to Meerza Yadgar Nasir, inviting him to go with him, saying that he should expect to see him on the road. On Tuesday the 18th of Jumadee-ool-Awul, 948 (A. D. 1541), the king went to the house of Meer Abool Buga, sending him to Meerza Yadgar Nasir, giving him advice to quit the paths of rebellion, and follow those of friendship. Meer Abool went as ordered, and with much trouble brought Meerza Yadgar Nasir within the ring of bending his head in submission. The following day Meer Abool was returning, of which circumstance the men in Bukkur becoming cognizant, they sent some of their people in boats in his front, who showered their arrows upon him. In this attack Meer Abool Buga received many deep wounds. The next day he passed from this world of death to the world of life. From his death great sorrow came upon the king. The following Wednesday, Meerza Yadgar Nasir, crossing the river, came to the presence of Hoomayoon, finding fortune by his interview with him. At that time the king gave his permission for the departure of Meerza Shah Hoosain's ambassadors, Shaikh Meeruk Pooranee and Meerza Kasim, sending by them a Firman, on which he wrote with his own hands— "After Salaam to Meerza Shah Hoosain: In this matter I will agree to your proposition, when you come to my presence with a clean heart. My Salaam to you. Enough!" Meerza Shah Hoosain was inclined to visit the Badshah, but the wisdom of the Urghoon nobles was averse to such a proceeding. Shah Hoosain considered much on the subject, thus delay occurred; so much so, that the king, leaving Meerza Yadgar Nasir near Bukkur, returned towards Sehwistan, close to which his standard full of victory came. At that time Fuzl Beg, the brother of Momain Khan, and Tursoon Beg, with about twenty followers, going on a boat, preceded the king; seeing which, some of the men in the fort sallied forth against them, who, disembarking, attacked and drove them back to the Killa.

On the 17th Rujub, Hoomayoon Badshah encamped round the place, where there were no buildings, trees, or shade for the sepoys; as, previous to his arrival, those who had charge of it, namely Meer Sultan Koolee Beg, Meer Shah Mahomed Urghoon, and others, had cleared away all the gardens and buildings about it. The king having beleaguered the fort, the inhabitants became much confined— their affairs were overturned. Hearing of this, Shah Hoosain, marching from Tatta, came to Sunn, where he made entrenchments, and collecting many boats, he encamped there, sending Meer Abeek Urghoon to Sehwistan, who in the nighttime, with some men, passing through the royal army by the bazar road, reached the fort. The news of his having arrived reached the king's forces, after he had gained the fort: he went so secretly, that information of his approach did not precede him. In the morning, Hoomayoon gave orders for mines to be sunk: in short, one bastion was blown up: but the garrison, as it fell, threw up another defence.

The king then knew that the resources of the Urghoons were full of strength. Besides this, the apparatus for opening the fort was not present. In short, having besieged it for seven months, the time of the inundation, and the season for bad winds, were approaching; moreover, Shah Hoosain had closed all the roads by which supplies could come. For these reasons many sepoys had deserted; and even some of the men of consequence, such as Meer Tahir Sudur, Khwaja Ghuyas-ood-deen Jamee, Moulana Abdool Bakee, had left, and gone over to Shah Hoosain, who gave them much honour, and then sent them to Tatta. Meer Kasim, and Hoosain went off to Meerza Yadgar, and the king heard that they would go off with him to Kandahar. After the king left Yadgar Nasir near Bukkur, the men in that fort twice went forth, and attacking his troops when unprepared, slew Mahomed Ali Kaboochee, and Shere Dil Beg, besides killing and wounding many others. These two affairs were conducted by Kokuh Turkhan, Dost Mahomed, and others. The garrison sallied forth a third time against their enemies, falling upon them on the sandy ground, near Roree; but this time Meerza Yadgar, going forth himself, stretched forth his hand in such a manner, that the attacking party turned their faces in flight, some throwing themselves into the waters of the river. Many got on boats, which they loosed, and allowed to go with the stream. When the news of this defeat of his men at Bukkur reached Shah Hoosain, he sent Ameer Koolee Mohurdar to Meerza Yadgar, shaking the rope of friendship, sending this message to him: "I have become old, and with the exception of one daughter, I have no other children. I make the betrothal of her with you; for a short time I may have to live, and after my death all this country will be yours. I will give you much wealth now, and both of us, uniting, we will go and conquer Guzerat." In short, Meerza Yadgar Nasir from this deceit of Shah Hoosain, becoming misled, turned his heart in enmity towards Hoomayoon, who, seeing the ruinous state of his army, had sent many successive times to call him; but he always sent back the messengers with some excuse or other. When the news of his enmity reached the king, he at once left Sehwistan, proceeding towards Bukkur, and on the way Hunbur Beg Urghoon, leaving him, returned to Sehwistan, and many sepoys, from getting nothing to eat, quitted the royal army. Hoomayoon, arriving at Roree, encamped there. Meerza Yadgar Nasir, being helpless, paid his respects to the king, giving up to him all the grain he had; but this was not sufficient to satisfy the cravings of the royal host. When the extremity of hunger came upon them, the king sent some of his confidential people to Sultan Mahomed, who came in front to meet them, giving Khilats to Mahomed Bukawul, and the other servants of the king, and presenting money and grain to the attendants, he gave them their leave. After the departure of these chiefs, the nobles of Meerza Shah Hoosain, assembling in the reception-room, discoursed on the scarcity of grain in the royal camp, each saying what he thought. Sultan Mahomed afterwards sent 300 Kurwas of grain for the use of the royal household; but the people, from getting nothing, left the king's camp, dispersing over Sind. Many of these parties followed one route, numbers perishing from hunger. The royal troops often came in contact with the men of Shah Hoosain, who were always beaten; but as there was no appa??tus for opening forts, on this account he could not conquer these. When the will of God's power, the wish of the Eternal Wisdom, (which shows the countenance of misfortunes in the midst of happiness, and which brings in the midst of these the apparatus of happiness,) agreeably to the desire of the king, had not placed upon the stool the painting of his wishes in the country of Sind, and upon the test of fortune the gold of Hoomayoon had proved counterfeit, he saw the infidelity of his army, and the unkindness of his brethren. Then he wished to place upon himself the dress of separation from others, and placing his foot on the road of those who love to walk after God, to go and seize the knocker of the door of Kunbuh (the Temple of Mecca), and there to remain sitting in a corner. But his confidential nobles represented, that although this wish which had entered his breast was very proper, yet the king was aware how much hardship and distress had befallen his people; that with these evils they were still at his stirrup; that if he placed his foot on that path, they would be entirely deserted and ruined, and that with so much distress they could not accompany him to Hijaz. Their opinion was, that he should remain where he was some days.

The king, on account of the absence of grain, determined to leave that place. At that time a petition reached him from Mal Dewe, the Raja of Jodhpoor, saying:— "Unknown to you, I place the ring of submission to your orders in my ear. I wish that the fortunate foot of the king may come to my house. If the royal army will do honour to this country, by coming to it, I will attend in service to you with 20,000 Rajpoots, and wherever the king goes, I will be present with my life and fortune." After the arrival of this petition, on the 21st Mohurrum, 949 (A. D. 1542), the king marched upon Ooch, and passing over the intervening space, he arrived there. On the 20th Rubee-ool-Awul of the same year, he proceeded, and, on the, 14th Rubee-oos-Sanee, he reached the fort of Dilawur, and on the 20th of the same he arrived and encamped at Beekanere. Some of the royal troops went into this city, and returning from thence, they informed the king that the language of respect was not heard among the inhabitants. Upon this, the king sent Sumundur Beg to Raja Mal Dewe, before whom he arrived, and returning with great expedition, he represented to Hoomayoon, that "Although Mal Dewe openly speaks strongly of friendship, yet underneath he does not place the light of truth." Then the royal army, going by the way of Phutodee, went on two or three marches, and encamped on the banks of a tank. From this place the king sent spies to bring intelligence. These returning, showed the perfidy of the Raja, to the effect that, at the instigation of Shere Shah, and seeing the strength of his forces, Mal Dewe was sending an army to loot that of the king. Hoomayoon, on hearing this, became much astonished, and full of anxiety. Spreading before his chiefs the carpet of deliberation, he then decided that it was necessary by all means to turn the bridle of their intentions from Jodhpoor.

In short, the king retreated towards Phutodee, from whence he was going to Sambur, giving orders to his chiefs whom he left behind to bring up his rear, to take care that the Raja's army did not come upon him. But another force from another direction encountered the king, when he himself mounting, and going against the enemy in person, with only a few men, showed such bravery that he routed and dispersed them. He then with great expedition turned his face in the direction of Jaisulmere, where he arrived on the 1st Jumadee-ool-Awul, 949 (A. D. 1542). Here the Ameers, whom he had left behind to bring up his rear, closed up, and joined him, but many of their people had perished. Sonkurun of Jaisulmere, from badness of disposition, forbad their taking water from the tank, placing his men on the banks for its protection; thinking that, as the king's army had come dragging hunger with them from the jungle of mirage, it was better for them to die there for want of water. The nobles and sepoys, collecting, attacked and drove off those men, encamping on the banks of the tank, and the thirst of the royal host left them there.

After remaining some days, Hoomayoon marched towards Omurkote, reaching it on the 10th Jumadee-ool-Awul, with great difficulty and distress from the want of grain. Rana Bereesul with his men came forth in front with his people to meet the king, finding riches by kissing the royal stirrup. He evacuated the fort for Hoomayoon to reside in it, but he remained some days outside, placing in it Humeeduh Banoo Begum.

One day, the sun of glory arose from the horizon of good fortune; that is to say, on the night of Sunday the 5th of Rujub, in that same year, the shadow of God, the king of kings, Julal-ood-deen Mahomed Ukbar Badshah (Oh God, do you always preserve his country and his rule!) was born. Mahomed Badshah Hoomayoon was highly pleased, and greatly increased in size on the birth of this child.

In the early days of Mohurrum of this same year, Meerza Yadgar Nasir, depending on what Shah Hoosain had said to him, becoming seditious, left the royal camp, and crossing the river, went to Sukkur; but that promise on which he trusted had not the strength of a rotten thread, and nothing came of it. Such guns as he had, he sent to Meerza Shah Hoosain, by Haluh, and Omur Shah, and other nobles who were with him belonging to the Meerza. When Shah Hoosain heard that Badshah Hoomayoon had marched upon Ooch, he came with great speed to Bukkur. The nobles went out in front to meet him, and on the 24th Mohurrum he entered the fort. He became very much displeased with Sultan Mahomed Khan, for having given away his grain; he hung Moolla Durwesh Mahomed Anbardur, superintendent of grain, in front of his (Sultan Mahomed's) house, and he skinned alive Haluh and Omur Shah, between the two gates of (in the centre of) Sukkur. All who had remained at Roree after the departure of the king fled. Meerza Shah Hoosain, in the beginning of Rubee-oos-Sanee, went to Sehwistan, remaining there a week, repairing the broken parts of the fort. He then proceeded to Sunn, where he stayed some time. On hearing that the king was coming back again, he quickly went to Tatta.

On account of the country about Omurkote being unable to supply the royal host with the necessary supplies, it appeared advisable in the wisdom of the nobles to go to Sind, and in a few days the whole went to Joon, the cultivation of which is on the banks of the river. There are many gardens there, such as the heart rejoices in, with fruit trees, on which account it raises its head above all the other towns of Sind. There are many other things pleasing to the heart there. Hoomayoon remained at this town a long time. Shah Hoosain, with his forces, came and encamped on the opposite side of the river. About that time the king was informed that there was much grain and other supplies in a fort in the Purguna of Buthoruh, and that it would fall into his hands without much trouble. The king sent Shaikh Ali Beg, Taimoor Sultan, and Turdee Beg Khan against this fort. Shah Hoosain, hearing of this, named Meerza Eesa Turkhan to go there, but he had not the mind to agree to this, because he was aware that people had told the Meerza that he was favourably inclined to the king. Shah Hoosain did not insist upon his going, and called Sultan Mahomed Khan, who was sitting in sorrow on one side, by reason of the displeasure of his chief, and giving him much encouragement, he sent him on this expedition to aid Moolla Boohlool and the garrison in this small fort. There was constant fighting between parties of the royal troops and those of Shah Hoosain about Joon. The forces of the latter were assembled on the land, and in boats opposite to that place, ready to attack the enemy.

By chance, one day, Taimoor Sultan Shah, Ali Beg, and Turdee Khan, arrived with their men at this fort where the grain was, but Sultan Mahomed had previously reached it, and he had assembled the Lunduruhs, the Munduruhs, and the Sakurs. The royal troops approached, without having heard of this, coming upon them unknowingly. Fighting commenced, in which Turdee Khan behaved negligently. Shaikh Ali Beg, with his brethren, fixed his foot firmly on the battle-field, falling there. Shaikh Taj-ood-deen was mortally wounded, and many gallant men of the royal army in that battle took the apparatus of their lives to the other world. Of Shah Hoosain's people, there were also many slain. When the news of the destruction of Shaikh Ali Beg, Taj-ood-deen, and his other brave men, reached the king, he became full of sorrow. Other matters pressed heavily upon him also; thus his heart cooled towards Sind, and he strengthened his determination to go to Kandahar. About that time, on the 7th of Mohurrum, 950 (A. D. 1543), Buhram Khan came alone to the king from Guzerat: he placed salve on the wounded heart of his royal highness, and he brought about negotiations for peace between him and the Meerza, who, deeming this good fortune, became satisfied in his heart. He sent to Hoomayoon Badshah one lakh of Misgalees (about 6 annas each), 300 horses, 300 camels, and other requisites for marching, and he threw a bridge over the river opposite to Joon. At the time of making peace, and when this bridge was completed, Hoomayoon became aware that 950 Urghoons had vexed his royal highness and his imperial troops, as to subsistence in Sind, for the space of two years. By reason of this making of peace, the Urghoons were so pleased, that they extended their hats of happiness to the heavens, looking upon it as an unexpected blessing, making many excuses for their conduct, and sending all things needful for marching to the Badshah. On the 7th of Rubee-oos-Sanee of this same year, the king, leaving the town of Joon, crossed the river by the bridge. This occupied two days, and on the 9th, he commenced his march upon Kandahar.

AN ACCOUNT OF THE EXPEDITION OF BUKSHOO LUNGAH AGAINST BUKKUR.

When Bukshoo Lungah had built a fort in Mooltan opposite to Junpoor, he caused the city of Mooltan to be deserted, gathering people of all descriptions in that fort, such as the men of Lungah, Beloochees, Nahurs, and all kinds of factious men were collected within his ring. Then, making up his mind to attack Bukkur, he was constantly sending spies there; so much so, that at length a succession of these arrived, bringing intelligence to him of the unprotected state of that fortress, and that Shah Hoosain was at Tatta, with all his nobles and troops. On hearing this, Bukshoo Lungah, placing his men on board boats, he started, sending fifty of these in advance, ordering them to arrive at Bukkur in the middle of the night, and by some device to convey themselves upon the walls, and, by breaking down the gates, to open a road for him to enter by. When these arrived at midnight of Friday at the foot of the fortress, they lighted a fire beneath the gate opposite Sukkur, and commenced shouting. The people in the fort, hearing this, were aroused, and mounting the towers and walls, commenced throwing stones and arrows. There were but few sepoys there. At this time the mother of Sultan Mahomed Khan, coming over the gateway, having had a large mat soaked in oil, cast it down upon the heads of the assailants, who by this were separated and broken. Meer Janee Turkhan, Humzuh Beg, and Kazee Eesa the son of Kazee Kazin, exerted themselves greatly, so much so, that some of their enemies were burnt, many drowned, and a few, throwing themselves into the boats, thus escaped. Early on the following morning, Bukshoo Lungah, with Nugarahs beating, approached, with the thought that his men had taken the fort; but when he drew near, and the garrison commenced firing cannon and guns upon him, he then knew that his people had not succeeded in their work, so he turned and landed near Roree, where he remained three days, looting the country of Bukkur, after which he retired. When Meerza Shah Hoosain received this news, he sent Shah Mahomed Urghoon, with Kazee Kazin, to take care of Bukkur. The above attack occurred on the night of the 14th Jumadee-oos-Sanee, 950 (A. D. 1543).

AN ACCOUNT OF THE COMING OF MEERZA KAMRAN TO SIND.

When, in the beginning of the year 951 (A. D. 1544), on account of the unkindness of his brethren, Hoomayoon Badshah proceeded to Irak, then Meerza Kamran sent Shaikh Abdool Wuhab Pooranee, Meer Eelah Dost, and Baba Chochuk, on a mission to Meerza Shah Hoosain, making known his wish to form a connexion with his daughter. Shah Hoosain agreed to this, giving leave to the messengers to return.

When Hoomayoon returned from Irak to Kandahar, Meerza Uskuree retired to the fort, becoming submissive to the king, who then marched towards Kabool. Meerza Kamran stood up in enmity, but his chiefs deserting him, went over to the king. Thus his strength to fight left him, so turning the bridle of his intentions from war, he put his face in the direction of flight, and by the way of Herat he came to Sind. Hearing of this, Shah Hoosain made a place of residence for him at Pattur, sending Durwesh Mahomed in front, to meet and escort him. Arriving there, Kamran shook the cord of marriage. Shah Hoosain sent Meer Furookh to make the arrangements in this matter, and he gave in marriage to Meerza Kamran, Chochuk Begum, the chaste daughter of Meerza Shah Hoosain. Three months after his marriage, Kamran left Sind, proceeding towards Kabool, Shah Hoosain sending with him 1,000 well appointed horsemen, repairing and furnishing whatever was required by him. Meerza Kamran first went to Ghuznee, which he took; he then marched against Kabool, reaching and entering it without the knowledge of the garrison. At that time the king was away at Budukshan.

Six months afterwards, Shah Hoosain's horsemen returned to Sind. Subsequently to this, the king with many men came back to Kabool, throwing his forces around it; at which Kamran becoming alarmed, he left it, going towards Hindoostan. He had an interview with Islam Shah Afghan, asking his aid; but he meant to seize him, hearing of which he fled, going to the men of Kokur, who protected him for a long time. At length, when the king heard that he was concocting mischief in his head, he had him caught, drawing a Mil (a wire instrument used to blind people) over his eyes.

In the year 957 (A. D. 1550), Meerza Kamran arrived at Bukkur. Shah Hoosain gave to him for a residence the small hill of Shad Beluh, which stands in the midst of the water, to the westward of Bukkur. He afterwards settled upon him for his house expenses the Purguna of Buthoruh, giving him Futeh Bagh for a residence. After remaining there some time, he left for Hujj (a pilgrimage to Mecca), and Chochuk Begum prepared to accompany him, sending to her father for his permission; but he made denial to this, enlarging upon it. Nevertheless, Chochuk Begum, without her father's consent, went on board a boat, wishing to go alone to Meerza Kamran; but Sultan Mahomed Mohurdar, and others, coming in front, turned her back. At that time Shah Hoosain arriving, went on board her boat, reasoning much with her; but she was not affected by this, saying: "When Meerza Kamran had his eyes right, you gave me to him; now that he is blind, do you intend to separate me from him? The world will say the daughter of Meerza Shah Hoosain at such a time turned her head from associating with her husband, and they will give me reproach!" The Meerza was pleased at this, and giving her valuable things, allowed her to depart.

Meerza Kamran and Chochuk Begum, after performing the pilgrimage to Mecca and Medina, lived at the former place two or three years. One year, on the day of Hujj, after standing on Urfat (a mountain near Mecca), and before sunset, the sun of his life went into the corner of death. Seven months after his death, Chochuk Begum passed from this world to the world everlasting. This occurred in the year 964 (A. D. 1556).

AN ACCOUNT OF THE URGHOONS AND TURKHANS BECOMING REBELLIOUS, AND OF THE DEATH OF MEERZA SHAH HOOSAIN.

In the latter days of Meerza Shah Hoosain, he was struck with the palsy. At that time many men of low origin were his confidants. The Urghoons, the Turkhans, and all men of character, being excluded from his presence, remained in their own houses; and those low people day by day ascended in degree, acting without respect and with oppression towards the Moguls. In the year 960 (A. D. 1552-53), Urabee Gahee had charge of the treasury at Tatta, and Ismael Bhuttiryuruh issued all orders to the country and Ryuts. Whatever truth or falsehood these men spoke, it was approved of by Shah Hoosain. On this account all the men of respectability sat sorrowing in corners. Things came to such a pass, that the sons of Urabee Gahee stretched forth the hands of oppression upon the Urghoons and Turkhans. One night, one of these kicking a woman of the Urghooneeyuhs who was in the family way, caused her to have a premature delivery. The Urghoons conveyed this to the ears of Shah Hoosain, who paid no attention to it. When they greatly enlarged upon it, the Meerza wrote a note to Shaikh Meeruh Pooranee, the chief of Islam, at the time in Tatta, saying: "Inquire into this quarrel agreeably to the law, and after it has been proved, punish whoever is worthy of punishment." Shah Hoosain gave charge of the fort of Musrutabad to Shunbahand Rufeez, who were his purchased slaves, and he himself turned the bridle of his intentions towards Bukkur, and in the early part of Zilhuj of this same year he arrived at Baburloe, remaining there twenty-five days. On the 7th of Mohurrum, 961 (A. D. 1553-54) he entered Bukkur, sitting in the Hall of Audience from morning till evening.

All the Urghoons and Turkhans, seeing the predominance of the men of low birth about Shah Hoosain, became full of vexation; they were thinking that the only medicine for their affairs was the destruction of these. They and all the other nobles assembled in the house of Meer Shah Mahomed Beg Lar, who was the Hakeem of the fortress, placing before him the state of affairs, good and bad, backbiting the slaves and attendants of Shah Hoosain; declaring that it was necessary for them either to leave the country, or else to destroy these people. They asked for counsel in this subject, viz: "That now Shah Hoosain is sick with the palsy, he has not strength to ride, going about in a travelling throne: we will place him in this fort, leaving our families to do his service, and slay all the men of low birth about him." Meerza Janee Turkhan, a Sirdar of consequence, said: "Meerza Shah Hoosain is like the sun on a hill; it does not seem proper to me to bring myself into bad repute in his last days. As you have borne this burthen for so many years, continue to do so for one or two more, and carry on your affairs with trouble: see what comes forth from the curtain of the invisible world."

They did not place their ears upon this, and some of them, rising from the assembly, went outside with the purpose to go to the Hall of Audience, and kill and wound all the attendants they might find near the Meerza, and to place him under surveillance; but before they reached the hall, Shah Hoosain, having gone on board a boat, had proceeded to a garden, from whence in two or three days he went to Tatta.

Meerza Shah Mahomed Beg, the Hakeem of Bukkur, after this wrote on the page of his heart the picture of rebellion, collecting the Booldee Beloochees. At that time the mother of Sultan Mahomed, a woman of great goodness and wisdom, hearing of this, sent a man to call Meer Mulik Mahomed, and Meer Lootfee, who were in the districts of Oobawruh and Matheluh, who, on her summons, quickly conveyed themselves to Bukkur, when they called Mihr Ali and the other servants of Shah Hoosain, also the Kotwal, &c. who had joined Meer Shah Mahomed, and greatly frightening them, they went away, and dispersed. They then wrote the circumstances to Shah Hoosain, who quickly sent Humzuh Beg and others to Bukkur, and he despatched Meer Humeed-ood-deen Mahomed Sarban, with a Purwana, to call Meer Shah Mahomed, saying: "I have recollected you: when you see my writing, come here." Shah Mahomed found no other medicine but to obey; so he went with Meer Mahomed-ood-deen, arriving in the presence of the Meerza opposite Sunn, receiving much kindness from him. At that time Sultan Mahomed Khan was at Seebee. When he heard of Shah Mahomed becoming rebellious, he proposed to go quickly to Bukkur, because his mother and near relations were there: so, leaving Seebee, he arrived at Gunjabah, where his people brought a letter from his mother to him, the contents of which were as follows:— "Meer Shah Mahomed was bringing bad thoughts into his head, but before he could do anything, he was called to the presence of the Meerza. Oh my son, keep your mind at ease, doing that which you have to do!" Upon this, Sultan Mahomed determined to return from thence. His chiefs, becoming aware of this, came before him, asking the reason of his returning: he produced and showed to them his mother's letter, on reading which they exclaimed: "Moobaruk (congratulation) to you on becoming the Hakeem of Bukkur: it is now necessary for you at once to advance your foot, and talk on the way." Sultan Mahomed said: "To me it does not appear proper to go there without being called." They replied: "It seems fit for you to convey yourself speedily into the fortress; for if Shah Mahomed was in it, it would be difficult for you to find an entrance: now he is dismissed, it is necessary for you to go there immediately, and from thence write a petition to the Meerza, saying, that having heard of what had occurred, you had arrived there, requesting his instructions."

Some days before his arrival at Bukkur, a Firman had arrived from Shah Hoosain, appointing as Hakeems there, Meer Mulik Mahomed and Meer Lootfee; upon hearing which Sultan Mahomed became greatly vexed, and he was attacked with diarrhœa. The governorship being entrusted to these two, they were dividing the Purgunas of the country between them; so Sultan Mahomed, with jealousy, sent a man to them, saying: "In these arrangements do not forget me, for I am in the fort." Hearing this, Mulik Mahomed said to his sons: "Take the keys of the fort to Sultan Mahomed." Meer Lootfee remarked that it was better not to act hastily, but to remain under the orders of the Meerza. Meer Mulik was a man of wisdom; he did not attend to Meer Lootfee, and he sent the keys of the fort to Sultan Mahomed.

On the 1st of Mohurrum, 962 (A. D. 1554), all the Urghoons and Turkhans in Tatta, being of one mind, agreed to obey the orders of Meerza Eesa, and they turned their heads away from listening to the commands of Meerza Shah Hoosain. They slew Urabee Gahee, Shunbuh, and Rufeeg, seizing and confining Mah Begum, the Hurum (wife) of the Meerza; and extending their hands to the treasury, they distributed much money to the sepoys. Shah Hoosain had appointed Meer Shah Mahomed to the governorship of Tatta, but before his arrival all the people had agreed to obey Meerza Eesa, bowing their heads before him; and Shah Mahomed, being helpless, likewise became submissive to him. Hearing of this, Shah Hoosain was much afflicted: he sent a messenger to Sultan Mahomed, directing him to seize all the Urghoons and Turkhans in Bukkur country, and to send them as prisoners to him. After being attacked with the palsy, the Meerza constantly drank wine, remaining intoxicated. At this time his attendants were backbiting the Urghoons, saying: "They are very Neemukhuram (faithless), because they have killed all your followers, who had passed their lives in your service, committing no offence: it is advisable, for the preservation of your government, to give us orders to destroy them, and to seize and confine Ahmed Wulee, the head of this dissension, and he is now present here in your force." They then began crying and lamenting. The Meerza had Ahmed Wulee seized, sending him to Sehwistan in charge of Mustee Sarban. He killed Ali Hoosain, who was the near relation of Ahmed Wulee, and placing his head on the point of a spear, had it paraded on all sides. Hearing of this, the rebellious enmity of the Urghoons increased. Seeing their disposition, Shah Hoosain gave the charge of Bukkur to Sultan Mahomed, directing him to slay all the Urghoons and Turkhans who were there. Sultan Mahomed took this Firman to his mother, telling her of its contents. She said— "I give you Moobaruk on being made Governor of Bukkur; but instead of having these killed quickly, it is better to seize and send them to the Meerza, who will do as he pleases with them."

Sultan Mahomed confined Meer Janee Turkhan, Ahmed Turkhan, and others, who were in Bukkur, to take to the Meerza: he put to death Yadgar Mahomed Kotwal, who had incited Meer Shah Mahomed to rebellion, and he turned out of the fort the family of Kazee Kazin, and all who were on the side of Shah Hoosain, and making over the charge of Bukkur to his mother, he proceeded to Meerza Shah Hoosain. At his second march, he met Syud Janfur, and other Syuds, who had come from Musheed: these gave to him a pair of Nugarahs, which had been sent for him by the superintendent of the Rowzah (tomb) of Emam Moose Reiza at Musheed. Sultan Mahomed was very happy at this, receiving it as an omen in favour of the Sultanut, and he gave much money to the Syuds.

He then collected twelve pair of Nugarahs, and nine pair of Korkuhs; and making successive marches, on the 22nd Mohurrum of that year, he arrived in the presence of the Meerza, to whom he showed his forces, and being much pleased, and getting confidence, he marched on Tatta with warlike intentions. On his arrival at Suyat, the forces of the two parties met. There were two or three battles between them, in which many men of both sides were slain. In this state of affairs Meerza Eesa sent secretly to Sultan Mahomed, saying: "By necessity we are fighting against each other: why should we fight between ourselves, the people being killed every day? If I and you have an interview, showing to each other the good and bad in our affairs, and consult about our own business, it will be well." The two met at midnight, and there was much friendly conversation between them, bringing their talk to this point, that Meerza Shah Hoosain is a visitor in this world for but a short time: it is better to take the road of peace; because, after his death, there will be no one but us two, when, in such manner as we may determine upon, we will make arrangements for the country, and we will not disturb that which we may agree to. No one knew of this meeting.

At that time Ameer Sultan and Meer Abool Khair, taking some of the Sodahs, &c. went to the Berar ferry, where there was a Belooch Chokee, under Beg Mahomed. A serious affray took place, many of Meerza Eesa's men being killed, the heads of whom were brought before Shah Hoosain. By chance, amongst these there were some heads of Moguls, seeing which the water came into the eyes of the Meerza. Upon this, Sultan Mahomed, who was sitting near, went before him, saying: "If any men of our side are killed, you become sorrowful, and if those of the opposite party are slain, you bring water into your eyes: I am vexed, and much distracted in finding a medicine for this." At that moment Shaikh Abdool Wuhab Pooranee, and Meerza Kasim Beg Lar, came between them, speaking in extenuation of the faults of Meerza Eesa. Then Sultan Mahomed Khan and others, finding the opportunity, said: "Meerza Eesa is much ashamed at the behaviour of the Urghoons and Turkhans towards your servants: if the pen of forgiveness is drawn across his errors, and if the Turkhans in confinement are released, he will without doubt present himself before you as a suppliant."

Meerza Shah Hoosain assented to this, and Meerza Eesa, releasing Mah Begum and the slaves, conveyed them to his army. This occurred in the last days of Sufur, in that same year.

On the 1st of Rubee-ool-Awul, Shaikh Abdool Wuhab Pooranee, and Meerza Kasim, asked forgiveness for the errors of the Turkhans, sending a letter on this subject to Tatta. On the 2nd, there was a meeting between Meerza Eesa Turkhan and Sultan Mahomed Khan, when each of them, placing a hand on the Koran, agreed as follows— "That they would be of one heart, keeping enmity at a distance; that as long as Meerza Shah Hoosain lived, they would both remain obedient to him; that they would not enter into any dissension during his lifetime; that when the Meerza shall depart from this to that other world, then they would divide the country of Sind into two parts, when that above Lukhee should be in the hands of Sultan Mahomed, and that below Lukhee should remain with Meerza Eesa."

Both of them, agreeing to this, they wrote an agreement, to which were affixed both their seals, and those of their men of consequence. They then embraced each other twice, and separated. After this, orders were given for the men of the two armies to go into each other's camp, so that the idea of enmity might be removed from the minds of all. The following day, Meerza Kasim Beg Lar, going to Tatta, brought Mahomed Saleh Turkhan, the son of Meerza Eesa, to Shah Hoosain, before whom he placed many valuable presents. From this side (Shah Hoosain's) Abdool Wuhab took Ameer Sultan the brother of Sultan Mahomed to Tatta, for an interview with Meerza Eesa. Meerza Shah Hoosain, presenting a Khilat to Mahomed Saleh, gave him leave to depart, and he sent a pair of Nugarahs to Meerza Eesa. The next day he presented to Sultan Mahomed a standard of Meer Zoonoon's, and his own seal. On that day Ameer Sultan came back from Tatta. After this the sepoys of the two forces went to and fro with confidence.

Shaikh Abdool Wuhab, who was learned in medicine, from observing the countenance of Meerza Shah Hoosain, became aware that his long standing disease was increasing its head: he therefore deemed it proper, now that peace was made, that he should go to Sehwistan, and that the troops should be allowed to depart to their homes. Sultan Mahomed proposing this to the Meerza, he assented, and that morning he marched; but his malady gained strength that day, increasing every hour. On the 11th Rubee-ool-Awul, he encamped at the village of Nalee Potruh; the following day, Monday, in the afternoon, the bird of his life heard the sound of— "Do you come to your God with much pleasure!" (Koran), and fled towards the Garden of Paradise. At that time Shaikh Abdool and Meerza Kasim were sitting at his head, and they sent to call Sultan Mahomed, who, coming on board the boat, and seeing what had occurred, tears of affliction came into his eyes, and a minute afterwards, uncovering the face of Shah Hoosain, he wept much, and kissing his feet, sat down there, saying: "Oh Shaikh Abdool Wuhab! Oh Meerza Kasim! You are my witnesses to God, that during the lifetime of Meerza Shah Hoosain I committed no act of enmity towards him. I have always been faithful to him; so much so, that see, I now sit at his feet— no one else besides myself has found this good fortune."

Shaik Abdool, taking him by the hand, went with him to Mah Begum, desiring them to sit together, and that he would do what was customary. Having performed these duties in the early part of the night, he placed the corpse on a bed, reading over it the funeral prayer. Sultan Mahomed took a little of the treasure, and much of the property, which was then belonging to Shah Hoosain. He said to Mah Begum: "God forbid! but the Urghoons and Turkhans at Tatta may commit errors with respect to your honour: on this account do you come to Bukkur, taking with you the corpse of Meerza Shah Hoosain." To this Mah Begum replied: "It is necessary to convey his remains near to those of Shah Beg at Mecca, which is nearer to Tatta— it is far from Bukkur." In short, Mah Begum did not approve of going to Bukkur; she determined to take the body to Tatta the following morning, accompanied by Shaikh Abdool, Meerza Kasim, and Khwaja Mahomed.

The next morning Sultan Mahomed marched on Bukkur, and on that day the news of the death of the Meerza reached Tatta, when Meerza Eesa, with a large force, started after Sultan Mahomed, near whose camp he assembled his troops. Sultan Mahomed then sent a man to him, asking what his wishes were, saying: "If war is your intention, tell me, and I will come to the field of battle." Meerza Eesa replied: "I have come, because the Urghoons had heard that you were taking the corpse of Shah Hoosain and Mah Begum to Bukkur: it would not have been proper to do so, because Tatta was his; but now it has become known to me that Mah Begum has conveyed his remains to Tatta, do you go at your pleasure to Bukkur." Sultan Mahomed then, marching quickly, reached Sehwistan. At that time Meerza Shah Musnood, and others there, came to the determination, that as Tatta had gone into the hands of Meerza Eesa, and Sultan Mahomed had obtained Bukkur, it would be advisable for them to hold the possession of Sehwistan. Sultan Mahomed argued much with them, but they would not deliver over the fort to him, keeping it themselves, agreeably to what they had agreed upon. Sultan Mahomed, by encouragement, called from the fort Meer Abool Khair, and Meer Abdool Humeed, and he then turned the bridle of his intentions towards Bukkur. Meerza Eesa, who was following him march by march, on arriving at Sunn, heard that the men of Sehwistan had shut the gates upon, refusing admittance to Sultan Mahomed; so he sent a large body of men in advance under his son Mahomed Saleh, to surround the place, and he himself arriving shortly after, kept tightly confined the men in this fort. At that time my (the historian's) grandfather, Syud Meer Kulan, coming between them, peace was made. After this, the men in the fort asking for quarter, evacuated it, Meerza Eesa taking possession. The chief men of the place, being greatly ashamed, asked for, and obtained leave to depart, for the purpose of going to Hujj; but they went to Guzerat *viâ* Barguh or Barkuh. From thence they went to Hindoostan, where they took service under Moonim Khan. Meer Abdool Humeed, also, having obtained permission from Sultan Mahomed, went to Hindoostan.

When the corpse of Meerza Shah Hoosain reached Tatta, it was conveyed to the house of Meer Ahmed Wulee, on the bank of the river, and a tomb was erected for it on the Mokullee hill. Three months afterwards, Meerza Eesa coming, took it from the house of Meer Ahmed, and buried it there, Meerza Eesa, and all the Urghoons and Turkhans, wearing the apparel of affliction. One day they all went to his tomb to read the Eatihuh (prayer for the dead). Two years afterwards, the remains were taken up from thence by the nobles, and conveyed to Mecca, by whom they were placed on one side of those of his father Shah Beg, erecting over them a very handsome tomb, which is well known.

A SUMMARY OF THE LIFE OF MEERZA SHAH HOOSAIN.

Meerza Shah Hoosain was the son of Shah Beg, the son of Meer Zoonoon. He had no equal in bravery from his youth, till he was seized with disease. He was victorious in all the battles he fought: in these his arrangements were good. He was born in the year 896 (A. D. 1490); he died in the year 962 (A. D. 1554), having lived sixty-six years. From childhood he was anxious to attain knowledge, and all praised him for the extent of his wisdom. His mind was always intent upon that which was good; his knowledge of all ancient traditions was great; he understood poetry well— sometimes the result of his thoughts came forth in verse. His titular name was Siyahee, and I (the historian) have possession of some of his poetry in his own handwriting. He always showed honour and distinction to the Soduts (the Syuds), the priests, and to all men of learning: whatever allowance was settled by him on these, there never was any mistake in it; he gave to all according to their condition. In his time, the hand of oppression did not reach the humble; he did not wish to injure any one. His arrangements for the country were good. For the space of thirty-four years he sat on the throne. In his youth, he went from Kandahar to Babur Badshah at Kabool, remaining with him two years. Babur always spoke in praise of him, saying: "Shaikh Hoosain Beg has not come to me for service, but he has come to learn the customs of kings." During his life he married two wives— the one Mah Begum, the daughter of Meerza Mahomed Mokeem Urghoon, who was his uncle, by whom he had one daughter, whom he gave in marriage to Meerza Shah Kamran, who, after coming to Sind, went to Mecca, accompanied by her, where she died. Mah Begum was married in the first instance to Kasim Kokuh, by whom she had one daughter, name Naheed Begum, through whom her descendants have continued. After the decease of Shah Hoosain, Mah Begum was married to Meerza Eesa. From her enmity towards Meerza Mahomed Bagee, she was placed in confinement, in which state she died. The other wife was Goolburg Begum, the daughter of Meer Khuteefuh. She remained married to the Meerza two years, but after that, as they did not agree, they became separated. She went to Hindoostan, previous to Badshah Hoomayoon's first coming to Sind. She gave the ready money of her life into the hands of the treasurer of death at Delhi, the leaf of her life falling before the hot wind of death. Meerza Shah Hoosain had one son, named Meerza Abool Munsoor, but he died when two years old, so none remain of his family.

AN ACCOUNT OF THE SODUTS, THE MEN OF LEARNING, THE PRIESTS, THE JUDGES, AND THE POETS, IN THE TIME OF MEERZA SHAH HOOSAIN.

Amongst these the first is Meerza Mahomed (known by the name of Shaikh Meeruk), the son of Meer Aboo Suneed Pooranee. His genealogy extends back to Arab Shahee Sodut. The mother of Meer Aboo Suneed was the daughter of Shaikh Julal-ood-deen. Shaikh Meeruk gained praise above all the Soduts by his charity, his devoutness, abstinence, and wisdom. He remained a long time in Sind at the head of the priests of Islam. All who came and went, all travellers, found bread at his house; all men of learning, and studying, gained much wisdom from his exertions; these took the ball from those who studied elsewhere. He wrote a very good hand, particularly the Nustungleek. In the month of Mohurrum 962 (A. D. 1554), he died.

Shaikh Meer Mahomed and Shaikh Abdool Wuhab were the two sons of Meer Bayuzeed the son of Meer Aboo Suneed. They were cousins to Shaikh Meeruk, after whose death they were superior to all. The habits and character of the latter were very good: he was of a happy temper, giving life to large assemblies. He understood poetry well; he restrained himself much, walking in the ways of God; with all his power he showed the proper path to men of consequence, exerting himself much to do away with oppression, and to put a stop to all the introduction of novelties in the exercise of religion. These two brothers died in the year 970 (A. D. 1562). The Jamin Futawa Pooranee, a work on law well known at Tatta and Bukkur, was written by Shaikh Abdool Wuhab.

Shaikh Kootb-ood-deen Mahomed, the son of Shah Mahomed, the son of Shah Tuyub, was the chief of the Soduts of Khorasan. He came to Sind after the quarrels of the Toorkomans, living at Bukkur. Every Friday he spoke in public, giving advice to the people. He was a man of great abstinence and piety. He died in the latter end of the year 977 (A. D. 1569).

AN ACCOUNT OF MUKHDOOM ROOKHN-OOD-DEEN, COMMONLY CALLED MUKHDOOM MUTOO.

He was successor to Mukhdoom Bilal. His heart was always given to piety; those who walked in the path of austerity looked upon him with reverence. He was well acquaintad with traditional sayings. The Shurh-i-Urbueen, the Shurh-i-Kaidanee, books on religion and law, and other works, are the result of his knowledge. His death took place in 949 (A. D. 1542), at Tatta.

AN ACCOUNT OF KAZEE KAZIN.

He was the son of Kazee Aboo Syud, the son of Kazee Zain-ood-deen Bukree. His ancestors lived in Sehwistan. One of these, a very devout man, came to and remained at Bukkur. Kazee Kazin was very virtuous; he was well skilled in incantations, in interpretations of the Koran, in the traditional sayings of Mahomed; also in all that related to religion and law, and the contemplative sciences, he understood, reading the Koran in a proper tone (Ilm-i-Kirat); no one surpassed him in writing. He exerted himself greatly in penitence to God. He made the pilgrimage to Mecca and Medina; he travelled much. He was a disciple of Syud Mahomed Juwun Poree, who was commonly known by the name of Mehran Muhdee,* on which account the Moolvees of the Mahomedan religion taunted him. After the death of Shah Beg, Meerza Shah Hoosain looked upon him with the eye of kindness. He was the Kazee (Judge) of the city of Bukkur, displaying great ability in settling all disputes. He died in 958 (A. D. 1551).

AN ACCOUNT OF KAZEE ABDOOLLA, THE SON OF KAZEE IBRAHIM.

He was one of the chief men of learning, and very virtuous. He attained knowledge from Mukhdoom Abdool Uzeez Abhuree; he had a strong mind, full of piety. In his youth he lived in his country, Durbelah. When Shah Beg took Sind, he lived some time at Baghbanan. In the year 934 (A. D. 1527), he went to Guzerat; from thence to Medina, where he took the apparatus of his life to that other world. He had two devout successors, Shaikh Rehmut-ool-lah, and Shaikh Humeed Ooch. There was no one equal to the first of these two. In his day, he wrote three works relating to the customs of the pilgrimage, and these are now adhered to. His tomb is at Jerusalem (Urz-i-Mokuddus).

Shaikh Humeed Ooch was ornamented with the dress of virtue; he was a proficient in knowledge of all kinds, especially in the interpretation of the Koran, and in the traditions of Mahomed. When Moozuffur Khan, the son of Sultan Mahomed Khan Guzeratee, took Ahmedabad from Shuhab Khan, who was one of Ukbar Shah's nobles, Nuwab Khan Khanan, with a large force, went there, driving out Moozuffur, and placing the country under Ukbar Shah. At that time I was among the nobles who were with Khan Khanan. I received virtue from the Shaikh, whom I went to see, making an offering to him of a complete book called Mishkat, with some other works, all containing the sayings of Mahomed (Hudees). I then took leave of him. Shaikh Humeed afterwards went on a pilgrimage to Mecca, with Nuwab Moostitab Khan Auzum, and he still reads the sayings of Mahomed there.

AN ACCOUNT OF MUSLUH-OOD-DEEN LAREE.

This was a man of great understanding, well acquainted with Arabic; he instructed Meerza Shah Hoosain for some time. In 961 (A. D. 1553-54) he went to Hujj. The results of his clear mind are a work explaining the Shumayul-i-Nubuwee, and marginal notes to Tafseer Baizawee (an interpretation of the Koran); also a commentary on Farsee Muntik; besides others.

AN ACCOUNT OF SYUD TAJ-OOD-DEEN.

He was amongst the good Soduts of Bukkur. He was their Sirdar, possessing goodness of all kinds. At present the Sirdaree is held by his descendants, who are numerous.

AN ACCOUNT OF THE MOST PERFECT, THE MOST ELOQUENT OF POETS, SHAH JAHANGHEER HASHIMEE.

He was descended from Tuyub Hurwee (of Herat). His writings were very sweet. He came to Sind from Khorasan, in the beginning of the reign of Meerza Shah Hoosain. He was without equal in knowledge of poetry. The results of his genius are the Muzhur-ool-Anware, a reply to Toohful-u-Ahrar, and Dewan Hashimee (a book of poems). In 946 (A. D. 1539), he went to Hujj by Kutchee Mukran, drinking the sherbet of martyrdom at the hands of highway robbers, whilst on his journey.

Meer Shah Hoosain Nukduree, Meer Shah Musnood Sudur, and Moulana Fukr-ood-deen Hurvee, were also great poets. The former was proficient in poetry, and chronograms. The Rorezut-oos-Sulateen was written by him. The latter wrote Sunaiyn Budaiyn (a work on versification).

Moulana Haidur Kakh was the Sirdar of all poets. He wrote a book of poems: this is an extract from it:—

"Oh my heart, be free from the confinement of the world-like Mujnoon.
"Take the road of the jungle of bearing trouble, turning your face towards the plain of sorrow."

He came from Khorasan to Sind: his tomb is at Puttur.

AN ACCOUNT OF MEERZA EESA, THE SON OF MEER ABDOOL ALI TURKHAN.

In his youth he found instruction from Meerza Shah Beg, being in the rank of his nobles. When Meerza Eesa was with Meerza Shah Hoosain in Mooltan, Ameer Amranee came to Tatta, looting the people. The nobles then wrote to Meerza Shah Hoosain, acquainting him of this. Meerza Eesa, placing the foot of bravery in front, asked for leave to go and punish the intruders. He arrived with great speed near Tatta, where he fought well, slaying many of them. The survivors dispersed.

After the return of Meerza Shah Hoosain, Ameer Amranee, with 40,000 men, came, and putting in order a field of battle, an action was fought, in which 10,000 of his men were slain. After the death of Meerzá Shah Hoosain, in Jumadee-ool-Awul 962 (A. D. 1554), Meerza Eesa sat on the throne of the government. The Urghoons and Turkhans approved of him as their ruler, placing in his hands the power of tying and loosening, of gathering and distributing.

Meerza Eesa was a good man in every sense of the word, always being indulgent to the Ryuts and sepoys. One year after he had sat on the throne, at the instigation of the Urghoons, he became at enmity with Sultan Mahomed Khan, marching on Bukkur with a large force, intent on war. In the month Rubee-oos-Sanee 963 (A. D. 1555), he encamped opposite to it, but Sultan Mahomed Khan was inside the fort. There were two fights between them.

At that time a body of Furinghees, whom Meerza Eesa had called to his assistance, came to Tatta, which they looted and burned, seizing some of the people, whom they carried away. The day previous to their looting Tatta these Furinghees threw some spirits into the river, when the water of it became ignited.

When this news reached Meerza Eesa, he went there with haste, being followed as far as Sehwistan by Sultan Mahomed, who destroyed all the Rubee (spring crops) of that country. Syud Meer Kutan, coming between, a treaty was made, and Sultan Mahomed returned to Bukkur. Some time after this, in the year 967 (A. D. 1559), Meerza Mahomed Saleh and Meerza Mahomed Bagee, the two sons of Meerza Eesa Turkhan, were fighting between themselves. The father gave his countenance to the former. The latter, being defeated, went to Wungub, where the Sodahs are. Those Urghoons who had accompanied him, agreeing to remain with him, they went to Omurkote. Thence, by the way of Jaisulmere, they came to Bukkur, where they had an interview with Sultan Mahomed, who took them into the armpit of his kindness, placing them at Sukkur. Meerza Eesa sent the children of Mahomed Bagee to Sukkur, to please Mahomed Saleh. Meerza Mahomed Bagee wished much to go to Hindoostan, but Sultan Mahomed Khan would not allow this, because he thought that if he got there, he would return with a large force, which would have to go through his country, by which much damage and annoyance would fall upon his people.

In 970 (A. D. 1562), Sultan Mahomed begged of Meerza Eesa forgiveness for the faults of Mahomed Bagee, agreeing to which, he sent a mission to Sultan Mahomed to make arrangements, saying how happy he was that he (Sultan Mahomed) had received and interceded for his son. Sultan Mahomed then sent Meerza Mahomed Bagee to his father, presenting him with all things befitting the son of a king.

Mahomed Bagee, arriving at Tatta, had an interview with his father, who gave him Sehwistan in Jageer, allowing him to depart. After this, the Urghoons quarrelled with Meerza Eesa's people. Peace was made between them, but as the Urghoons were crossing the river, they opened fire upon, and slew many of them. On this account, they reached Bukkur in a bad state, showing their circumstances to Sultan Mahomed, who seized and confined the whole of them. After some time, on the intercession of his mother, he liberated them, and giving to each a horse and Khilat, he sent them with his other people against Sehwistan, the fort of which they surrounded, attacking it two or three times, but they could do nothing.

When the river was very full, Meerza Eesa came with many troops. A fight took place at the Rufyan ferry, when many of Sultan Mahomed's men fell. Meerza Eesa encamped opposite the town of Dunbeluh, where Sultan Mahomed sent his forces. They were preparing for action when Shaikh Abdool Wuhab Pooranee, and Mah Begum, the well-wishers of both parties, made peace between them. Meerza Eesa then returned to Tatta, and the forces of Sultan Mahomed went back to Bukkur. In 974 (A. D. 1566), when Meerza Eesa drew near death, he proposed to seat in his place his youngest son Meerza Jan Baba; but Mah Begum said: "Meerza Mahomed Bagee is the elder, it is proper to place him on the throne." Meerza Eesa, shaking his head at this, replied: "He has violence in his heart, giving oppression to the Ryuts, and the families of others of God's creation, and you will come to your death at his hands."

When Meerza Eesa died a natural death, the event was concealed, to prevent discord, until Meerza Mahomed Bagee had come to Tatta from Sehwistan. On the morning of that day, the body of Meerza Eesa was placed in the tomb.

After this, Meerza Mahomed Bagee ascended the throne, placing all the affairs of state in the hands of the Urghoons. But these were without fear, conducting themselves improperly. The cause of this was this: Meerza Mahomed Bagee had only just ascended the throne; fear of him had not entered their hearts, although he had strongly remonstrated with them. In short, he saw that the only arrangement for the country lay in their destruction. He therefore issued orders for all to slay the Urghoons, to loot their property, and that their wives and children were to be taken by those who pleased to do so. In this manner numbers of them were killed, and those who escaped the sword fled to Bukkur.

During the first year of the reign of Meerza Mahomed Bagee, Naheed Begum came from Hindoostan to visit her mother Mah Begum. In the same year, at the instigation of the Urghoon nobles, Sultan Mahomed went forth to make war against Mahomed Bagee. On reaching Nusurpoor, he laid siege to it. He then heard that Huzrut Badshah (Ukbar Shah) had arrived at Shaikh Fureed-ke-Puttun (the Pak ferry), with the intention of making a pilgrimage to the shrines of the saints at Mooltan. Sultan Mahomed became very thoughtful upon this, and burning all his boats, by successive marches he retreated.

Meerza Jan Baba, the brother of Meerza Mahomed Bagee, and Meerza Shadman (a brave man, the son-in-law of Mahomed Bagee, and a descendant from Sultan Ali, the brother of Meer Zoonoon Urghoon), being displeased with Meerza Mahomed Bagee, left him, and went to Bukkur. Sultan Mahomed received them with much kindness, presenting to each, money, a horse, Khilat, and other valuable things. He also gave them Jageers. On their requesting his assistance, he gave them a large body of good troops. When they arrived at Tatta, they dug a ditch in front of the forces of Mahomed Bagee, but the Urghoon Sirdars did not make friendship with Jan Baba— they were against him. On this account he left them, going to the men of Sumejah. From the rising of the river, the troops of Sultan Mahomed were not successful, and they retreated. After this, in 976 (A. D. 1568), Meerza Mahomed Bagee, giving his daughter in marriage to Ukbar Shah, he sent her with Mah Begum and Naheed Begum, and everything of every kind that the king could approve of, he forwarded by these. He appointed Yadgar Miskeen Turkhan to go in charge of them, with intimate friends of the family, and men of trust, and he himself determined to accompany them some way.

Previous to this, Meerza Mahomed Bagee, having become friends with Naheed Begum, married her daughter Buchuh Begum, who was formerly the wife of, but had separated from, Nigat Khan. Thus Meerza Mahomed Bagee's heart was at ease with respect to the king, through Naheed Begum. When these arrived at Lukhee Alvee, they met there Meerza Jan Baba, who, coming with a force of Sodahs and Sumejahs, made a night attack upon Mahomed Bagee, who threw himself from the stern of his boat into the water, from whence he got into a small boat and escaped. The Sumejahs, boarding his vessel, slew Buchuh Begum. For this reason, the departure of the bride was deferred. A year afterwards, Mah Begum, Naheed Begum, and party, made a fresh departure, accompanied by Yadgar Miskeen. Meerza Jan Baba met the Begums, and having an interview with them, he said: "What is the meaning of your departing from Sind, leaving Meerza Mahomed Bagee to rule for himself." On hearing this, Mah Begum became his friend, uniting with him. They destroyed the marriage presents and dowry, distributing them to the sepoys, preparing to resist Mahomed Bagee. They got a field of battle ready, in which, in the first instance, Mah Begum raised on high the standard of war. By the order of God, the breeze of victory struck the banner of Meerza Mahomed Bagee, and being defeated, the forces of Mah Begum fled.

At the commencement of this flight, Jan Baba and Yadgar Miskeen fled to Kukraluh, which is on the salt sea side, belonging to Jam Muhr. Mah Begum was confined; Naheed Begum, with some followers, escaped to Bukkur. After this victory, Mahomed Bagee returned to Tatta, being much incensed against Mah Begum. In those days, Sultan Mahomed Khan arrived at Tatta, with a large force, when Mahomed Bagee sent to him Syud Ali Tuttuvee, the head priest there, and he made arrangements between them.

Mahomed Bagee, by some artful design, induced Meerza Jan Baba and Yadgar Miskeen to come in to him, when he killed both of them. Mah Begum died in her prison.

After this, Sultan Mahomed, with a numerous army, again marched on Tatta, encamping opposite one of the gates. Meerza Mahomed Bagee, having cut his own legs from under him, was unable to fight. He placed guns on the bank of the river Rein, to protect the city. There was constant fighting between the two parties, in which Fakeer Mahomed Turkhan, the son-in-law of Meerza Eesa, was slain, as also Sultan Mahomed Turkhan. When Sultan Mahomed Khan was encamped at Berar, he heard that Tursoon Mahomed Khan had laid siege to Ooch. Having taken possession of the neighbouring country, it did not seem wise to remain where he was after this, so he turned the bridle of his intentions towards Bukkur.

In 978 (A. D. 1570), Meerza Mahomed Bagee sent his daughter, with numerous handsome things as her dowry, to the king, accompanied by Shaikh Abdool Gufoor, the son of Shaikh Abdool Wuhab; but she did not receive the honour of being accepted by the king, and she was brought back to Tatta.

In his latter days, Meerza Mahomed Bagee showed kindnes to the Urghoons, taking them under his shadow: such of these who had gone to various parts of Sind were collected together, salaries being fixed upon them, and he gave them Jageers according to their merits.

In 979 (A. D. 1571), Meerza Mahomed Bagee, becoming out of his senses, with the intent of self-destruction, he wounded himself with his sword and knife, giving his life to the owner of it.

After his death, great ease and happiness came to the people of Tatta, and the country.

The nobles and chiefs chose placing themselves under the authority of Meerza Janee Beg, in preference to any of the sons of Meerza Mahomed Bagee. He, by strength of his fortune, ascended the throne in the early days of his manhood.

He distributed amongst the people like Abr-i-Naisan (vernal rain) the gold and jewels which his ancestors had collected with so much trouble.

All the people found much comfort under the shadow of his rule. Those whose eyes during the reign of Meerza Mahomed Bagee had not seen happy sleep, under his government slept in the swinging cradle of ease.

AN ACCOUNT OF THE MEN OF LEARNING IN THE TIMES OF MEERZA EESA, AND MEERZA MAHOMED BAGEE.

Meeruk Abdool Bagee and Meeruk Abdool Rahman were the two sons of Shaikh Meeruk Pooranee. They were well versed in all knowledge; their minds were quick and good; their means were much limited, yet still they were so charitable that all the poor about, and all travellers, received bread from them. Good dinner was cooked in their kitchen; but there was one dish, called Mahichuh, which they made a mixture of sweet and sour, of such a flavour that no one else could attain. They also made preserves, in which they excelled. I myself learned how to make them from them. The elder Meeruk was well versed in the theology of the east. The younger understood all kinds of knowledge, particularly that of the human body, and astronomy. They gained much wisdom from Moulana Abdool Kalig Geelanee, when he visited Tatta, and some things which were beyond his comprehension they mastered. The younger Meeruk made additions to the Tahrir Ukledus (Euclid's Elements), and he was a good poet. The death of Meeruk Abdool took place in 983 (A. D. 1575), and that of Rahman in 991 (A. D. 1583).

AN ACCOUNT OF MIYAN SYUD ALI.

He was of the Syuds of Shiraz, from whence his ancestors came to Hindoostan. He was very devout, giving much away in the name of God. Every year, in the beginning of Rubee-ool-Awul, for twelve days, he cooked much food, which he gave to the Fakeers in the name of Mahomed. He was in the habit of visiting and remaining at the tombs of the Mokullee saints, taking musicians and singers with him. The Kazees (Judges), Mooftees (superior Law Officers), and Mohtusids (Censors), were always dissuading him from this practice, but he did not attend to them.

AN ACCOUNT OF SULTAN MAHOMED KHAN, FROM THE BEGINNING OF HIS LIFE TO HIS DEATH.

Sultan Mahomed Khan was the son of Meer Fazil, the son of Meer Nadil Khwaja Ispahanee. His ancestors lived at Khwasgan, in the Purguna of Ispahan. When Saheb Kiran Ameer Taimoor Goorgan went to take the country of Irak, the Bulookats of Ispahan ceased bending their heads under his orders, so he issued directions to loot and seize them, and a strong force was sent for this purpose. In this expedition, Ahmed Khwaja, the father of Nadil Khwaja, fell into the hands of Meer Husun Busree, the father of Meer Zoonoon, who placed him in his family, showing him great kindness. The family of Nadil Khwaja goes back three generations to Mulik Mahomed Nandih, well known at Ispahan for his charity: from this he was called Nandih. He counts back nineteen generations to Udee, the son of Hatim Taee. Ahmed Khwaja had two sons, Adil Khwaja and Agil Khwaja. The first of these left a son and a daughter, Meer Fazil, and Sultan Bejuh. Meer Fazil had five sons, Baba Ahmed, Sultan Mahomed Khan, Meer Abdool Futeh, Ameer Sultan, and Ameer Abdoolla. All of these were by different mothers. The mother of Sultan Mahomed Khan was of the daughters of the Kashee Afghans of Shawul and Pishing. In his youth, when fourteen years of age, he appeared to all to be good in everything, and he came under the kindly eye of Shah Beg. When Shah Beg went against Baghbanan, Kahan, Tuluhtee, and Tatta, he was always in the front. On returning to Kandahar, Shah Beg wished to leave some one at Bukkur. All his nobles refused to remain, when Sultan Mahomed, though so young, volunteered to do so. For eleven months, he took care of that fort with 70 men: there was such bravery in his heart, that no fear of his enemies came upon him, and frequently, taking a few men, he sallied forth, attacking the Dharejas and Sodahs, on all of which occasions he was victorious. When, in the year 927 (A. D. 1520-21), Shah Beg died, and Meerza Shah Hoosain sat in his place, Sultan Mahomed displayed great valour in the war against Ameer Amranee, smiting with the sword in the presence of all. He also showed gallantry towards Ooch, at Dilawur, and Mooltan.

In 940 (A. D. 1533), taking a large force against the people of the fort of Sathulmere, and having plundered it, and seized some of the people, he retreated. He remained one night on the road, when his enemies made a night attack upon him, rescuing the prisoners. Sultan Mahomed was awoke from his sleep by the noise, and rushed forth on foot, when, his Pugree falling from his head, one end of it remained in his hand— the other was seized by Jugmul, the Sirdar of the Sodahs. Sultan Mahomed began twisting his Pugree round his head: when he came near the end held by Jugmul, seeing him armed, and having no weapon himself, he caught up a handful of sand, which he threw into Jugmul's face, who, letting go the Pugree to rub his eyes, Sultan Mahomed escaped. Sultan Mahomed has himself told me, that at that time he fell in with one of his men who carried horns, whom he ordered to sound his instrument, when his sepoys collected about him, and Husun Ali Pooranee, dismounting from his horse, Sultan Mahomed got on him, when he attacked and slew numbers of the Kafirs, recovering the prisoners, and all the stolen property. He showed great bravery in Guzerat and Khangar. In no battle was he ever known to be idle. When Hoomayoon Badshah came to Sind, he displayed valour and skill in the defence of the fort of Bukkur. He also distinguished himself in the action on the hills near Roree, with the king's troops, under Taimoor Sultan and Shaikh Ali Beg; so much so, that he slew with his own hand the latter chief.

When, in 950 (A. D. 1543), Meerza Shah Hoosain appointed him to the charge of Seebee, he took several forts, which had been held by Beloochees for many years. He severely twisted the ears of those vicious people of Kohistan, bringing them under subjection.

In 961 (A. D. 1553-54), when the Urghoons and Turkhans were opposed to Shah Hoosain, he came from Seebee with a large force, and by his endeavours these were brought back to subjection.

When Shah Hoosain was seized with the palsy, becoming powerless in his limbs and body, Sultan Mahomed made an agreement with Meerza Eesa, by which discord was prevented. In Rubee-ool-Awul 962 (A. D. 1554-55), after the death of Meerza Shah Hoosain, having lamented for him according to custom, he took possession of Bukkur, and its country. This had been much destroyed by the violence and oppression of the Beloochees, but very soon after his coming there, by the arrangements he made, it became fruitful, and by these arrangements the disturbers of the peace remained quiet during his rule.

In the latter days of 963 (A. D. 1555-56) he seized Shah Abdool Munallee, confining him in Bukkur for seven months. When the prisoner came for his release, he gave him his liberty, sending him to the king (Ukbar Shah) by Mooltan. In 964 (A. D. 1556-57), Meerza Eesa, at the instigation of the Urghoons, came against Bukkur with a large army. For fifteen days he remained encamped opposite Miskeen Turkhan's terrace. There were two or three combats between the parties in this space of time. The friends of Sultan Mahomed advised him not to go forth from his fort to fight, saying that if he did so, many of the Sirdars with him would go over to Meerza Eesa, and Mah Begum had also written to him on this. Therefore he did not leave his fort. Such of Meerza Eesa's men who fell into his hands were slain, whilst the Meerza saved and liberated those whom he took. After their last engagement, Meerza Eesa sent Meer Muksood as ambassador to Sultan Mahomed, writing a letter to his mother, saying: "Tell Sultan Mahomed to meet me, that enmity against him may leave my breast, and that I may depart." But Sultan Mahomed, being confident in his strength, wrote a harsh reply. About that time, through the slander of Moola Mohib, Sultan Mahomed Vukeel, Meer Lootfee, Durwesh Mahomed with his son, Ahmed Ghuznuvee with his son, also Moola Moonshee, were killed, and at this same time, some Furinghees, whom Meerza Eesa had called to his aid, arrived at Tatta on a Friday, when all the people had gone to the Jamin Musjid, which these Furinghees entered, throwing gunpowder about in it, and in the streets, which they set on fire, by which all those in the Musjid were destroyed, and many in the town were burnt. They looted the whole place, and then went away. Meerza Eesa was much dejected at hearing of this, and returned. One week after he had left, Sultan Mahomed, having collected men, followed him as far as Sehwistan, destroying the spring crops of that country on both sides of the river. He wished to do the same by the gardens, but he withdrew his hand from this on the representation of Syud Meer Kulan, my (the historian's) grandfather.

When Sultan Mahomed was returning to Bukkur, Shaikh-ool-Islam Abdool Wuhab Pooranee arrived as ambassador from Meerza Eesa. Finding Sultan Mahomed near Durbeluh, he strengthened the roots of peace and friendship. Agreements were drawn up, to which the seals of each being affixed, they were exchanged, so that from that date there should be no alterations made in this treaty.

In the latter days of that year (A. D. 1556-57), Khwaja Mouzzum was sent by the agent of Hirum Khan to Bukkur. In six months he had leave to proceed to Guzerat. In that year Shah Mahomed Khan Kandaharee made Kandahar over to Sultan Hoosein Meerza, he himself going to Hindoostan. In 965 (A. D. 1557), Wulee Beg, the father of Khan Jehan, came to Bukkur, with whom Sultan Mahomed made great friendship. In this year he married Gonhur Taj Khanum, the daughter of Shah Boordee Beg. At this time he received a standard, Nugarah, a waistcloth, &c. from king Tuhmasp (of Irak). In 965 Moola Mohib went as his ambassador to the king, who, taking Ooch, Jujhuhwahim, and Bhittee Wahun, from the Beloochees, gave them to Sultan Mahomed.

A quarrel arose this year between him and Khan Nahur, about rent and taxes, so in 966 (A. D. 1558), Sultan Mahomed went to Seetpore (near Ooch), besieging the fort for two months. Many of the enemy fell, and all in the place became much distressed; when Khan Nahur was induced to go on the walls with his sword suspended around his neck, and to beg for pardon submissively. He paid down four lakhs of Tuh-i-Larees. Peace being made, Sultan Mahomed returned to Bukkur.

In the latter days of that year, having suspicions of his brother Ameer Sultan, he sent him to Hindoostan, where he was followed without leave by his relative Meer Abool Khair. This year he heard that Hirum Khan intended to go to Mecca by Bukkur, therefore he destroyed the Char Bagh at Baburloe, thinking "that on account of the happiness Hoomayoon Badshah enjoyed there he remained so long, that grain became so scarce that pearls were given for jowaree; numbers had perished from hunger, and with affairs in this state, his heart had still no disposition to leave the place. God forbid that this place should so please Hirum Khan that he should remain in this manner!" Hirum Khan, hearing of what had taken place, went to Mecca *viâ* Puttun. In 968 (A. D. 1560), Meerza Mahomed Bagee Turkhan, being displeased with his father, came to Bukkur, when Sultan Mahomed received him kindly, giving a good place to him to reside in.

In 969 (A. D. 1561), Huk Boordee Beg came to Bukkur as ambassador from Shah Tuhmasp, bringing a ruby ring, a crown, a waistcloth covered with jewels, a Khilat, a bow, a Zaighuh, and a sword, with many other things. Sultan Mahomed Khan went in front to meet him, showing him all honour. He kept him one year; the next he sent him to Irak, with Abool Mokarim, with great gifts. Shah Tuhmasp again sent them back to him, with other presents, giving him (Sultan Mahomed) the title of Khan Khan.

In 970 (A. D. 1562), Meerza Mahomed Saleh, the son of Meerza Eesa, was killed by a Belooch; therefore Sultan Mahomed sent confidential men to sympathize with Meerza Eesa. Through these he asked for pardon for Meerza Mahomed Bagee, which Meerza

Eesa granted, and he sent men of trust to Sultan Mahomed, who allowed Meerza Mahomed Bagee to return with those, giving him rich presents.

In 973 (A. D. 1565), the Urghoons were at enmity with Meerza Eesa. They remained in this state for one month, when it was arranged to settle some Purgunas upon them for their subsistence. As they were crossing the river, Meerza Mahomed Bagee fired upon them, by which many were slain; the rest, being exiles, went to Bukkur, when Sultan Mahomed confined them, but at the intercession of his mother he afterwards released them, giving them horses, and other presents. At their instigation, he sent them with a force against S??hwistan, to which they laid siege, when Meerza Eesa, coming with many troops, raised the siege. There was a battle between the parties at Rufyan, in which Sultan Mahomed's forces were defeated with great loss. Meerza Eesa, expecting more fighting, entrenched himself at Durbeluh. After this, letters passed between him and Sultan Mahomed, peace was made between them, and Meerza Eesa returned to Tatta.

I have previously given an account of Meerza Eesa's death, and of the succession to the throne of Meerza Mahomed Bagee. I have also related, that Mah Begum was taken by Mahomed Babur Badshah from Kandahar to Kabool, where she had a daughter called Naheed Begum, whom she left at Kabool when she escaped to Kandahar.

When Julal-ood-deen Ukbar Badshah Gazee had taken the whole country of Hindoostan, Naheed Begum proposed going to Tatta to her mother; so, obtaining the king's permission, she went there with her daughter. She met her mother there, and she married her daughter to Meerza Mahomed Bagee. She was killed in the night attack made by Meerza Jan Baba, the brother of her husband.

Meerza Mahomed Bagee sent his daughter to the king with Naheed Begum, but at that time the Urghoons were rebellious, and these met her on the road, and, taking her with them, they went to Tatta, where they fought with Mahomed Bagee, and being defeated by him, they went to Bukkur. Meerza Mahomed Bagee then seized and placed in confinement Mah Begum, giving her nothing to eat or drink; so much so, that on this account she died.

Sultan Mahomed Khan said to Naheed Begum: "If you will get a Firman from the king, I will go and take revenge for you against Meerza Mahomed Bagee." Therefore, on her return, she related to Ukbar Shah all these circumstances. The king wrote a Firman to Sultan Mahomed, with which Naheed Begum went back towards Bukkur. She did not ask the king for any troops, trusting entirely to what Sultan Mahomed Khan had said; but at her request, the king sent her husband Mohib Ali Khan, and Mojahid Khan with her, having given to them in Jageer Futehpoor and Goohrore in Mooltan.

Sultan Mahomed having suspicions against the Urghoons, turned them out of Bukkur, sending them to Hindoostan. These met Naheed Begum, and her friends, who took them into service. Sultan Mahomed, hearing of this, became much incensed. He was in this angry mood when letters came to him from Naheed Begum, and her companions, to this effect: "We are coming, having confidence in you." Sultan Mahomed replied to this in harsh, angry terms; at which Naheed Begum, Mohib Ali, and Mojahid Khan fell into much astonishment, saying to each other: "It is wonderful! On what he said we have come, without bringing with us any of the royal troops; and here he is opposed against us." Calling their attendants, and the Urghoons, they consulted with them as to the course to be pursued: these said it was better now to go to Goohrore, and to send a petition to the king, asking his assistance. Kuluch Khan Oozbuk, who had lately came from the north, and joined them, was present at this council. His opinion was asked, when he replied: "I am a traveller; whatever you decide upon doing, I am willing to agree to it." They asked him a second time, when he said: "I am a sepoy; give me some men, and I will go in advance, and have one fight with Sultan Mahomed Khan: if I am slain, do you retreat; if I am victorious, that which you desire will be in your hands." Mojahid Khan, being a brave man, approved of what he said, declaring that it was very proper; that he had spoken like a sepoy; that in his heart he himself had held that opinion, and that he was now ready to advance. In short, 30 men had offered to proceed in advance, the remaining 200 were to follow in a body. They then left Oobawruh, marching towards Matheluh. On hearing of this, the 2,000 men who were then under Moobaruk Khan, a slave of Sultan Mahomed, went forth from the fort, prepared for battle. Mojahid Khan and Kuluch Khan, with their 30 men, meeting these, fell upon them with such vigour, that God gave them the victory before their main body had arrived. Moobaruk Khan with his troops, running away, got into the fort.

"In many places, by God's assistance, small numbers of men overcome great numbers!"

Moobaruk Khan remained in his fort, making a petition to Sultan Mahomed, relating all that had occurred. So he sent Zain-ool-na-bideen Sultan, with two or three thousand horse, to assist the Matheluh people. When he arrived at Lunjaree, 18 kos from Bukkur, the news of his coming reached Mojahid Khan, who sent Meer Abool Khair, who was related to Sultan Mahomed Khan, and who had first lately joined them from Mooltan, with 150 horse, to fight Zain-ool-na-bideen, who heard of his approach as he was preparing to leave Lunjaree; so, quitting his baggage there, he advanced one or two kos to give him battle. They met, but his men did not fight properly, and turned their faces in the direction of flight. Their leader stood alone, with a few men: amongst these there was one named Haidur Beg, a relative of Sultan Mahomed, who fell there, after having greatly distinguished himself. Zain-ool-na-bideen, finding that all the Juwangurs, the Buranqurs, and Moguls, had fled, retreated to Lunjaree. Mojahid Khan's men, having gained the victory, sent him news of their success; and hearing of this, the men of Matheluh lost all heart, and on the 1st Sufur, 980 (A. D. 1572), Moobaruk Khan asked for quarter, and evacuated the fort, which was entered by Mojahid Khan, who took possession of all that district.

On the 20th of that month, Moosnid Wulee Juatmad Khan, who had been sent by Mahomed Ukbar Shah to bring him the daughter of Sultan Mahomed, arrived at Bukkur, bringing a Khilat befitting a king, a waistcloth, and sword set with precious stones, a horse with caparisons, and four elephants, as a present from Ukbar Shah for Sultan Mahomed Khan; who in return prepared many valuable things fit for the king as his daughter's dowry, such as handsome robes of silk, various kinds of jewels, gold articles;

and with much pleasure he spread out the cloth for a festival, to which he invited every one, expending much money in different things for eating and drinking. The cloth was spread twice a day for fifteen days; 500 animals were cooked daily in the kitchen during that period. At the party, on the day of the wedding, many Soduts, men of learning, priests, and nobles, were present, to all of whom Sultan Mahomed made presents according to their degree. To Juatmad Khan he gave 30,000 rupees, and many other things as a present. On the 15th Rujub, he sent his daughter to the king by the way of Jaisulmere, accompanied by Zain-ool-na-bideen, Nouroz Khan, and many other confidential men.

At that time Ukbar Shah was hunting in the country of Nagore, having sent Meer Mahomed Khan Utkuh against Siroee, when the news arrived that a Rajpoot, disguised as an ambassador, had wounded Mahomed Khan with a knife. Hearing of this, the king quickly turned the bridle of his intentions there, and from thence he went to Guzerat.

Sultan Mahomed Khan, after sending away his daughter, placing great confidence in Moobaruk Khan, who held in his hands all the affairs of the country, gave him 1,500 well armed horsemen, with whom he sent him to Alore, thinking that, by his being there, the faces of his enemies might be turned away. But it was the will of God to cause the fall of the mansion of Sultan Mahomed Khan's authority; therefore that force joined his enemies, and became opposed to him.

AN ACCOUNT OF THE DISSENSIONS IN THE GOVERNMENT, AND OF THE DEATH OF SULTAN MAHOMED.

Living in this world is like the sun; the evening comes upon it. The sun of the government of the world is like ice, which melts with a little heat. When it is the will of God to destroy the government of any ruler, he is not able to retain it with many sepoys. When it is the intention of God to disperse the force of any king, it is not to be collected again by the councils of learned men. "When the will of God wishes to ruin the property of any one, wisdom and deliberation are of no avail!"

When the fate of God was prepared to destroy the house of wealth, and the existence of Sultan Mahomed Khan, he was unable to put it off with numbers of sepoys, and much counsel.

After Sultan Mahomed had sent his daughter to the king in charge of Zain-ool-na-bideen, and Nouroz Khan, the chief Sirdars in his country, he placed all the affairs of state in the hands of Moobaruk Khan, and his son Beg Oghlee. Moobaruk Khan's wife, who was a good, clever woman, had gone with the bride. Beg Oghlee was always drinking wine, associating with drunkards. These used to say to him; "Sultan Mahomed is old: after his death you will be the ruler of the country." Beg Oghlee, becoming faithless, proposed in his heart the death of his chief, and he got many of his servants to come over to his side. After a time this got abroad, when a Tumachee, a Hindoo servant of Sultan Mahomed, told him of what was going on. By chance Beg Oghlee heard of this; so at the time of evening prayers he conveyed his wife and sister out of the fort by the Khwaja Khizur gate, which was under his charge, and travelling in the night, he joined Moobaruk Khan at Alore, telling him that Sultan Mahomed proposed killing them both; discovering which, he had left Bukkur; and adding, that it was now necessary to have a care for themselves. Moobaruk Khan intended going to Nagore, and from thence to join the Badshah; but some men persuaded him to mount and go to Bukkur, and all being on his side, to seize and place in the Harem, Sultan Mahomed, and then to take the government of the country into his own hands. He approved of this, and in the morning, with Nugarahs beating, he arrived at Roree, and formed up his troops opposite Bukkur.

Sultan Mahomed Khan wrote a Purwana to him, saying: "I purchased you for 200 Laree-i-Sigah; I have raised you to your present position; are you now become faithless? It is better that you go to Mecca, and there beg pardon for your fault." To this Beg Oghlee wrote a harsh reply. After this, some of Sultan Mahomed's servants, who were with Beg Oghlee, leaving him, went across the water to the fortress, and he, being himself confounded, determined to go to Guzerat. He went to Alore, accompanied by some sepoys. On the 22nd Rujub, 980 (A. D. 1572), he joined Mohib Ali with some men, telling them of the enmity of Sultan Mahomed, and making friends with them. The following morning Mojahid Khan marched to Roree, when Moobaruk Khan came in advance to meet him. His troops after this encamped at Roree. Sultan Mahomed, hearing this, bit the back of his hand with his teeth: he called all his troops into the fort, which became filled with men. At that time Nuwab Suneed Khan, coming with speed, arrived at the distance of a cannon-shot above and from Roree. The Urghoons, holding their hearts full of the blood of enmity against Moobaruk Khan and his son, said to Mohib Ali and his companions: "Suneed Khan has come at the call of Moobaruk Khan, who this very night will leave you, and join him, when your affairs will not come to pass." Mohib Ali at once seized and confined the two, plundering their property. At this time Khwaja Munaj's son fled from Roree, going to Mukhsoos Khan, so they confined him (Munaj). Suneed Khan looted Kundruh. Sultan Mahomed wrote to him, asking— "What is the reason of your coming here?" He made some excuse, and went towards Mooltan. Mojahid Khan made great preparations to war against Sultan Mahomed, who sent forth his nephew Mahomed Koolee Beg. By chance, as the battle was raging, a fire-ball thrown by the enemy fell into his magazine, by which he and numbers of his men were blown up, and his troops met with a wonderful defeat. Some time after this, Mojahid Khan, with some troops, crossed the river at Puhnwaree, 5 kos from Bukkur. He arrived at Sukkur. Having made a bridge across the river, all the army came to Sukkur. Some Toorks, with Mahomed Ruheem (an ambassador sent to Sultan Mahomed by Sultan Hoosain Meerza Kandaharee) went forth to fight. Sultan Mahomed was in the bastion, called Boorj; Sultan Ameer on the eastern side. Some of his troops also went to fight. They did so bravely, but there was no Sirdar at their head, fortune was not with Sultan Mahomed, and they were driven back with heavy loss.

Seeing this, Sultan Mahomed closed the gates, and would not permit his men to go outside to fight again: he prepared everything for war in the fort.

After a long time, disease attacked his men; many were prostrated, numbers died: to those who were much afflicted he gave leave to quit the place, wishing their recovery. Provisions in Bukkur became so scarce, that one seer of meat fetched 2 rupees, a seer of ghee the same, and a seer of fish 30 Tunguhs.

Moobaruk Khan, his son, and Khwaja Munraj, the cause of this discord, were killed by Mohib Ali's men.

When Sultan Mahomed Khan's people arrived at Ajmere, finding the king there, they delivered to him the presents and Harem. Ukbar Shah was much pleased, approving of the offerings. He wrote a Firman, appointing him the Wabee of Bukkur, sending it by Meer Haig Tumachee; but Mohib Ali and Mojahid Khan did not listen to this Firman.

In the beginning of Rujub 980 (A. D. 1572), Sultan Mahomed became dropsical: he had taken much medicine, but all without avail; so, helpless, he turned his heart in the direction of death, writing a petition to the king, requesting him to send an agent, to whom he might deliver over charge of the fort.

When the greatest distress came upon him and the garrison, Meer Abool Khair, whose sister was married to Sultan Mahomed, with 30 horsemen, went by the way of Seetpore to Gunjabah, where he collected many men, and materials for war. On his getting there, Mojahid Khan became full of anxiety, and deeming it best to go against him, before taking Bukkur, leaving Mohib Ali there, he marched against him. At that time the mother of Mojahid Khan, Said Begum, committed great atrocities, ripping open the stomachs of the sick who came from Bukkur, and filling them with chaff. The garrison, seeing this, strengthened their hearts to remain and die where they were.

Sultan Mahomed's disease had been of long standing, when his doctors advised him to drink the wine of grapes: he called the Soduts, and the men of learning, to whom he said: "For forty years I have forsworn wine; now it is preferable, in my opinion, to keep it at a distance." In short, he did not partake of wine. His hands and feet became swelled; this reached his heart, and at midnight of Saturday the 8th Sufur, 982 (A. D. 1574), his life went from this perishable world to the world eternal.

On hearing of this, Mohib Ali, with many boats, surrounded Bukkur; but the garrison drove them away.

The nobles, the Soduts, the men of learning, the priests, and all the men of consequence in Bukkur, took oath that they would not give it up to Mohib Ali, but that they would deliver it over to any one sent to receive charge of it by the king. All having agreed to this, they issued pay to the troops from the treasury, taking great care of the fort; so much so, that on Monday the 12th Jumadee-ool-Awul, 982 (A. D. 1574), Keshoo Khan approached from the Badshah. When he was 10 kos from Bukkur, Mohib Ali sent a boat across to bring him to him, instead of his going to the fort, that, after an interview, matters might be settled; but Keshoo Khan wrote a letter to the Sirdars in Bukkur, who sent a force to escort him, and, as they did so, they had fighting with Mohib Ali's men.

After Keshoo Khan's arrival in the fort, day by day happiness increased in the faces of all there.

Mojahid Khan took the fort of Gunjabah, and made peace with Meer Abool Khair, whom he afterwards killed. Hearing of the arrival of Keshoo Khan, he quickly turned the bridle of his intentions from Gunjabah.

A continuation of the circumstances I write in the IV. Chapter.

A SHORT DESCRIPTION OF SULTAN MAHOMED.

Sultan Mahomed Khan was a ruler with many excellent qualities. He was very brave, and very charitable. From the days of his youth, until his death, he lived in plenty; but his temper was so passionate, that when he became angry he could not control himself. He shed blood without care. If he ever suspected any one of evil, he would ruin his family. He himself would commit violence, but in his country no one else could do so. The sepoys and Ryuts were happy under him. During his life he read the Koran entire 1,001 times.

He took great trouble in building and laying out in proper form the town of Bukkur. He was born in 898 (A. D. 1492), living eighty-four years. His strength was such, that many times, at the order of Meerza Shah Hoosain, he put irons on his legs, and with these on, threw himself from the bastion of Meerza Shah Hoosain's receiving-room, into the waters below, where there was a very deep dangerous whirlpool, from whence he would come out near the rocks with the irons broken. Many people have witnessed this— they looked upon it as a sight.

END OF CHAPTER III.

CHAPTER IV.

AN ACCOUNT OF SIND COMING INTO THE HANDS OF THE AGENTS OF JULAL-OOD-DEEN UKBAR SHAH.

I have before said that Keshoo Khan came to Bukkur in Jumadee-ool-Awul 982 (A. D. 1574). He brought a Firman to this effect:— "Divide Bukkur equally between Mohib Ali Khan and Mojahid Khan; then you are to go to Tatta, and seize Meerza Mahomed Bagee." At this time Mojahid Khan was at Gunjabah. Hearing of the arrival of Keshoo Khan, he quickly went towards Bukkur, but before his arrival Keshoo Khan had determined to turn his friends out of Sukkur. Mojahid Khan's men said they would not leave before his return, but Keshoo Khan did not approve of this, and sending some of his men there, they quarrelled with those of Mojahid Khan, near a wall which he had built, when several were killed and wounded on both sides. Three days after this affray, Mojahid Khan came, and taking his men to Roree, Keshoo Khan occupied Sukkur, and the neighbouring country. Mohib Ali and Mojahid Khan held Roree and Tiggur, but their men were heartbroken. About that time, some of the Urghoons, deserting them, came to Bukkur, when they were put to death by Keshoo Khan, through the backbiting of Shah Baba, the son of Meerza Jan Baba Turkhan. Keshoo Khan had a bad disposition: one day a Tumachee, who was inconsiderate in the assembly, he put in irons. Two months after his return, Mojahid Khan went against Tatta, leaving the families at Roree with Mohib Ali.

At the instigation of the men of Bukkur, Keshoo Khan determined to send a force against Roree. On Friday the 3rd Ramzan, 962 (A. D. 1554), he divided his army into two divisions: one of them he sent down towards the gardens below Roree, the other he directed across above by the shrine of Khwaja Khizur. Mohib Ali's men, mounting, went towards the Eedgah. Keshoo Khan's men set on fire Mojahid Khan's boats, seeing which, Mohib Ali Khan's troops returned in the direction of the ground they had left. At this time, the division which had gone below Roree came in front of these, and commenced throwing fire-balls, by which the town was fired in several directions. Mohib Ali Khan, then mounting his horse, pursued the road of flight. The men of Bukkur, having surrounded Roree, plundered it till near sunset, capturing the standard and Nugarah of Mohib Ali Khan.

When Mojahid Khan heard of this, he quickly returned with much dejection, and for fear of the king he did not attempt to molest Keshoo Khan, who sat in his government, conducting himself improperly.

When Ukbar Shah heard of what Keshoo Khan had done, he gave Bukkur in Jageer to Nuwab Tursoon Mahomed Saif-ool-Moolk, some of whose Sirdars came to Roree in Mohurrum 983 (A. D. 1575). They sent a copy of the royal Firman to Keshoo Khan, who in the first instance put these off, but many people coming between, he sent some of the priests with them to these chiefs, to give them advice. The Sirdars, requesting them to sit down, said: "For the sake of God, write and acquaint the king of our condition." The priests replied that they could not do so, unless Keshoo Khan was present. The Sirdars said: "Keshoo Khan's Vukeels are present; write the truth before them: we do not ask you to do more." Upon this, they began to write. Keshoo Khan, hearing of this, became alarmed, seeing that his affairs would be ruined; therefore he sent word that he was willing to give up the fort, and there was no necessity for writing to the king. The chiefs sent back word to him, that the letter for the Badshah was written, and that the seals of the priests would be affixed, and that it would be despatched, if he did not at once deliver up the fort. Keshoo Khan, being helpless, these Sirdars entered the fortress.

Keshoo Khan had received the royal order to take an account of the property of Sultan Mahomed in company with these Sirdars, and the chief priests, whose seals were to be affixed to the account. This was done. Agreeably to the orders of the king, the family of Sultan Mahomed Khan prepared to leave Bukkur. His senior wife, the sister of Khan Jehan, went to Lahore, as directed. Certain confidential servants of Ukbar Shah came for the rest of his family, and for the treasure. They intended leaving on the 1st Rujub, 983 (A. D. 1575), and to go by the way of Nagore.

When Nuwab Tursoon was preparing to start for Bukkur, having taken his leave, some of the nobles said it was not proper to place the family of Saif-ool-Moolk on the borders of the country. The king, agreeing to this, removed him from Bukkur, making him the Governor of Agra. A royal order was sent to Bunwaleedas, directing him to superintend Bukkur, and to make arrangements for the country. After this, to increase his confidence, Ukbar Shah sent Meer Syud Mahomed Uadul to govern Bukkur. He also made him chief of the priests there, because he was a Syud, and a man of learning.

He arrived on the 11th Ramzan, when he was received with much distinction by the priests, and every one else. He gave 50,000 Beegas of land to the Syuds, the men of learning, and the priests, for their subsistence: these were very happy during his time. He marched a force to Seebee.

The Mungnejuhs of Gagree becoming rebellious, opposed his men, for he oppressed the Ryuts more than usual, appraising with the Kunkoot (the rope measure) the good and the bad land equally, making the Ryut pay five maunds of grain for each Beega alike. The overseers or watchmen conducted themselves harshly, with a tight hand towards the cultivators. Meer Uadul's men got into a small fort between Gunbut and Vejuran, where the Mungnejuhs, without respect, shot arrows at them, killing several. In this fort there was one well, into which they cast the dead bodies of both Musulmans and Kafirs. They then filled it up with earth.

Meer Uadul, hearing of this, was much enraged; and calling his troops from Seebee, he sent them to take revenge on the men of Gagree, who fled, leaving their country before they had received much punishment. Syud Meer Uadul's son, Syud Abdool Fazul, who commanded the troops, followed them some way, and then came back to Bukkur. Shortly after this, Meer Uadul was bled in the arm. Much blood flowed from the wound: he was in a bad state of body, and on the 8th Shaban, 984 (A. D. 1576), he died.

After his death, the king appointed his son, Abdool Fazul, to the government of Bukkur, who the following year seized and confined the chief men of Gagree, destroying one or two of them, by having them trampled under elephants. On the 2nd Zilkad, 985 (A. D. 1577), Tutumad Khan, a eunuch, and a confidential servant of the king, came to govern Bukkur. He was of bad disposition; he did not take proper care of the sepoys, Ryuts, and men of consequence. Many of the priests, being displeased with him, were going to the Badshah. He sent people to persuade them not to go, but these were not listened to, and proceeding, the holy men arrived before and made their complaints to the king. Ukbar Shah said, that if Tutumad Khan had behaved as represented he will be killed; and so it was. In this manner Tutumad Khan was always in the habit of jesting and talking lightly, speaking with levity before men of consequence. His conduct towards the sepoys was improper, a few of whom, collecting on the 10th Rubee-ool-Awul, 986 (A. D. 1578), in the reception-room, killed him there.

After the death of Tutumad Khan, the king gave Bukkur in Jageer between Futeh Khan Muhawut and Raja Purmanund. These, arriving in Rujub, each took possession of his share of the country.

Two years afterwards, Purmanund, being appointed to the palace guard, he went to the king. The Dharejas, quarrelling with the brother of Purmanund, Madhodas, assembled in the fort of Alore, prepared for war. There were two or three engagements between these parties, in which many of both sides were slain. Many unruly men then joined the Dharejas; therefore Futeh Khan sent his men to disperse them, which they did. During that year, Futeh Khan visited the Badshah, who received him with great honour, promoting him in his degree, and he assigned the whole of Bukkur to him. Futeh Khan was a man of simple habits, fond of money, giving thanks with the tongue alone. His conduct towards the people was good, giving food to those entitled to receive it. He had a Vukeel named Shuhab Khan, a Zemindar of Sumanah, a man without experience, new to business. At the instigation of one Fureed, he took a force against the fort of Kum, which was in the hands of Ibrahim Khan (Khan Nahur). A severe battle was fought there, in which many of Futeh Khan's men were killed. Amongst these were Shuhab Khanund, and his brethren.

On this news reaching the king, he deprived Futeh Khan of Bukkur, giving it to Nuwab Mahomed Sadik Khan, who received orders to take Tatta. He arrived at Bukkur on Tuesday the 12th Rubee-ool-Awul, 994 (A. D. 1585-86), when the priests and men of influence went out in front to meet him, whom he received with much honour.

He remained some time, putting the affairs of Bukkur in order, and in Zilhuj he marched against Sehwistan. Previous to this, there had been several encounters between his men and those of Meerza Janee Beg, in which many of the latter were slain, and taken prisoners; the breeze of victory in all these affairs striking the standard of Sadik Khan.

When Sobhan Koolee Urghoon heard of Sadik Khan's coming, he collected materials for war, in a fort on the bank of the river, underneath which he assembled many boats, large and small. Sadik Khan's force arriving near this, the enemy, getting into their boats, went to fight him, when they met with defeat, and Sobhan Khan was captured alive. Sadik Khan was much pleased at this victory. He then besieged Sehwistan. Some time passed in this way, when his men, having sunk a large mine, blew up a gateway, and the curtain before it. Sadik had directed that none of his men were to enter the fort without his orders, when the dust and smoke had subsided. The garrison instantly threw up another defence, and began firing cannon and guns. Those men who had been blown up from the roof of the gateway, and the walls, by the force of the gunpowder, fell to the ground entire, without hurt.

At that time Meerza Janee Beg, bringing a large force by land, and the river, arrived at Muhran, 6 kos from Sehwan.

Sadik Khan, raising the siege, went to fight him. On arriving parallel with the Lukhee hills, the boats of Meerza Janee Beg came opposite to, and opened with cannon against him. They fought equally for some days, when the Badshah's Firman arrived, saying: "Meerza Janee Beg has sent many presents: with his tongue he speaks submissively, and in a friendly tone. It is proper for Mahomed Sadik Khan to return to Bukkur." Sadik Khan then retreated to Bukkur, and some time afterwards he went to the king. One year after his departure this Jageer was taken from him. During the two Kureefs, when Sadik Khan held Bukkur, the locusts came, devouring the whole of the crops; so much so, that he got nothing. Severe famine fell upon the country; the people leaving their houses, dispersed, and the Sumejahs and the Beloochees looted both sides of the river, leaving nothing.

In Rubee-oos-Sanee, 996 (A. D. 1587-88), Nuwab Ismael Koolee Khan received the Jageer of Bukkur, and his son Ruman Koolee Beg arrived there. He was a man of great wealth; his behaviour was good; he gave food to those who were entitled to receive it, showing much kindness to the country-people; so much so, that through his exertions and management the face of cultivation again appeared.

When Ismael Khan left Mooltan, going to the king, Bukkur was taken from him, and assigned to Sheroyuh Sultan, who came there in Mohurrum 997 (A. D. 1588). He was always drinking wine, giving himself up to ease and pleasures, leaving the country in the hands of his slaves, sitting in the Audience Hall but seldom; the food and subsistence hitherto given to the Fakeers and Soduts was stopped. He once sent his son Mahomed Hoosain to Seebee, where the Afaghinuhs opposed him. He was in advance with the Boordee Beloochees, who ran away at the first encounter, when the Afaghinuhs, without thought, fell upon the Moguls, who, being routed, fled. Numbers of them were killed and taken prisoners; many died from thirst in the mirage, and those who escaped were a long time recovering from the effects of the heat they had experienced.

Sheroyuh Sultan, having attained the height of his oppression, God listened to the complaints of the poor people, and they escaped from his wickedness, becoming happy, for Mahomed Sadik Khan again received that country.

On the 12th Rubee-ool-Awul, 998 (A. D. 1589), his son Meerza Mahomed Zahid arrived. He showed much kindness to the Ryuts, the Soduts, and all, placing ointment on the wounds of those who had been oppressed. He was of a very happy disposition, frequently sitting with men of learning, and giving according to the Sunuds of Mahomed Sadik. He turned the hands of violence from the heads of those whom they oppressed.

Khwaja Mahomed Munsoom was Mahomed Sadik's Vukeel. His conduct was good; he was capable of managing great and small affairs. The Bukkur people, being happy, began cultivating, but from the displeasure of heaven, the Rubee crop of that year was destroyed; every thing became scarce, and Mahomed Sadik Khan made no collections.

The phœnix of the government of the Badshah threw its fixed shadow over Lahore. Meerza Janee Beg then began to follow the example of Meerza Shah Hoosain, not placing his neck under the rope of obedience, but boasting of independence. Hearing of this, the perspiration of jealousy burst forth on the body of the king. He determined to take Tatta, and to arrange matters with the Beloochees through Nuwab Khan Khanan. At that time I (the historian) went from Guzerat to the presence of the king. By good chance my mother had sent some curiosities, which I laid before him. With much kindness and great condescension, he asked me how long I had been absent from my mother. I replied twenty years; the king then told me to go and visit my mother, and then to return to him. An order was given to the minister of finance to write me a Jageer as pay. At that time Sadik Khan, with great kindness, remarked, that if the Jageer was named in Bukkur, it would be preferable, as I was going there. The king said that all Bukkur had been assigned to Khan Khanan, who being there, said: "If the king pleases to give him a Jageer in Bukkur, I shall be happy to point one out to him, but I shall be in hope of receiving another from the Badshah in exchange." The order was issued at once to give me a Jageer in Bukkur. The financial minister, by direction, settled upon me in Jageer, Durbeluh, Gagree, and Chandooka. On this being arranged, the king gave me a boat for my conveyance, and one of his own Posteens. He allowed me to depart, repeating this single line of a verse— "To sit down and travel thus is very good."

I arrived at Bukkur on the 14th Sufur, 999 (A. D. 1590). The Nuwab Khan Khanan also arrived there at that time. The winds were hot, and the river was rising. The Nuwab remained there some time.

When the star Canopus appeared, he sent me with others to Sehwistan; he himself overtook us there. He gave me an audience. The men of Sehwan had strengthened this fort. The Nuwab held council with his nobles as to what was best to be done— whether it was preferable to go at once against Meerza Janee Beg's head at Tatta, or to take this fort first.

It was the opinion of all, that as Sehwan was on the line of road by which our boats and forces came, it was desirable in the first place to take it.

This having been agreed upon, the water was crossed, and batteries were distributed to the several Sirdars, encircling the place. News then arrived, that Janee Beg had left Tatta, and that he was coming to fight: upon this, the siege was raised, and we went to meet him. Hearing of this, he built a strong fort at the village of Roree, on the bank of the river above Nusurpoor.

On Khan Khanan arriving at 6 kos from this, Janee Beg sent against him 200 large boats, with many small ones, under Khosrow Khan, and other chiefs. He gave directions to his forces to attack Khan Khanan from two directions. Hearing of the approach of the enemy, we advanced a short distance to the bank of the river, where Khan Khanan threw up batteries of earth, on which to place his cannon, covering 5 or 6 Jureebs. This temporary fort was in this way: it commanded a part of the river where, from the formation of a large sandbank, all boats were obliged to come closer to it. At midday the boats arrived, and perceiving the sandbank on one side, and our works on the other, they stopped, and the battle began on both sides.

The following night Khan Khanan sent some troops over to the sandbank opposite. During this night Janee Beg's forces attacked our position, but it was strong, and they could do nothing.

The next morning, the boats turned against the force on the sandbank. Our cannon opened upon them, but the balls going over, fell amongst our friends, killing some of them. After this, the muzzles were depressed; so much so, that the shots falling into the water on this side, rose, and then passed through eight or nine of these vessels, killing many men. But they had carpenters in every boat, who repaired the damages. In this manner the fight was carried on that day— on one side was the fort, on the other the sandbank. The enemy, being helpless, remained stationary between. Many were killed by our cannon.

Seeing that their boats could not advance, and that numbers were slain, they turned their faces in the direction of flight, and our boats went in pursuit of them. Khosrow Khan, ordering all his boats to proceed, he himself remained in the rear; but some of their vessels having on board sepoys and some Furinghees, fell into the hands of Khan Khanan. The king's boats came up with Khosrow Khan, when by accident fire fell into the royal magazine, by which many men were destroyed, and on this account he and others escaped, but the hand of victory remained with the king.

The following day we marched against the fort in which Janee Beg had taken refuge, surrounding it; but around this there were isolated hills, on which account it appeared a difficult matter to take it. Much time had thus been spent, and the Killa was not won. The Ameers, seeing this, that nothing was done, made a simultaneous attack upon it; but because of its strength, this attack was of no avail. Khan Khanan then determined to take possession of the country of Tatta: he said that he himself would hold Sehwan, Tatta, Budeen, and Futeh Bagh, and he directed Shah Beg Khan to go to Shahghur, which was built by Shah Kasim Khan Urghoon.

According to this arrangement, Nuwab Khan Khanan marched to Tatta, sending troops to Futeh Bagh, Budeen, and Jhoon; Shah Beg went and surrounded Shahghur.

Syud Buha-ood-deen, myself, and others left for Sehwan, and arriving there, we sat down around it. When the garrison became much distressed, they wrote to Janee Beg, saying: "If you are coming to us, well and good; if not, this fort passes from our hands." The Meerza, seeing this, marched with expedition. When he had arrived at 20 kos from us, we had information of his movement. Consulting what was best to be done, all agreed that it was preferable in the first instance to go against him; and raising the siege, we marched in his direction.

Khan Khanan, hearing of Janee Beg's march, sent a force under Mahomed Khan Niyazee, and other chiefs, who joined us near the Lukhee hills, where our entire force amounted to 1,200 horse.

Meerza Janee Beg had with him 10,000 horsemen; numbers of footmen archers were coming by the way of the hills, and on the river he had boats with cannon. With all this force he arrived at 6 kos from us. Our Sirdars saw, that if they remained where they were, they could be attacked on all sides; that Janee Beg would fall upon them in front, the archers from the hill side, the boats from the river, and the garrison of Sehwan from the rear, and that thus their affairs would be desperate: they therefore deemed it preferable to advance at once, and attack the Meerza. Having agreed upon this, they quickly prepared their troops, and went in his direction. At that time spies gave information of our movement to Janee Beg, who would not believe them, saying: "How many men are they, that they should come and attack me?"

He then saw our dust, and quickly arranged his men. At midday the forces met, when some of our men, in advance, turning, fled, reaching our main body, pursued by the enemy, and then the fight became general. There were several severe attacks. In short, defeat came upon the men of Meerza Janee Beg, who, fixing his foot firmly on the battle-field, fought with great bravery; but when this availed nothing, he placed his face in the direction of flight. Many of his men were killed, and taken prisoners in this action. He retreated to Oonurpoor, 20 kos from the field, where he had built a small fort, in which he remained secure. The wishers of prosperity to the sovereignty of the king went there, and surrounded him. Some days afterwards, Nuwab Khan Khanan arrived, who advanced the batteries. There was daily fighting; men of both sides being killed. At length, our men, digging approaches, brought these close to the ditch of the fort. Upon this, Janee Beg became hopeless, and proposed to make peace in this manner:— "I will give you 30 (gun) boats of large size, and the fort of Sehwan; I will now go to Tatta, and I will come and meet you at a future time."

Khan Khanan consulted with his Ameers upon this proposition, all of whom were of opinion that Janee Beg was anxious for peace, being unable to fight; and that as they had brought matters to their present state, his affairs would be settled in a day or two. They also said that from his proposition it seemed to them that he had some sinister intention, and that probably he would change his tone when he arrived at Tatta. Khan Khanan said: "If I do not make peace, and attack his fort, of course men will fall on both sides, and his family will fall into the hands of men of violence, and from this bad repute will ensue. I will make peace, and I will obtain for him, from the king, the command of 5,000 men, similar to myself."

Without doubt, Nuwab Khan Khanan's judgment was of a good nature.

An ambassador then came from Meerza Janee Beg, making over the 30 large boats; he also sent a man to Sehwan to deliver up that fort, and he himself went to Tatta.

Khan Khanan passed the season of the inundations at Sunn. At the commencement of the cold weather, he marched on Tatta. When we reached Futeh Bagh, Meerza Janee Beg came in front to meet us, and he had an interview with Khan Khanan, who, leaving him there, he himself proceeded to Tatta, arriving at which place, he divided all that he had with him at that time, amongst the sepoys and nobles, giving a handsome festival. He then went to the Luheree Bunder,* where he saw the salt ocean. When he marched from thence he left there Dowlut Khan and Khwaja Mokeem. Previous to his leaving this, he received a royal Firman to this effect:— "Bring Meerza Janee Beg with you, and come to me." Therefore, taking the Meerza with him, Khan Khanan went with expedition to the king, receiving honour by kissing his foot. At his representation, Mahomed Ukbar Shah showed much kindness to the Meerza, confirming to him the country of Tatta. He had confidence in his service, and he nominated him to the command of 5,000 men. He also displayed other good will towards him; so much so, that he decided that Kosroo Shah should become his (the Meerza's) son-in-law.

When the king went to the Deccan, conquering Ahmednuggur and Asseerghur, at that time, on the 22nd Rujub, Meerza Janee Beg died from inflammation of the brain, and his son Meerza Ghazee Beg received the country of Tatta, at the representation of Nuwab Ullamee.

THE END.

Translated by G. G. Malet, most ably assisted by Peer Mahomed, Government Moonshee, attached to the Resident at the Court of His Highness Meer Ali Morad Khan Talpoor; to whom, and to two other Native friends, my acknowledgments are due, for their kindness in lending me original copies of this work.*

(Signed) G. G. MALET, Captain,
3rd Bombay Cavalry,
Resident at the Court of H. H. Meer Ali Morad Khan Talpoor.

Residency, Khyrpoor, Upper Sind, 21st September 1846.